Men in political theory

Published in our
centenary year
⁓ 2004 ⁓
MANCHESTER
UNIVERSITY
PRESS

Men in political theory

Terrell Carver

Manchester University Press
Manchester and New York

published exclusively in the USA by Palgrave

Copyright © Terrell Carver 2004

The right of Terrell Carver to be identified as the author of this work has been asserted by him in accordance with the Copyright, Designs and Patents Act 1988.

Published by Manchester University Press
Oxford Road, Manchester M13 9NR, UK
and Room 400, 175 Fifth Avenue, New York, NY 10010, USA
www.manchesteruniversitypress.co.uk

Distributed in the United States exclusively by
Palgrave Macmillan, 175 Fifth Avenue,
New York, NY 10010, USA

Distributed in Canada exclusively by
UBC Press, University of British Columbia, 2029 West Mall,
Vancouver, BC, Canada V6T 1Z2

British Library Cataloguing-in-Publication Data
A catalogue record for this book is available from the British Library

Library of Congress Cataloging-in-Publication Data applied for

ISBN 978 0 7190 5914 8 paperback

First published by Manchester University Press in hardback 2004

This paperback edition first published 2009

Printed by Lightning Source

Contents

		page
	Acknowledgements	vi
	Introduction	1
1	Plato: men/women and order/disorder in *The Republic*	11
2	Aristotle: men, masculinities and metaphors	34
3	Jesus: masculinity and the 'son of man'	58
4	Augustine: confessing like a man	80
5	Machiavelli: discourses on masculinities	105
6	Hobbes: materialism, mechanism, masculinity	130
7	Locke: overtly and covertly gendered narratives of political society	153
8	Rousseau: fantasising men	177
9	Marx: (non)critique of the gender categories	205
10	Engels: men behaving naturally	227
	Conclusion	252
	Bibliography	255
	Index	262

Acknowledgements

I am grateful to the Arts and Humanities Research Board of the UK for financial support under their Research Leave Scheme (Award Reference: RL/AN 2500/APN 14812) and to the Department of Politics, University of Bristol, for a matching period of study leave during the academic year 2002–2003. I am extremely grateful to the academic faculty and administrative staff at Pitzer College, of the Claremont College Consortium, California, for the use of facilities that sped the production of this book and contributed greatly to the content.

While I owe a huge vote of thanks to individuals and audience-participation in the thoughts that have gone into this work – far too many to list – I would like to single out Nancy Hirschmann, Raia Prokhovnik, Anne Phillips, Jeff Hearn, John Seery and Sharon Snowiss for kicking in with ideas and support at crucial stages.

For copyright and other permissions I would like to thank the following:

Manchester University Press, with respect to my updating of material (in Chapter 9, 'Marx: (non)critique of the gender categories') that first appeared in Chapter 10, 'Women and gender: Marx's Narratives', of my book *The Postmodern Marx* (1998), pp. 206–33.

Lynne Rienner, Publisher, together with *masculinities* and *History of Political Thought*, with respect to the reproduction of my material (in Chapter 10, 'Engels: men behaving naturally') that has previously appeared as follows:

- Chapter 2 ('Theorizing Men in Engels's Origin of the Family') in *Gender is Not a Synonym for Women* (1996), pp. 37–53.

- 'Theorizing Men in Engels's Origin of the Family', *masculinities* 2 (1994), pp. 67–77, copyright © Sage Publications Inc. Reprinted by permission of Sage Publications.
- 'Engels's Feminism', *History of Political Thought* 6 (1985), pp. 479–89.

For feminist friends

Introduction

But isn't political theory already about men anyway? Certainly the answer to this is 'yes' in several senses. Political theory rests on an established canon of 'great texts' by 'great authors', from which contemporary political concepts derive their genealogical origins and from which contemporary political theorists (and politicians, sometimes) draw their argumentative ammunition. Traditionally all these great authors have been male (and white and of European extraction – the apparent exception is Augustine, who was born and lived in North Africa, but he was hardly 'African' in the way that this cultural modifier is understood today). Since the 1970s the canon has been enlarged to include women writers; the 'Cambridge Texts in the History of Political Thought' now lists four women out of approximately one hundred total authors, and the series is now closed. Rather less successfully, there has been pressure to include in an updated canon non-Western authors and non-Eurocentric perspectives, of which the Cambridge series lists none. There are, of course, prior questions as to what constitutes a canon, and indeed what constitutes political theory. For the present study I leave those questions largely aside. Those who teach and research in this area, and those who sit in classes (and occasionally in other venues) to read these classic works in a 'political theory' way, will recognise the canon and the familiar DWMs (dead white males). Indeed they are occasionally to be seen arranged as busts or escutcheons in celebration of this particular branch of the academy.

Feminists and cultural theorists have critiqued these widely studied texts and demonstrated their androcentric and Eurocentric suppositions, content and limitations. The limitations relate to the exclusion, denigration and marginalisation of women and non-European peoples, cultures and perspectives (taking Europe to be Greco-Roman, Christian and 'white', which it isn't uniformly so, by any means, neither today, nor historically). Needless to say, these works contain economic (that is, class-oriented), religious and oftentimes anti-democratic and anti-egalitarian assumptions, arguments and judgements that pose interesting challenges to readers and students today. Moreover all these works, in their different ways, represent some kind of intervention into the politics of the author's time, even when these are confessional works written in (apparent) withdrawal from the world. That again makes them challenging with respect to their interpretation and value-in-politics today, and challenging in terms of rival claims that such works embody timeless truths, or contrarily that they are purely of their own times, and not ours. These again are problems that I note, and address *passim*, but they are not the focus of the book.

This study is focused on how male theorists present men in political theory *as men*. This takes a little unpacking, and indeed it may seem odd to approach men as problematic *in gender terms* at all. This is because 'man' in political theory (and generally) has been until recently taken unproblematically (at least by most male and many female readers) to represent the generic human individual of – as a famous textbook title had it – 'Man and Society'.[1] *Men in Political Theory* builds on feminist re-readings of the traditional canon of male writers by turning the 'gender lens' onto the representation of men in these widely studied texts. It explains the distinction between 'man' as an apparently de-gendered 'individual' or 'citizen', and 'man' as an overtly gendered being in human society. *Both* those representations of 'man' are crucial to a clearer understanding of the operation of gender as a power structure of difference and domination. However, it is not the case that women and 'the feminine' are ignored or marginalised in this book, or at least that is not my intention. In terms of the literature cited, the questions raised, the issues discussed and a gender politics involving both men and women, I am hopeful that many feminists will find this work valuable as a whole, or at least in parts.

This project arises within the context of feminist critiques of political and social philosophy, beginning with landmark works such as Okin's *Women in Social and Political Thought* (1979), Pateman's *The Sexual Contract* (1988) and Coole's *Women in Political Theory* (2nd edn,

1992), all referenced in the chapters below, along with many others. Through textual and philosophical analysis this work traces out the foundational discourses of political theory that have been instrumental in producing the extensive political exclusion of women from public life and full citizenship. Feminist critique has rightly attributed this discourse to men, to male interests and to the reinforcement of masculinity. Building on this, the newer disciplines of men's and masculinity studies have produced a theoretical framework of plural masculinities. Landmark works such as Brod's *The Making of Masculinities* (1987), Hearn's *The Gender of Oppression* (1987) and Connell's *Masculinities* (1995), again, all referenced in the chapters below, along with many others, have shown that there are structures of dominance of men over men, as well as men over women, and that these structures have important consequences for both.

This book is the first to use the 'men's studies' and 'masculinities' literatures in rethinking the political problems that students and specialists in political theory must encounter: consent, obligation, equality, legitimacy, participation and life-cycle. It does this by re-examining the historical materials from which present-day concepts of citizenship, individuality, identity, subjectivity, normativity and legitimacy arise. The ten chapters on Plato, Aristotle, Jesus, Augustine, Machiavelli, Hobbes, Locke, Rousseau, Marx and Engels show the operation of the gender lens in different ways, depending on how the theorist deploys concepts of men and masculinity to pose and solve classic problems, albeit unselfconsciously for the most part. I show how these conceptions of men and masculinities form a hierarchy through which men as political subjects are themselves categorised and disciplined. The book draws on newly theorised concepts of dominant and subordinate masculinities that are co-defined with concepts of race/ethnicity, class, sexuality, religion, nationality, language-use and similar markers of 'difference' and subordination.

The chapters can all be read independently and are as suitable for those just making the acquaintance of these classic writers as for those with specialist knowledge and interests. This book does not cover the basic historical and contextual background easily obtained elsewhere, nor does it introduce readers to an author's political theory as such. Rather the chapters are analytical demonstrations that the gender lens, applied in the way I have indicated above, generates new insights into the political theory of that writer as understood through that text, new insights into the methodologies and analytical techniques appropriate to political theory, and new problems for further consideration both in political theory and in gender studies, broadly conceived. Thus this book presumes some acquaintance already with the texts and authors of the classic canon, and an interest in how they have previously been handled, especially by recent scholarship in political theory and allied disciplines in the humanities and social sciences. But I have striven to make the content accessible to the non-specialist, even if not the absolute beginner.

My working definition of gender is 'ways that sex and sexuality become political'. This is not supposed to legislate what gender is ('always and already', as the phrase goes). Rather it is intended to alert readers to the ways that the term can be useful in identifying power-relations that are binary and hierarchical, as Butler argues in *Gender Trouble* (1990), referenced below, along with other works that have revolutionised our understanding of sex, gender and sexuality in recent years. In my view, using gender to mean merely sex or M/F is in effect an attempt to erase or silence the complexities of sexuality, and to disguise the ways that these and other factors are constitutive of gender-relations. Highlighting sexuality in considering gender is not only a matter of adding marginalised sexualities to 'the heterosexual matrix', as Butler puts it. Rather we should also remember that heterosexuality is a sexuality, albeit an under-theorised and under-investigated one. It denies its own variousness. Much the same could be said with respect to men as gendered beings, and with 'straight' ones in particular. By posing as the norm, they become unproblematic, and invisible to scrutiny. This book works against that kind of discursive politics.

This study thus addresses the following questions:
- How have male political theorists presented men, considered as gendered beings, in the classic texts of political theory?
- What do theories of masculinity/ies, developed within gender studies and feminist thought, reveal about the classical terms and conceptions of political theory?
- How does this consideration of political theory contribute to contemporary gender studies and feminist political and social theory?
- What does the distinction between apparently de-gendered and overtly gendered discourse in classic theoretical texts contribute to political theory?

Obviously the ten chapters of this work represent only a small selection of texts and authors in the traditional canon. My selection criteria were dual: currency and importance of the thinker/book, and historical coverage of the major periods. There is, of course, a certain arbitrary personal element involved, too, and I hope that readers will be patient with it. I did not aim to produce a large but flighty overview of (almost) everyone and everything, nor a formulaic book that stated a thesis and demonstrated it in every case (whatever the cost). The cost that I have run up in my approach will possibly be paid by the reader, as each chapter has a somewhat idiosyncratic range of categories, ideas and enthusiasms deployed by me, and I am braced for a certain amount of puzzlement from reviewers and emailers (t.carver@bristol.ac.uk). To keep the book to a manageable size, and to avoid straining anyone's patience and perseverance too much, I have tried to write chapters that are engaging but varied, show new things about the gender lens and demonstrate the vitality of the enterprise that is political theory.

Why are there no canonical women authors considered in this book? Wouldn't it be worthwhile to consider their view of men, as well as of women and the generic human individual (if, indeed, they think there is such a category)? The answer again is 'yes', but I have kept the focus tight in this work on how *men* present men *as men*, rather than on how men *are presented* as men (by men and women). The presentation of men by women is a further project, and one in which I have no small interest. But I have chosen to keep the active voice here, as it registers the politics involved – men are not presented *as men* in these texts through some impersonal and de-gendered process. The political answer to the question posed at the head of this introduction is that political theory is already about men anyway, in so far as the men writing the texts presented their view of men (as both apparently de-gendered 'man' and as overtly gendered husbands, fathers, sons and lovers etc.) *selectively*. Each text considered below consists in a pastiche of assertion, selection and silence, building up the kind of picture that the author wants us to have. Some of these pictures are rather more subversive of traditional gender norms of masculine domination (over some men and over women generally) than one might expect. But most are not. Indeed, that is the political question at issue here: how do men do it?

Chapter 1, 'Plato: men/women and order/disorder in *The Republic*', takes seriously the well known fact that the text itself is couched in a dramatic form with a central character who is *not Plato*. The absence of a stable authorial presence or voice in the text makes it difficult to read the author's politics or 'teachings' off the text, yet this has not deterred generations of commentators from doing so. Instead of following this interpretive model, I focus on the interactions between the (entirely male) cast of characters and then re-interpret the rightly famous discussions of gender equality in that light. This not only de-centres any firm doctrine or conclusion arising out of the text, but also re-values for us what is actually and variously said in the dramatic situation, given the masculinised character of the interchanges.

Chapter 2, 'Aristotle: men, masculinities and metaphors', examines the authorial search in the *Politics* for fixed points of certainty. These are read as tropes making up a concept of nature such that social distinctions (famously, the male citizen elite, women, 'barbarians' and slaves) can then be read out again as natural. This results in a gender hierarchy in the wide sense (race/ethnicity, class, culture and sex) that establishes a hegemonic masculinity. Historically this Aristotelian 'ideal' has been widely admired and imitated as quintessentially (but falsely) 'Athenian' and 'Greek'. Femaleness, for Aristotle, functions as a point where human difference and hierarchy are at their clearest, whereas other boundaries and distinctions that he wishes to establish among males require recourse to animal and machine metaphors to make them (supposedly) visible to 'observation'.

Chapter 3, 'Jesus: masculinity and the "son of man"', explores the gospel accounts, reviewing well-established but often disregarded hermeneutic difficulties concerned with authorship, narration and historicity. Taking the narratives as a set of ambiguous but dramatic scenes and encounters, I focus on the reactions that other characters in the set pieces have to Jesus, and his reactions to them. This exposes the extreme novelty and disturbing quality that Jesus' teachings have on his interlocutors, variously, according to who they are and what (else) they want. Moreover it also reveals that his teaching and example recommend and perform an inverted masculinity that runs quite opposite to any recognisable hegemonic conception, of his time or ours, without making Jesus feminine, or woman-centred as such. He emerges as an enigmatic theorist of an other-worldly politics, inexplicably acted out in this world, and a notable exemplar of gender transgression. While many 'canonical' courses in political theory deal with the Christian tradition, few deal with directly with its sometimes eponymous, possibly fictional and perhaps – whatever the actual circumstances – unwitting founder. This chapter argues that Jesus represents an interesting challenge in political theory, as he is so literally 'something else'.

Chapter 4, 'Augustine: confessing like a man', views the surviving surfeit of autobiographical material about this man as a disadvantage to political theorists who generally need to conceptualise an 'author' for their readings of his texts. The chapter is thus more about the way that biography is handled within the political tradition, than the political theory of Augustine himself, as we read it today. Given the understandable proclivity of commentators to bring an author in political theory to the aid of their legitimately held values and views, I note the way that Augustine has been somewhat normalised away from the wilder images of himself that abound in his work, and the stranger aspects of his life and loves as he relates them in his confessional writings. Reading Augustine for what he writes about himself as a man could make the vagaries of masculinity visible and problematic today in interesting ways. However, this runs against the need to create a 'friendly' author for classic texts, such as the *City of God*, who exhibits few such disturbing challenges, and thus fits smoothly into the canon.

Chapter 5, 'Machiavelli: discourses on masculinities', observes that he is indeed the ultra-theorist of the alpha-male but focuses instead on his use of subordinated or 'failed' masculinities. These are deployed to make his conception of *virtù* visible, intelligible and vivid. This has the effect of making 'man' a complex category, in order to view more directly the political structures within 'men's world'. Modern liberal readings of Machiavelli drive towards the generalisation of a republican ideal of citizenship, thus erasing or limiting what there is to be learned about men, as differently masculine, in his writings. Reinforcing modern-day sociology of masculinities, Machiavelli's analysis argues that access to, and prowess in, sporting and military activities are crucial to the establishment of hierarchical masculinities of men over men. Conversely priestly males who preach the Christianised moralities that Machiavelli claims are politically disastrous are traitors to masculinity, as well as Italy.

Chapter 6, 'Hobbes: materialism, mechanism, masculinity', aligns Hobbes's materialism, his use of mechanical metaphors and his political theory with early modern conceptions of masculinity. These famously contrast the calculating, 'rational' man of commerce and government with older, less egalitarian conceptions. To explicate this, Hobbes chooses a colourful language of metaphor that apparently works against his materialist literalism, yet I argue that his consistent materialism is so bizarre that these outlandish tropes are required to express it. Ultimately Hobbes outlines a dominant masculinity that is mechanistic at the level of individual reasoning and behaviour (e.g. in aligning morality with predictable self-interest), at the level of collective action (e.g. in armies and the like) and at an ontological level (e.g. in his conception of god and the cosmos).

Chapter 7, 'Locke: overtly and covertly gendered narratives of political society', makes the substantive claim that in his *Two Treatise of Government* his egalitarian arguments relating to gender are tempered with a residual patriarchalism, his objections to Filmer's (allegedly) extreme version notwithstanding. This residual patriarchalism appears clearly in two concepts of fatherhood that he deploys favourably, one historical and one contemporary, over and against a timelessly bad fatherhood that he attributes to Filmerian patriarchalists. This has consequences for his theory of legitimacy based on consent, in that he requires two contrasting forms of tacit consent, both of which contrast with the familiar concept of express consent. In the contemporary world his residual patriarchalism is effected through a mingling of archaic and modern traits and values explicated through the masculinities of fatherhood that are both 'good', but are also contrastingly tender/solicitous and rational/bureaucratic.

Chapter 8, 'Rousseau: fantasising men', examines him as the political theorist with the most extreme view of gender rooted in sexual difference between men and women, namely that this is both physical/natural and yet secured in society through education and politics. Taking a cue to explore the opposite view, namely that there is no difference between men and women, and that contemporary society demands this, I analyse a recent film that crosses the final frontier of sexual difference: male pregnancy and childbirth. Parting company with commentators who take as read Rousseau's claim that males and females have identical lifestyles in the most animal-like and least human condition at the dawn of the state of nature, as he depicts it, I argue that he is just as guilty as other state-of-nature theorists in projecting 'civilised norms' onto the human animal. Rousseau's vision of 'man' in his earliest state is profoundly andromorphic, masculinised, and homosocial, because it expresses and reinforces persistent hunter/warrior fantasies about men that are generative of, and deployed in, contemporary armed conflict.

Chapter 9, 'Marx: (non)critique of the gender categories', looks again at Marx's scattered and inconclusive comments on sexual difference and gender equality, in a presumed natural state of proto-human existence, in civilised but class-divided societies and putatively in communist societies. I see a narrative and political strategy of masculinised evasion at work in which he makes presumptions about women and thinks little about men. Compared with his thoroughgoing and relentless criticism of the economic categories of the time, this is poor stuff, but unsurprising. Read against some of the feminisms of his day, though, some of his comments about women have a greater resonance with contemporary values of gender equality and even female-centred perspectives than has been noted. The value of Marx's work in this area, though, is not in resurrecting him as any kind of proto-feminist but in aligning his silences with current masculinised cowardice and his comments on women and 'the family' with our own agendas of unfinished business.

Chapter 10, 'Engels: men behaving naturally', notes the contrast between Marx and his 'other half', Engels, in terms of involvement with gender issues. Engels's *The Origin of the Family, Private Property and the State* famously outlines a history of female oppression and gestures at gender-liberation under socialism. Yet in focusing on women in his narrative, Engels effectively disguises the role he assigns to men, that of historical agency rooted in a naturalised and dominant masculinity that is singular and universal. In overtly theorising women, Engels covertly theorises men. In exploring female victimisation, he shifts from gender to class as an explanation, once he crosses the boundary between the historical and modern worlds. This is a deeply masculinised explanatory strategy, precisely because it removes men from political scrutiny. What they do is either 'natural' in a simplistically 'Darwinian' pastiche, and cannot be helped, or it is an effect of a dominant class, rather than a dominant gender order, which benefits men *as men*. Engels thus reinscribes masculinism within an apparently feminist, or seemingly feminist-friendly, theory of history.

In my Conclusion, I review what I think has been achieved, but readers may beg to differ!

Notes

1 John Plamenatz, *Man and Society: a critical examination of some important social and political theories from Machiavelli to Marx*, 2 vols (London: Longman, 1963), rev. edn, 3 vols, ed. M.E. Plamenatz and Robert Wokler (London: Longman, 1992).

CHAPTER ONE

Plato: men/women and order/disorder in *The Republic*

Dialogues and investigations

Any reader of *The Republic* is confronted with formidable challenges. It was written almost 2400 years ago, and the structure and content seem hard to grasp.[1] It is unclear to us now why any philosopher would have chosen a dialogue structure in order to expound views on justice, rulership and the good society. Surely 'the message' could emerge much more simply and directly? In any case there is quite a large imaginative exercise involved in developing a personal engagement with concepts and contexts that seem remote, even opaque. Moreover much of the 'contextual evidence' cited by modern commentators and critics is necessarily literary, and this raises large problems to do with representation in a genre, and everyday social experience. Or to put it simply, literature is not by definition or very often in practice a way of mirroring 'reality'. For most readers these difficulties are compounded by translation, in that any modern language, say English, must either make some sense but sound anachronistic, or sound archaic but miss out on intelligibility.

Then there are the unknown accidents and scholarly problems connected with the transmission and establishment of the text in classical Greek. The text was constructed, of course, from copies of copies of copies of … what? We do not actually know. Moreover there are serious difficulties not so much about authorship as about 'authorial voice'. While there is a biographical tradition, at least, about Plato, and about his mentor and teacher Socrates, the attribution of an authorial voice to Plato in the text itself is made unusually tiresome by the text itself.

Socrates as a character in the dialogues features as a gadfly, just about as annoying to his readers in the present as to his interlocutors in the dialogues. Among other things, this authorial tactic rather reverses the usual presumption that teachers influence students. As the Platonic dialogues are almost our only source of information about the views of Socrates the philosopher, perhaps this is a case of a pupil creating the teacher as the kind of influence he really wanted – a 'true' Socrates, better than the original. Or perhaps not. Maybe Plato was portraying the Socrates he knew with all the accuracy he could muster. Possibly he was portraying a Socrates whom no one else would recognise as such, and one that he knew was false – but more useful or entertaining than the original. Notoriously we have no idea whether Plato is reproducing what he learned from Socrates by creating a character 'Socrates' who speaks a quirky philosophy, or conversely whether Plato is inventing a philosophy for someone who conveniently left, and was evidently known to leave, no other textual traces. There are certainly scholarly theories on this subject, and it may be that Plato was doing some (or all) of these things in the different works we have, and possibly his focus was different at different times. We don't know for sure.

Finding the philosophy in *The Republic* is no easy task anyway. The dialogue form makes finding Plato's authentic 'view' about as likely as finding Shakespeare's politics in the history plays, his ethics in the problem comedies, and his sexuality in the *Sonnets*. What is the status of Socrates and the rest of the cast of characters, anyway? There are some historical suggestions that the characters are real people, or rather that there were real people who are characterised by Plato in the dialogues. Were Plato's readers thus to be confronted with a docu-drama or re-enactment? If so, why? Surely any verbatim account of friendly bandinage is a long way round to a philosophical thesis. Or were Plato's characterisations aimed back at the real people as barbed comment, as a kind of satire or poison-pen? Or were they projected forward, as it were, towards engaging his readers with lifelike personalities on the page? (Were they even aimed at readers? or instead at listeners?) Either way, as a satirist or as a dramaturge, did Plato do a good job? Most people would say so. But have they always asked themselves exactly what *they themselves think* he was doing?

Whatever the status of the characters and strategy of the author (was Plato a gifted amanuensis? a Stoppard-like playwright?), the dialogues do seem to tell us something. The tradition of commentary began with Aristotle (Plato is extensively reviewed and critiqued in *The Politics*[2]). Yet in *The Republic* views are argued, points made, questions resolved, discussions concluded and topics advanced, so there is perhaps somewhat more point in trying to discern a 'message' than the Shakespeare analogy suggests. However, some of the banter in the dialogues could well be ironic in an important way, as John Seery has argued, in that one 'message' might be that reading will only go so far, and hearing 'messages' only do so much.[3] There may be an authorial strategy here that was intended to impel readers towards judgement and action. Following that view further, we might begin to see the Platonic dialogues as more political intervention than as classical entertainment. That interpretive strategy might get us closer to what was really going on in Athens of the late fourth century BC. But we will never know. Indeed opinion at the time could well have been mixed or contradictory on quite fundamental points.

Those who find such a deconstructive and sceptical line on *The Republic* extravagant and anachronistic might well ask themselves, then, what they think the dialogues were actually supposed to be in the first place? Down through the ages there is no doubt that the Platonic corpus was treasured as great philosophy and lively literature, lacking perhaps the majestic and reverberant dramaturgy of the great Greek tragedies. Everyone agrees, though, that the dialogues rate more highly than the plays on engagement with recognisable issues, especially those to do with the way that language can be wrapped into abstractions and worked into generalisations. The great tragedies, while eminently powerful on the stage even today, have an enigmatic quality that seems quite beyond recovery. They do not mirror modern conceptions of religion, religious belief and religious practice, in ways that we readily understand, nor are they historic or domestic or psychological in ways developed in dramatic writing since the Renaissance that we find reasonably familiar. Possibly they are more 'civic' than any of our more individualised aesthetic categories suggest. In other words, while exciting and powerful, they are decidedly distant and 'other', and the Greek comedies are even more so.[4] Perhaps if we really understood the jokes in Aristophanes' *The Clouds*, which is self-evidently a satire on the philosophers and philosophies that Plato knew, we would really know quite a lot more about *The Republic*, and why it is cast in dialogue form. Humour, however, is super-subtle and context-dependent, does not travel well through the ages, and is possibly much more 'knowing' and difficult than philosophy, anyway.

Today we make imaginative efforts to contextualise the great Greek tragedies (and occasionally the comedies) and to develop some hazy ideas about how and why they were staged, and what they could conceivably have meant as cultural productions to their contemporary public. Yet for the Platonic dialogues as cultural productions there is no comparable tradition and no effective theorisation. Was the dialogue a common form of writing? of recitation? of circulation? Were there other similar efforts? We have some fragments and possibles, but not much to go on. Or were Plato's works a one-off? eccentric? disturbing? annoying? Were they deadly serious? tongue-in-cheek? satirical? flippant? ironic? The initial answer is bound to be 'probably all of these things', but that then begs the question as to the content of the form: why were all of those things crammed into such a startling succession of ever-provocative and sublimely rewarding masterpieces? Who was the reading (or listening?) public, and what were their reactions? Probably it is just as well that we have no idea, though with the recent archaeological identification in Athens of what is said to have been Plato's Academy, this blissful ignorance may yet be challenged with some Globe Theatre-like reconstructions and 'Plato-in-Love' style film scripts for *The Symposium* (with everyone involved safely over the age of consent).

This may seem an unusually and hermeneutically circuitous route to another reading of *The Republic*, yet I hope the reader will now be alerted to my view that important interpretive principles are at stake. These are really crucial to any credible discussion of a text-in-context. Both text and context are scholarly constructions involving choice and judgement, and in that way both text and context inevitably mirror the scholarship involved, perhaps more than they really mirror 'how things were at the time'. Even then, whose reality was it? No one really wants to claim that 'the Greeks' had no concepts or practices relating to class, race/origin and gender – far from it, given what scholars and readers can quite reasonably infer from the contemporary histories, inscriptions and documents available. While 'Greek society' (or rather too often an 'Athens' writ large) is taken rather smugly by modern commentators to be divided and inegalitarian, the 'man in the agora' that commentators employ as Plato's assumed audience is always an elite figure, rather like the people behind the voices in the textual dialogues with Socrates. Yet these were not the only subject-positions available in Athenian society in Plato's time, and we know this, not least from the dialogues themselves, where other kinds of people are mentioned (though not given direct speech). Plato as author could no more determine who his audience was, and what exactly they made of his productions, than authors of our own day and age. My point here is that commentary on Plato draws its notions of context from a particular way of reading his texts, a way that makes assumptions about authorship and readership that are simplifying rather than challenging, closing down on interpretation rather than opening it up. Even simpler are the 'Plato for Beginners' type of popularisation, and 'Let's start with the Greeks' accounts of 'western civilisation' that feature in undergraduate teaching and TV overviews. It surprises me how much of this view is taken as read (as it literally is in college survey courses) when commentators examine Plato as a political theorist on the assumption that 'his ideas' are still of interest. Something between *Shakespeare in Love* and *Amadeus* would at least clear the air (and make us laugh, itself an excellent aid to learning).

When it comes to telling us 'what Plato said in *The Republic*', too much commentary has simply proceeded by quotation from the printed page without sufficient attention to what those words were doing in dialogical terms within the ebb and flow of argument and conversation, and indeed within the terms through which the characters as dramatic entities are constructed. In brief, it matters in *The Republic* who says what to whom – all the time. Sometimes it seems as if commentators are taking the characters seriously; certainly commentators turn their attention carefully to what each character says, and to how Socrates knocks it down. However, there is little else in this line of analysis, as traditionally pursued, than seeing the characters as themselves mouthpieces for philosophical ideas – rival philosophies to the one that is presumed to lie there waiting for us in *The Republic*. Surely the author wants us to have this 'great philosophy', and that is the point of the text! If we were certain that Socrates really was Plato, and that Plato really intended to use him to sum up – to stand and deliver the 'message' – then perhaps all would be well. But we can't, Socrates doesn't, and Plato won't. *Plato is not actually in the text at all!* In the text, dialogue gives way to something more like monologue, as Socrates does what his audience has challenged him to do, that is, say what he thinks. While he comes to function like a narrator, and appears in the (dramatic) text as a narrator (to an audience), he is still himself, and only by (wilful) deduction, 'the author'. Compared with almost any other work of philosophy, the authorial voice in the dialogues is deliberately and completely obscured, so there is no sense of a reliable narrator to tell us what is what, philosophically speaking. This is certainly a way of provoking interpretation and goosing lazy readers, or at least it should be.

It would be, if readers did not rely perversely on Socrates as Plato's authorial voice. That they want to do this is an indication of how much they think they need one, and how difficult it is even to begin to cope with a text that does not seem to work that way. Socrates never actually steps out of the dialogue and addresses the reader, something hardly unknown even then as a theatrical device. Nor does he enter sometimes as a kind of messenger with revelatory news from elsewhere or function as a chorus putting some agreed commentary on the situation to the audience – a device rather well sent up in Woody Allen's *Mighty Aphrodite*. In fact Socrates is thoroughly immersed in the dialogue as a kind of drama, whether fiction or reportage, and he never seems to make things easy for the reader. Instead he makes things difficult for the other characters, trying their patience and provoking them (famously, with Thrasymachus) into a rage. How exactly is this philosophy? And what relation does it have to 'the message'? The twists and turns of intellect and emotion in the dialogue tend to make these questions disappear. Should they? Is it just commentators that keep them visible?

After all, it is Socrates who is evidently in charge. Even when he apparently gives in to a polite rebellion (by Glaucon and Adeimantus) against his evident evasions, he merely changes tack. Obviously he is playing on all the other characters' emotions and intelligence (or lack of it), and at times he is saying things that he knows full well will outrage them, because he says as much. At other times he is cajoling them and giving in a little, saying things that will reassure them and get them on-side to hear the rest of the argument. Given that all these things are going on inside the dialogue, and given that Socrates never steps out of character to deliver an author's 'message' reliably (rather like Frankie Howerd mugging to the camera in *Up Pompeii*), it follows that any quotation from Socrates will have to be treated with great attention to the flow of ideas in a characterised context. The other characters in the dialogue are not all the same, nor are they foils to 'the message' in some abstract and stilted way. Rather they are all different in intellectual and emotional terms, and intriguingly they are all participants to differing degrees in a variety of commonplace beliefs, prejudices and views – just like real people!

They would have to be. Otherwise *The Republic* would not be about politics. What Socrates says at any point is not necessarily what he means as such. There is an elaborate language game going on within this imaginatively dramatised dialogue, and there may be no points whatsoever at which some propositional 'meanings' are expressed by Socrates, speaking as a philosopher. Whatever philosophy there is will have to adduced by readers from how – for them – the dialogue has gone, what were the high and low points, the climaxes and conclusions, the padding and 'the message'. Perhaps we are closer here to the 'novel of ideas' (maybe *The Magic Mountain* or *Lord of the Flies*), provoking thought and action, than to Shakespearian theatrical poetry. What do such heavy-weight authors tell us? What do their novels say?

On the one hand we seem happy with an infinite number of critical studies telling us different things about such works, and so we go on asking the questions; on the other hand, authors who give in to temptation and deliver an overarching philosophy and detailed commentary on their fictions tend to lose face because they kill off a productive ambiguity. When Plato delivered *The Laws* and advised Dionysus of Syracuse on how to rule his country, did he do us a service? Is that 'what he was getting at in *The Republic*'? I am resisting the idea that *The Republic* can be simplified into a philosophy and a politics by relying either on Socrates or on Plato's other works and deeds. Those who like things simple will find this perverse. Those who like *The Republic* for itself may find this quite helpful.

Over-arching historical accounts of 'the Greeks', their city-states and 'the Athenians' are well worn, and now, so it is persuasively argued, over-written with the assumptions and aspirations of the historians who constructed them. And in the reverse way most commentators still fall disturbingly into a line of contextualisation that mirrors a view of 'Greek society' that seems to them to emerge in the text itself. This happens when commentators find some degree of agreement in the 'commonsense' and prejudice that the various characters air. That 'commonsense' is then made general and said to represent what was taken for granted by 'the Greeks' at the time. Exactly which characters are gifted with this Everyman role, why those characters and not others speak these obvious (and therefore unnecessary) truths, and why this realm of prejudice counts as unchallenged consensus (in a dialogue, for heaven's sake!) are crucial methodological questions that many commentators find difficult to formulate, never mind answer. It does not take much imagination to see Plato's cast of characters as well-to-do, Greek and male. There is ample evidence from less fictive sources that other kinds of people in Athens thought other things (Thucydides is excellent on this in his highly political *History of the Peloponnesian War*), not all of them complimentary about the sort of characters that Plato recruited to his *dramatis personae*. Rather than confirming such upper-class people in their smugness, *The Republic* exposes them to scrutiny, perhaps in a cunning way. Perhaps they are all narrow in experience and unreliable in speech. Just like us. Perhaps the very security and normality of their situation is the issue?

This is not to say that I am advocating 'doubt everything' and 'believe nothing', but rather that I am appealing for flexibility and imagination in the way that Plato is approached today. Rather like the lion in Wittgenstein's *Philosophical Investigations*, if Plato could speak to us today, we could not understand him.[5] We have no assurance of agreement between him and us in either language or in forms of life. Nonetheless we also have no assurance that he is *entirely* like Wittgenstein's lion and that there are *no* points of contact between his writings and his culture, and all the various cultures today where he is read. We just have to be careful and open about saying what these points of contact might be, and why re-reading (and thus re-writing) *The Republic* is in principle a useful exercise. Rather more disturbingly, perhaps *The Republic* is *even more* like Wittgenstein's *Philosophical Investigations*, that is, written in a unique and puzzling way that makes it difficult for commentators to say just what the philosophy is and to find the reliable narrator to give us the philosophical 'message'.

As explained in the introduction above, the major point of interest in the present volume is the exploration of classic texts in political theory in order to see how men have represented themselves – constructed themselves fictively and abstractly – *as men* in relation to women, and to the other categorial elements (such as race/origin, class and age) from which gender is defined and enforced in society as a system of binary and hierarchical power-relations. Writing within this context I am simply going to take *The Republic* as a text that my readers will encounter in English translation. No doubt there are difficulties in some of these citations with the Greek that the translators found on their pages, in varying editions, and ultimately in differing manuscripts versions, imperfectly retained today from the *scriptoria* of the Dark Ages. Few political theorists involve themselves in that, and in any case it is likely that most of the arguments in a text like *The Republic* have a flow that is not too dependent on whether the odd word in Greek is X or Y. On the other hand, given the intricate subtleties of gender politics, it is probably quite important in many cases whether the odd word *in English* is X or Y. Given that many commentators quote selectively and briefly in aid of the generalisations that constitute their own contribution to 'the literature' and their own aspirations to a political view, it is always helpful to check the text in different translations in order to disturb these rather reductive tendencies. Plato is really too good to be whittled down to what are said to be the prejudices of his sex, class and period; if he were really like that, why would he have written works that draw attention in such a performative way to social and intellectual disruption?

Curiously even those who find Plato at least somewhat on-side for disruption cannot ever seem to conclude that he was really all that radical. Either he was half-hearted, or confused, or on the right track ... but not very far down the line. Most of the time history is said to excuse him – how could he have looked (properly) at class before Marx? at women before Wollstonecraft? and so on. Alternatively he is sometimes said to have made history go the way that it did by influencing (mysteriously) so many influential people with his 'ideas'. The chief suspects here are his views on authority and rulership, truth and creativity, collective requirements and individual choice. Perhaps *The Republic* is a monumental work of hypocrisy, flirting with disruption in a fictive context while attempting to obliterate it forever in reality. Among commentators, the pro-Plato community is not very pro-disruption, and the anti-Plato brigade is overwhelmingly hostile. For Plato's hostile critics, he is said to advocate an unattractive array of baldly stated views, abstracted from speeches in the text made by *characters* in the dialogue. These are then portrayed as a misguided critique of some aspects of 'Greek society' (e.g. philosopher rulers vs 'democracy'), while of course reflecting other aspects of it uncritically (e.g. 'slavery' and chauvinism). For selectively sympathetic critics, Plato is allowed some critical distance from what is taken to be his own 'community of prejudice', though in the right direction (e.g. women's equality). But because the participants in the dialogue are assured by the *character* Socrates, rather ironically, that this radicalism is not so far distant from their commonsensical views about women anyway, this supposedly ultimate authorial 'message' is deemed unsatisfactory, and so the promising aspects of the discussion are then regarded as lost or negated. Somehow the desired critical distance between the presumed authorial Plato and 'Greek society' always collapses, and the radicalism exhibited in *The Republic* gets drained away.[6] This applies just as much to commentators who demonise Plato as anti-democratic as to those who find him pertinent but flawed, such as a small number of feminist writers. Of course it is important to remember that for centuries Plato has been read in this way, and that as 'Plato' he has been influential in reinforcing prejudices of various kinds, or rather that many commentators have made it their aim to regularise his views in this direction by making sure that we always have our 'Plato' constructed in this way. Otherwise he might escape, and who knows what that would mean! I think it is worth freeing *The Republic* from *any* 'Plato', even the real one, as whatever it was in his own time, he did not control it anyway. Perhaps in *The Republic* there are some criticisms of democracy that it would be useful to air? Perhaps we could take these up without worrying that some anti-democratic 'Plato' might be a bad example. It might even be that some of characters in *The Republic* make other interesting points for us to consider. Do they have to be puppets for some 'Plato'? Could they not just *speak to us on their own*?

Besides asking a new question of the text – how does it construct men as men in a gender framework? – I am going to try a new approach. This will involve ducking almost all of the favourite issues that have occupied commentators for many centuries. Those are issues that can only be addressed by finding the authorial voice, and I have argued that in the case of *The Republic*, this is seriously reductive and blatantly philistine. Rather I am going to concentrate on *The Republic* as if it were a play or novel, and engage with the flow of ideas. After all, it is a dialogue, and I do not see why we should not dialogue with it. This will subvert the tendency to find the 'message' and then judge 'the author' on its merits, whether ethical, practical, political or intellectual – as if *The Republic* were a tract for eternity. There are plenty of tracts (for 'the times' and forever) in the political theory canon, but *The Republic*, for my purposes, does not have to be one of them.

Men

Exploring the ways that men and masculinities are represented in *The Republic* is a way of tracing out gender in a representation of social relationships. In itself it is not an exhaustive way, but rather a way into an area of what is today highly political scrutiny and debate. We have not made up our minds about these things, and neither have the characters in the text. The characters in the text are all male, though the way that they are characterised can be read as a writing strategy and potential critique, since after all they are fictive. Are there things about men and masculinity/ies that are displayed in the text as matters of concern? Given the disparate philosophical views of the characters, and their differing temperaments, this is certainly possible, and it may be that gender is introduced as an issue in the text long before the famous disruption concerning women and rulership that occurs very near the middle. Of course, the central and familiar sex binary is introduced early on as an idea – an idea developed by men in the fictive space they occupy while engaging in the dialogues that constitute *The Republic* as a textual construction. Whether this kind of single-sex gathering doing this kind of thing was or was not a general practice in the Athens of Plato's day is not really an issue here. The scenes that make the narrative dramatic are fictive, and they could either reassure readers (or whoever the audience was intended to be) by presenting familiar ground, or those same scenes could jar readers somewhat by presenting an ideal (of some sort) at odds with their experience. Recourse by commentators to vase paintings and to other works of literature merely reproduces the problem. Are those images and texts representations of commonplace realities, presentations of desired ideals, or evocations of mythical or otherwise idealised events? Or something of all three?

The exclusion of women from public life in ancient Athens is well documented, as are other exclusions from citizenship and civil rights based on 'birth' and wealth. Quite how this was played out in terms of everyday experience is somewhat vaguer territory. The women who appear, and *even speak in public contexts*, according to the classical texts that we have, cannot have been an entirely fictional creation! An Athenian Pepys would be useful here, or a Thucydides of everyday life (though there is quite a lot of that in the Thucydides we have left). My point here is that *The Republic* shows every sign of imagination and creativity on the philosophical side. It is not that this imagination and creativity should be projected into some other supposed aspect of the work, such as characterisation or dramaturgy, but rather that what constitutes the philosophy is far too narrowly construed. Many of the remarks that might be thought to constitute scene-setting, character quirks or extraneous events could well have something to tell us in philosophical terms about politics. Anyone who could develop the abstract theory of forms could probably do just as brilliantly with more concrete concepts and issues.

The all-male cast of characters may not, therefore, be an unthinking reflection of Athenian 'normality'; it may be a way of subverting it, or at least holding it up to question. Given that this actually happens with respect to the male/female binary in the text itself, the opening of *The Republic* may well be a build-up to this central episode. The text as we have it begins with a narration, spoken by Socrates to the reader, describing his recent activities and experience; the overall form is that of a memoir with verbatim accounts of conversation, or that of a novel in the (apparently reliable) first person. Certainly *The Republic* proceeds from one point of view, and the reader is encouraged to rely on the narrator. As argued above, though, every remark of the narrator, particularly when recounting his own speeches to other characters, can hardly be regarded as philosophically definitive, that is, a set of propositions reflecting some 'message' that 'the real author' is trying to impart, precisely because the interchanges have an emotionally and intellectually irritating quality that was apparently the point of the whole gathering. However, there is also a further issue of reliability here, in that Socrates, our narrator, is also a character, not a camera. As we get to know him we wonder what his agenda is, particularly since as the text is set up, he seems to drift in our minds away from reporting what other characters say, according to his (presumed) memory, into writing their speeches for us as he tells them what they really meant to say. Hence we as readers come to hear the text, rather than just read it, as the dialogue drifts towards staginess and the one-man theatrical evening. Or so we sometimes suspect. Are we being lulled into uncritical reliance, or alerted to suspicions that we should cultivate?

Perhaps it is worth noting that the opening narration introduces a wide range of character types. 'Woman' appears as goddess, there are 'native inhabitants' (as opposed to foreigners), and overall we are given a context of the leisured class (as opposed to the 'slave boy'). Succeeding passages also introduce some very well-characterised 'hegemonic masculinity'. The Socrates/Glaucon party is begged to wait by the Polemarchus party, whose line of persuasion is that there are more of them and that they are stronger, obdurate, deaf to reason and out for excitement and fun ('a torch race on horseback', 'an all-night festival'). They present themselves as young men, anxious to join up with others, and when they are named, they emerge as a mixed group by origin, residence and citizenship.

No doubt the bullying is somewhat facetious, but then facetious masculinity is no less masculine for that, and no less persuasive in masculinised contexts. The scene shifts abruptly to Polemarchus's home and to a more serious dialogue, in terms of personnel and content. Socrates encourages the aged Cephalus, who recounts how he disagrees with others of his age when they meet to bewail the loss of two other masculine preoccupations, sex (with women) and drink, indeed sensual excess in general. Masculine society is evidently age-divided into separate groups; *The Republic* constructs a mixed group (for a time ... the aged Cephalus does not stay), but Socrates does manage to engineer dialogue across the generations, and seems himself to be conveniently located in the middle, or at some ageless position.[7]

Cephalus's great age introduces a note of seriousness in the judgements and opinions offered, and his wealth introduces a class divide; most people, says Socrates, might say that contentment in old age comes not from good character but from being rich. Moreover Socrates introduces further class-gradations, between those who inherit wealth and those who make it, and the sorts of (masculine) characters engendered by these circumstances. This appears to be a convenient hook into the first try at 'justice', conceived as the terror felt by those who have done unjust deeds that they may, after death, have to pay for their misdeeds in the next world. Cephalus says that the 'greatest good' he enjoys from his wealth is not sensual excitement but assurance that he can make good his debts and obligations to gods and men before being called to judgement. Socrates then famously and teasingly offers his first, reductionist definition of justice ('speaking the truth and giving back what one takes'), Cephalus's son Polemarchus interrupts (another recognisable masculine strategy), and the reader is launched into a rather tedious dialectic of question and answer in which the generalisation is tested by analogy and objection.

Turning this passage inside out, however, reveals a catalogue of masculine occupations and implements, presumed by Socrates to be familiar to his interlocutors. Internal evidence and external conjecture tell us that this is 'a man's world', or rather a world as men see it: doctors, cooks, ships' pilots, soldiers, farmers, shoemakers, business partnerships, draughts players, housebuilders, musicians, horse dealers, wine growers, boxers – concluding in a friends/enemies binary.[8] This is not to say that everything recounted in the dialogical world was done by men exclusively, nor that all men were likely to do these things, nor that the list is even surprising. Rather that the characters' experiential world in *The Republic* is varied (within a gender binary) and far from rarefied. The gendered character of this world is invisible to the characters (there is no overt questioning or suspicion at this stage), and put to the reader so uncontentiously that it is nearly invisible to them, too. In the larger scheme of the book, however, the very familiarity of all this becomes a foil for a contrasting scheme introduced later on.

The opening of *The Republic* not only introduces all the characters and their masculinised world but also reaches the highest point of physical drama in the work. Moving from masculine facetiousness through interruption to terrifying outburst, the characters are hardly such as you would gather together for a quiet philosophical dialogue. As the world is recreated in thought about what is outside the gathering, so it is also recreated within the group of friends. Thrasymachus is restrained by companions who stop him from taking over the argument … until he can bear it no longer; he jumps at them like a wild beast, frightens Socrates and Polemarchus, and contributes to the discussion by shouting scornfully against ironists and proposing a contest with forfeiture as the penalty for the loser. Actually Thrasymachus is the ironist here in that he demands that Socrates come clean – knowing that he won't – in order to benefit everyone. Thrasymachus really wants his superior view to win the 'battle', trouncing his opponent, as competitive masculinities dictate.

After that build-up it cannot be much of a surprise that Thrasymachus's position is that justice is 'simply what is good for the stronger', since that is what he has just performed.[9] It is difficult to get much closer to hegemonic masculinity as we know it than his view that 'might = right'. In the course of the intensely hostile and eventually grudging debate, Socrates tames Thrasymachus; it is also possible that taming the wild beast is not merely personal here, but that Socrates, in silencing Thrasymachus, has also exposed the outer limits of masculinity – behaviour that is aggressive, physical, competitive, zero-sum – and then critiqued it with the kind of tediously scornful and rather juvenile philosophy it deserves.

At this point the dialectic of discussion moves up a notch, in that two of Socrates's interlocutors – the brothers Glaucon and Adeimantus – propose to act as devil's advocates, thus providing Socrates with what he seems to need, a better opponent. The overarching metaphor here moves from something like war to something more like sport; rather than a genuine fight to the death, the antagonism moves to a bounded and fictive opposition undertaken by mutual agreement, everyone living (physically and emotionally), to 'fight again another day'. The text is replete with evocations of supportive brotherhood and virtuous fatherhood, and no one shouts or interrupts.

The pair of brothers develop a fiction-within-a-fiction by producing a twin representation: the man who reaps the material rewards of injustice but – through clever deception – is regarded as just, and so is further rewarded in this world and the next; and the man who is the opposite, eschewing deception and hence losing out materially by being just, as well as suffering further scorn and disadvantage through an undeserved reputation for injustice. Rather similarly the masculinised strategies of the characters, and of the life-strategies that they conjure up, move into a different register. Animal force and physicality are interestingly retained but transmuted – the unjust deceiver uses force if necessary, 'relying on courage and strength', but also mobilises 'friends and wealth'.[10] In a nutshell the argument put to Socrates is that injustice *pays* better than justice, and that deception can be fully successful in this world and the next:

> And to get away with it, we shall form secret clubs and societies, and there are teachers of persuasion to give us the wisdom of the assembly and the lawcourts. With their help we shall sometimes use persuasion, and at other times force, and so come out on top without paying for it.[11]

Conventional moralism is discounted as sour grapes and *ressentiment* on the part of cowards and victims, because they are unable to pursue the deceptive (rather than merely forceful) strategies that produce 'success' in practices that are interchangeably characterised as masculinised and commercial.[12]

Of course what makes greed, deception and self-interest masculinised is not an essentialism that limits these motivations and activities to men, nor a mere reflection of the exclusion of women from this 'mindset' altogether or a disadvantaging of them within it, but rather the mutually constitutive character of deception as a strategy and the feeble hypocrisy of the moralising against it, together with the blatant 'money and sex' view concerning what is ultimately good and worthwhile in life:

> No one could bring himself to keep his hands off other people's possessions, and steer clear of them, if he was free to take whatever he liked without a second thought, in the market-place, or go into people's houses and sleep with anyone he liked; or if he could kill or release from prison anyone he chose, and in general go round acting like a god among men.[13]

What remains to be seen is the gendered character of Socrates's alternative, a defence of the truly just man who persists with justice and abhors deception. Is this a feminised subject-position that centres an alternative structure of non-commercial and unexploitative values? Will it structure a different approach to individuality as played out in material and sexual terms? The answer is a long time appearing, famously because Socrates himself moves the whole subject from an individualistic frame into a much more sociological one, by filling in the way that human societies do and could structure modes of individuality, beginning with storytelling (by mothers) and continuing through various patterns of occupational and intellectual training for differentiated roles within an economic framework.

The opening discussion of common human needs and the mutual advantages obtained through economising on time and labour – given diversity among humans in terms of talents and capacities – follows a pattern familiar to us of apparent gender-neutrality. Seemingly universal needs and diversity in ability are gender-neutral amongst the inhabitants of 'the city', but characteristically in this kind of discussion gender-neutrality is belied when specifically feminine (rather than specifically and overtly masculine) occupations are introduced. Interestingly this happens when Socrates moves – jolted by a scornful comment from his audience – from the 'simple' city of mutual sufficiency to the 'feverish' city of luxury and defensive/ aggressive warfare. Courtesans, stylish women, dressmakers, servants, wet and dry nurses and beauticians suddenly appear, not all necessarily female, of course. But the association between masculinised realms of commercialism (rather than just efficient community production) and feminised realms of subordination, consumption and objectification, is unmistakably drawn.

Perhaps the 'simple' city of family-style inclusivity – 'they and their children feasting together and drinking their wine'[14] – really was gender-neutral with respect to most trades and roles, precisely because masculinised commercialism was not presupposed. Or perhaps it was founded on exclusion and silencing of females from such positions of leadership and advantage as the 'simple' society permitted. As Socrates does not return to this somewhat transitional idyll, we will never know. However, it is worth noting that a sex/gender system, in Socratean terms, arrives on the scene with masculinised surplus production and self-interested commercialised consumption. It may be that Socrates's characterisation of the role of women in such systems is conventional and thoughtless. Or it may be that the text can be read rather more richly as a complex and developmental parable about the mutually constitutive character of unequal gender-relations in society and of states that are founded on commercial production. Dramaturgically it is possible that a considerable amount of careful if not overly challenging discussion makes a good prelude to the sudden clap of thunder concerning gender, for which *The Republic* is indeed famous and ever-problematic. Perhaps there is just a suggestion in the argument as Socrates puts it, and in the dramaturgy that animates *The Republic*, that gender-relations are far more sacred in conventional society than the supposedly sacred issues concerning justice and the 'just man' that his audience feel comfortable engaging in their familiar fraternal setting.

Women

Certainly the 'problem' of gender-relations as they bear on women, in relation to men, is the subject of a dramaturgical build-up in *The Republic*. In considering not the 'simple' and 'healthy' city, but the 'luxurious' and 'feverish' one,[15] Socrates outlines the familiar three-class society, focusing on the education of the 'guardians', some with the military power necessary for policing and security, and some with philosophical skills necessary for ruling and making judgements.

Moving swiftly on, he suggests that:

> If the guardians are well educated, and grow up into men of sound judgment, they will have no difficulty in seeing all this for themselves, plus other things we are saying nothing about – such as taking wives, marriage, and having children. They will see the necessity of making everything as nearly as possible 'shared among friends,' in the words of the proverb.[16]

This provides the occasion for drama in the dialogue, perhaps signifying the importance of the subject to all, and to both sides of the debate, as it were:

> I [Socrates] was about to embark on a systematic account of the way I thought the various categories developed out of one another, when Polemarchus, who was sitting a little bit away from Adeimantus, reached out a hand and took hold of his cloak up at the shoulder. Drawing Adeimantus towards him, he leaned forward and started whispering to him. All we could hear of it was: 'What shall we do? Shall we let it go?'

Adeimantus drags Socrates back, as it were, saying:

> We think you're taking the lazy way out. Short-changing us out of a whole line of thought – and an important one – in the argument, to save yourself the trouble of explaining it. You think that when it comes to women and children you can get away with a casual remark to the effect that friends will hold things in common, as if no one could be in any doubt about this.

Speaking for his brother and friends, Adeimantus comments: 'We think it's of great, indeed crucial, importance for our state whether this is done in the right way or the wrong way' – 'the production of children ... what their practice will be in this regard, and how they will bring the children up once they are born'. Obviously there is a certain conventional conception of 'woman' at work here. Socrates warns that engaging in this discussion will stir up a 'a verbal hornet's [sic] nest' or 'swarm of arguments', something that appeals to his masculinised and conflict-hungry interlocutors.[17]

Teasingly Socrates prolongs the build-up with further (alleged) difficulties concerning his own lack of certainty in what he is going to say, and possible references to other dramas in which the role of women is – for the characters – an issue.[18] Proceeding from the view that guard dogs are familiar, and analogous (enough), Socrates draws a contrast between a sexual division of labour there ('we use the females as weaker and the males as stronger') and a contrasting situation in which female dogs would have to 'stay indoors as though they were incapacitated as a result of bearing and rearing the puppies'. Tellingly, he comments that that would leave the males to do 'the work and have the whole responsibility for the flocks' (evidently these are sheep dogs, or dogs doing similar kinds of work with animals). After that Socrates takes his audience through the mind-bending consequences of educating women for rulership on an equal basis with men, subject to the weaker/stronger (presumed) distinction. In particular he admonishes them not to get stuck on the (apparently) funny and ridiculous aspects of physical training, as practices and normality (and therefore what is considered funny and ridiculous) in this area have shifted within recent Athenian history anyway.[19]

Socrates catches his audience out in a contradiction – they have admitted that female nature (on the guard-dog analogy) is much the same as male, but when asked to acknowledge this, Glaucon demurs, saying that of course female nature is different. Socrates tackles this with a suggestion that long-hairedness might be a criterion for being a shoemaker, which his audience readily admits is ridiculous, and then another (real? hypothetical?) 'skill' example comes up: 'a man and a woman whose souls are skilled in the doctor's art'. The audience admits that these souls have the same nature, and that conversely men in differing occupations do not have the same qualities of 'soul', either (e.g. 'a man doctor and a man carpenter').[20] Anyone with any experience of 'equal opportunities' and anti-discrimination legislation and practice will recognise the litany of 'comparator' jobs and professions, mapping out the criteria of demonstrable functional similarity and unacceptable discriminatory difference with respect to sex, race/ethnicity, religion and other statutory categories. The conclusion proffered by Socrates is very clear. Sexual difference is material to begetting and birthing, and nothing else:

> So if either the male or the female sex is clearly superior when it comes to some skill or occupation, then we shall say this occupation should be assigned to this sex. But if the only difference appears to be that the female bears the children, while the male mounts the female, then we shall say this in no way proves that for our purposes a woman is any different from a man. We shall still think the guardians and their women should follow the same occupations.[21]

The Socratic argument takes a rather strange turn after that. 'Can you think of any human activity', he asks his interlocutors, 'in which the male sex is not superior to the female …?' Glaucon, the male respondent, replies that one class [women] is quite dominated in everything by the other [men]. 'Plenty of individual women', he continues, 'are better at all sorts of things than individual men.' But in general men are the more skilled, so it seems, in all things. Discouraging and disparaging as this argument is for women, Socrates's conclusion is forthright:

> In that case, my friend, none of the activities connected with running a city belongs to a woman because she is a woman, nor to a man because he is a man. Natural attributes are evenly distributed between the two sexes, and a woman is naturally equipped to play her part in all activities just as a man is – though in all of them woman is weaker than man.[22]

In terms of sticking it to the male audience, this is actually quite a strong conclusion. Despite handing them the (apparent) bouquets that men (as a class) are more skilled at everything, and always stronger (as a class) than women (as a class), none the less, maleness in the end is no guarantee of occupational potential or ability (ruling included) nor is physical strength as such ever said to be relevant to how well any ruling job is done, military matters included. The 'woman is weaker than man' is thus somewhat double-edged, if weakness is no particular bar to the exercise of human talent, and so *a fortiori*, strength is no great qualification.

Dramaturgically Socrates's discourse is aimed at males, and highly masculinised ones at that. Following this through, by considering both what he says, and who he is speaking to, the argument reads rather differently from the way that conventional and feminist commentators have handled it. Conventional (male) commentators, of course, have little difficulty with the differential strength discussion, and no real problem with the 'exceptional woman' strategy as the way to keep 'equal opportunities' within the safe realm of tokenism. Feminist (female) commentators rightly complain that 'woman' is treated by Socrates as an object, not a subject, and that the generalisations about female strength and skills are untrue and unreflective, given the gendered history of social institutions and expectations.

My point here is that the Socratic argument says different things, depending on who you think the audience is. Virtually all commentators take the audience to be themselves, and give their reactions accordingly.[23] What I am suggesting is that consideration of the 'dialogue' as drama, given what we know about the characters, puts rather a different light on matters, once we factor in the dominant masculinity in which Socrates's interlocutors have a stake, and the wily way in which he challenges it on *their* home ground. The boys who were out for a good albeit metaphorical punch-up will wake up to find that their masculinist gender-privileging has evaporated, at least logically. This is because, as (male) individuals, they will be scrutinised (in a fictive Socratic community) for their skills *as individuals*, and their presumptions about men as a class will simply not be allowed to figure. Whether their (supposed) class superiority is a fact or an illusion will simply be irrelevant *in the decisions which will matter most to them*. This puts the radicalism back into the 'woman' argument in The Republic, not because it reads contemporary feminism into what Socrates says, but because it reveals the challenge he poses, argumentatively, to masculinist assumptions concerning the class superiority that 'naturally' attaches to males, including presumptions about not just the existence but the *pertinence* of physical strength, *even when defined in their own terms*. It is difficult to imagine a more thorough attack on masculinism, or perforce a more thorough subversion of the gender binary itself.

Of course, I am not saying that this is what The Republic 'says' or what its author wanted us to find in it. Rather this is a re-reading of The Republic in the light of previous commentary, which has proceeded within certain conventions and constraints. Loosening those constraints has made it easier to employ the gender lens in The Republic not just because issues about men and masculinity have been raised, but because taking the dialogic and 'absent author' format seriously has revealed a male and masculinised but mixed community of interest and opinion, indeed of subjectivities that appear to change as the arguments develop. Single-sex communities of gender-interest (and power, or the lack of it) are not an ideal or necessary feature of human existence; but they are certainly entrenched and worth evaluating. All-male and masculinised communities tend to disappear from scrutiny precisely because they have been normalised against absent females and in line with a presumed but false universalism as to what constitutes worthwhile activities (including leisured and scholarly ones) in 'society' as such. Feminist analysis has highlighted the absent women and the false universalities. In so far as the astonishingly prescient process of questioning and analysis portrayed in *The Republic* can be replicated in our own time, *whatever one thinks of any of the opinions proffered by any of the characters*, then that will be all to the good. It will also tend to validate a reading of *The Republic*, and a notion of philosophy itself, as at its best when it stimulates action and change, even though the process (and the text) may be replete with irritation and discomfort. Socrates as the gadfly is a famous image, and perhaps that is all that needs to be said about philosophy in *The Republic*.

Notes

1 I am indebted to George Klosko for his immensely helpful scholarly and very critical engagement with the arguments and details of this chapter.
2 Aristotle, *The Politics*, 1260b 27–1264b 25; trans. Ernest Barker (Oxford: Oxford University Press, 1946, repr. New York: Oxford University Press, 1962; hereafter 'Barker'), pp. 39–56; cf. trans. Jonathan Barnes, ed. Stephen Everson (Cambridge: Cambridge University Press, 1988; hereafter 'Everson'), pp. 20–9; and many other references.
3 This approach is outlined in John Evan Seery, *Political Returns: irony in politics and theory, from Plato to the antinuclear movement* (Boulder, CO: Westview, 1990).
4 For an excellent study that takes up this kind of question, see Sara Monoson, *Plato's Democratic Entanglements: Athenian politics and the practice of philosophy* (Princeton, NJ: Princeton University Press, 2000).
5 Ludwig Wittgenstein, *Philosophical Investigations*, trans. G.E.M. Anscombe, 2nd edn (Oxford: Blackwell, 1958), 223e.
6 See, for example, Julia Annas, *An Introduction to Plato's Republic* (Oxford: Clarendon Press, 1981), pp. 1–10; Nickolas Pappas, *Routledge Philosophy Guidebook to Plato and the Republic* (New York and London: Routledge, 1995), pp. 3–17; Sean Sayers, *Plato's Republic: an introduction* (Edinburgh: Edinburgh University Press, 1999), pp. 1–4.
7 Plato, *The Republic*, 327a–329e; trans. Tom Griffith, ed. G.R.F. Ferrari (Cambridge: Cambridge University Press, 2000; hereafter 'Ferrari', from which quotations are taken), pp. 1–4; cf. trans. and ed. Robin Waterfield (Oxford: Oxford University Press, 1993; hereafter 'Waterfield'), pp. 3–6.

8   Plato, *The Republic*, 330d–336a; Ferrari, pp. 4–13; cf. Waterfield, pp. 7–15.
9   Plato, *The Republic*, 336b–338c; Ferrari, pp. 13–15; cf. Waterfield, pp. 16–19.
10 Plato, *The Republic*, 361b; Ferrari, p. 41; cf. Waterfield, pp. 48–9.
11 Plato, *The Republic*, 365d; Ferrari, p. 46; cf. Waterfield, p. 53.
12 Plato, *The Republic*, 366d; Ferrari, p. 47; cf. Waterfield, pp. 54–5.
13 Plato, *The Republic*, 360c; Ferrari, p. 40; cf. Waterfield, pp. 47–8.
14 Plato, *The Republic*, 372b; Ferrari, pp. 54–5; cf. Waterfield, p. 63.
15 Plato, *The Republic*, 372e; Ferrari, p. 55; cf. Waterfield, pp. 63–4.
16 Plato, *The Republic*, 423e; Ferrari, p. 116; cf. Waterfield, p. 159: '…where wives and children are concerned, "friends share"'.
17 Plato, *The Republic*, 449b–d, 450a–c; Ferrari, pp. 144–5; cf. Waterfield, p. 159–60: '… their approach to procreation, and to discuss the whole issue of the sharing of wives and children …'
18 Plato, *The Republic*, 451a–c; Ferrari, pp. 146–7; cf. Waterfield, pp. 161–2; the references are possibly to Aristophanes, Ecclesiazusae, or perhaps Lysistrata. Issues, perhaps even movements, to do with the emancipation of women and the fundamentals of communal and private property, were evidently intelligible to the Athenian public.
19 Plato, *The Republic*, 451d–453a; Ferrari, pp. 147–9; cf. Waterfield, pp. 162–4.
20 Plato, *The Republic*, 454b–454d; Ferrari, pp. 149–51; cf. Waterfield, pp. 164–6: 'a man with a medical mind and a woman with a medical mind'.
21 Plato, *The Republic*, 454e; Ferrari, p. 151; cf. Waterfield, p. 166.
22 Plato, *The Republic*, 455c–e; Ferrari, p. 152; cf. Waterfield, pp. 167–8; note also that Socrates applies the principle of non-discrimination to childcare 'officials', who could be 'men or women, or men and women, since offices, I take it, are open to women and men alike [emphasis in original]'; 460 b; Ferrari, p. 158, cf. Waterfield, p. 174; '… they [officials] could be men, women, or some of each, since positions of authority are open to both men and women equally, of course …'
23 Annas, *Introduction to Plato's Republic*, pp. 181–5; Pappas, *Guidebook to Plato and the Republic*, pp. 101–6; Sayers, *Plato's Republic*, pp. 82–92. Of the three, only Sayers really allows Socrates something of the radicalism of the argument with respect to the position of women, though not with respect to the assault on masculinist views that privilege men as a class.

CHAPTER TWO

Aristotle: men, masculinities and metaphors

Observation, knowledge, judgement

Aristotle is known as the founder of political science, the proto-scientific 'observer' who noted what he saw, collected his evidence, made his judgements and contributed to knowledge. What he contributed, of course, was subject to revision by further observation and reasoning, though it was also venerated through the ages and used conservatively to keep knowledge within familiar bounds.[1] Moreover his analytical-developmental method announced the importance of having a method in observation and in presentation. This was a rather more rigorous and thorough-going affair than the rarefied 'dialectic' propounded by the character 'Socrates' in *The Republic*. Aristotle's method was linked to sensory observation, rather than to the abstract ratiocination favoured in Plato's famous dialogue. The Platonic 'dialectic' was related rather unspecifically to mathematics and logic, but clearly the more removed from sensory observation, the better, as Socrates developed the idea in the famous theory of 'forms'.[2] That realm of ultimate perfection and value, as he explained, was accessible only to philosophers who had been trained for it intellectually, and also emotionally, giving up sensory experiences and the (supposedly) mundane preoccupations of physical and social life, in order to pursue timeless truths. Those truths were in themselves not knowledge, but rather the logical and sole basis from which knowledge itself could arise. The more related this was to the physical world, the less timeless and universal this knowledge would be, and therefore the more imperfect.

Aristotle's preoccupations and methods were stated in *The Politics* to be the other way round, and were advertised by him as such, in direct and competitive contrast. Given Aristotle's emphasis on the physical world, and on a logic that seemed to arise from observation itself, his has been the more popular 'natural philosophy', not least because it seems more real-world and more practical. This is not to say that there was ever that much practicality in Aristotle, but rather that his thought concerned itself with familiar institutions and at least sounded 'practical', rather than abstractly logical, recondite, theoretical and hermetic. Compared with the overt radicality of *The Republic* (a critical task that Aristotle himself undertook[3]), his *Politics* was much more conservative in validating what he portrayed as peculiarly Athenian (and sometimes generally Greek) institutions and practice. Obviously there is a certain ideological drift here, in that the narrative mode in *The Politics* predictably favoured an idealisation of what were said to be Athenian and other Greek institutions and practices, always set against an 'other'.

The Republic, by contrast, has a ruthlessly critical thrust, starting at first principles of a very abstract kind, certainly not marked as Athenian or Greek (or otherwise), but as generically human. The dialogical reasoning then takes its course, mostly on the basis of personal experiences drawn from the interlocutors, rather than from any (supposed) collective wisdom of community tradition that is specifically Athenian or even Greek. Indeed the old saws of collective wisdom in Athens, and the Greek poets who purveyed them, come in for considerable Socratic scorn and derision. It is interesting to enquire, then, why most readings of *The Republic* through the ages still react to its Socratic content in much the same emotional and intellectual way as Aristotle did in his reading: the thinking is too generic, too abstracted, too radical, too impractical ... compared with the people and institutions that the reader is already familiar with. While apparently generic and transferable, *The Republic* is therefore read as abstractly 'nowhere' and populated by unrecognisable 'nobodies' – a utopia. Curiously, readers have been more willing to make a transfer of ideas and practices to their own worlds from what was for Aristotle, as he viewed and idealised it, local, Greek and unreproducible elsewhere.

Why should this be? The answer lies in the combination of a transferable method, indeed transferable to anything and everything, and the power of idealisation. This power of Aristotle's idealisations resides in the notion that knowledge has the form of hierarchies, and that these hierarchies are themselves the elements of judgements that 'naturally' follow from the knowledge that 'observation' establishes. Whether one refers to this as 'natural philosophy' or as 'science' matters less than the general outline of how nature and 'the natural' are constructed as propositions of knowledge, arranged in hierarchies that give rise to inescapable truths, from which good judgement cannot be separated (without violence to reason). Moreover there has been, down through the ages, considerable overlap in the content of Aristotle's idealisations about society and the kind of idealisations that have appealed to his readers. The Athenian ideal of citizenship (as presented by Aristotle) – the famous 'sharing in ruling and being ruled'[4] – is an example. It is apparently remote from the philosopher kings of *The Republic*; it is presented as a practical and functioning institution; and it is presented as naturally male (unlike the notorious introduction of women into the 'guardian' class – and indeed into all other classes in principle – by Socrates in *The Republic*).[5]

This male-ideal, and ideal-for-males, appealed to readers of a certain type, anxious to maintain the male position in the social hierarchy, and anxious to maintain the hegemonic position of some males within the masculine side of the gender binary. Indeed many male readers made practical use of Aristotle's *Politics* in constructing hegemonic masculinities in their own societies that would (allegedly) confirm, recreate and update the ideal masculinity that Aristotle had declared to be natural, and to be natural to rulers. Liberal arts education, civil services and commercial organisations have all, somewhat in the past now, had overt programmes of self-creation for (young) men, based on presumptions of male talents and capacities easily linked to Aristotle's discussion of the elements of the *polis*, and the distinctions that 'nature' makes amongst its constituent 'elements'. Most influentially, this was the contrast that Aristotle drew between his 'citizen' class, and its 'others' – slaves, barbarians, females, children, tradespeople – boundary lines of politicised difference.

Quite how much sharing in ruling and being ruled was meant to be operative in any of these reincarnated male ruling hierarchies is a rather different and further question. Aristotle himself carefully outlined the differences between being in the ruler mode, and in the ruled.[6] While it is possible to project Aristotelian ideals beyond the gender binary (or other binaries, e.g. race/ethnicity) that he himself envisaged, and thus to democratise the 'citizen' ideal and make it (somewhat more) inclusive, this has none the less been a difficult project, though one that has gathered considerable speed in the last 100 to 250 years or so. The difficulty is in establishing where the new boundaries are, and why they are there, even if one rejects some or most of the boundaries that Aristotle himself so painstakingly attempted to draw and so patiently tried to persuade us are 'natural'.

The Republic, of course, offered a number of notorious boundary lines (viz. the gold/silver/iron three-class society).[7] Moreover it offered a theory of genetic inheritance that rather oddly attracts more opprobrium from readers today than it did in Aristotle's time. The instability in genetic inheritance, as explained by Socrates, is rather closer to current views than Aristotle's 'natural' fixities by birth, yet *The Republic* is generally treated as a notorious example of genetic determinism. Aristotle's naturalism and determinism, though admitted by him to be unrealised in actuality in certain instances (e.g. the physical and even intellectual character of slaves as opposed to rulers[8]), is rather more easily and quickly dismissed, precisely because that dismissal in itself does not spur us to examine our own views and confusions on the subject. Dismissal is easy because Aristotle's views are so different from ours, and so we feel affirmed; the common reaction to Socrates on this subject is demonisation, because that displaces our critical attention from where it should really be, exploring difficulties that we would generally rather not face.

Socrates in *The Republic* suggests that some talents and capacities are inherited, indeed fairly predictably so, and that these provide a fit between people and occupations in society. This happens in roughly the trades/military/ruling triad.[9] The prime political goal that drives Socrates in *The Republic*, as I see it, is to de-link commercial wealth from both the military and ruling 'classes', precisely through the peculiar 'non-family' communism and equalised poverty of the guardians (who do not own property!). Indeed corruption comes when guardians begin to own property, and to hoard advantages for the children that they come (against the original practice) to know are their own.[10] However, all the occupational matching that occurs between person and job, at whatever level, is managed *individually*, according to what has been inherited, and that, according to Socrates, is on occasion *un*predictable.[11] While the apparent genetic determinism and proto-eugenic legislation of *The Republic* excites considerable loathing today, the principle of unpredictability in inherited talents and capacities is methodologically intriguing, precisely because it displaces boundary lines from bodily visibility into a realm of highly individualised talents and capacities that has, somehow, to be revealed. *The Republic* does not explain exactly how this works in practice, but in terms of ensuring efficiency and functionality, it makes a certain amount of sense in present-day terms, where the thrust of anti-discrimination legislation today is to turn attention away from visible 'markers' of (supposed) suitability (such as sex and race/ethnicity), back to other more individualised qualifications, tests and criteria for suitability. Because we expect to award some things to some people and not others, we discriminate, but within bounds that (for us) determine its 'justness'.

Individual choice is not highly valued by Socrates in *The Republic*, it is true, and from current liberal perspectives this is a crippling fault. However, I have developed a certain contrast between Socrates in *The Republic* and Aristotle's views in his *Politics* that will help disturb rather complacent readings that see the earlier work as utterly remote both from Athenian ideals (as idealised in Aristotle and elsewhere) and from our own. The situation is considerably more complex, and my point here in relation to Aristotle's method and to his institutional idealisations (which presumably had some political value for him and others) is that – unlike the talent-matching in *The Republic* – his science of politics does not operate at an important level of individualisation that was available to him, and now makes some sense to us. Aristotle's preoccupation with determining the relevant boundaries through which society is created, and through which it is preserved, operates at a rather different level of generality, legislating categories into which individuals are said to fit in virtue of their 'nature'. A close look at this will generate some interesting questions for us in critically considering what boundary lines we instantiate, how we determine who and what lie within them, and where indeterminacy, renegotiation and migration *across* those lines is permissible.

Vision, science and boundaries

Aristotle is a great visionary. It is wonderful what his observation shows him. In present-day terms, this hardly disqualifies him as a scientist, given the emphasis – since Thomas Kuhn's work – on imagination, creativity and revolution in the history of science. Kuhn's account famously balances the normalisation of a scientific 'paradigm' against 'shifts' that occur, often beginning in maverick and (apparently) nonsensical re-conceptualisations that challenge established frameworks. The 'other' to this Kuhnian outlook on the structure of scientific revolutions is a more traditional view that emphasises evidential and factual challenges to established frameworks, within an overall norm in science that welcomes such 'tests' for 'falsity'. Challengingly Kuhn focuses on conservatism within the scientific community, rallying round existing theories and concepts to protect them, and most importantly defending established notions as to what did, and did not, could and could not, constitute evidence against an existing scientific theory and its associated practices of puzzle-solving.[12] On a Kuhnian view, centuries of 'normal science' had been established within an Aristotelian framework, which was no criticism of Aristotle, rather the reverse. My point here is that in common with other great scientists, Aristotle articulated a framework within which observation, evidence and knowledge were codified to a necessary and functional degree, and that despite Aristotle's own claims, and the (supposed) literalness and practicality of his language, his framework was essentially, and necessarily, a vision.

That vision has a certain kind of structure to it, traceable through its organisational terms. It has certain processes represented within it that licence judgements of different kinds. And it also generates certain kinds of problems and contradictions, which Aristotle himself acknowledged and attempted (somewhat unsatisfactorily) to resolve. Parts of this vision, and elements of the reasoning that it encourages, sound familiar to us, and have an appeal. Parts do not, though obviously this varies with the readership. My project here is to make Aristotle's work in *The Politics* deliberately remote and to present it as a unity (which doubtless it does not achieve as resolutely as my reconstruction will suggest). This will then represent a challenge to our own visions of the world as we like to see it, and a way of capturing the visionary quality of our own assumptions and judgements. Calling our visions 'liberal' or 'scientific' restates rather than resolves the issue. The issue is how we distribute the metaphors of valued and gendered existence to create classes of humans, animals and things. This happens not only through exclusive identifications and boundary drawing but also through *comparative* ascriptions of similarity and difference. These work by projecting constituent metaphors *across* the boundaries that have already been discursively declared.

Aristotle's vision may seem more moralised than ours, and even religious in form, as it unfolds. I suggest that this is misleading, and that our own redistributions of metaphors like his, and our collective establishment of 'classes' in terms of valued and gendered existence, are in effect just as judgemental and prejudicial, despite our supposedly secular and universalised moralities. The difference now is that we have access to numerous debates over all these very issues, and competitive ascriptions of metaphorical similarities and differences that cause us – sometimes – to question the boundary lines that give our world its apparent stability. Aristotle's *Politics* itself tracks a number of debates that were current in his time, such as views contrary to his own on the naturalness of slavery and the equality of women. Those points in the text have been consistently under-valued in commentary, which tends to promote Aristotle as the reliable 'Athenian citizen' – though as a Macedonian alien, he was neither. It is apparent from Aristotle's account that others of his time and in his community had quite different views on, e.g. slavery and women. What we do not have from his text, or any others to a significant extent (*The Republic* being an important exception), is much rehearsal of what those other 'visions' actually were. While Aristotle reviews ideal and existing states with considerable critical acumen, we know where he is coming from and where he expects to go in his criticisms. What we do not have very much of is the other voices in the debates within which Aristotle was reacting. This line of argument suggests that we need to pull Aristotle's 'vision' firmly back towards Aristotle himself, however convenient it might be to let it stand for some larger, consensus view in Athens or in 'Greece' generally. It seems unlikely that no one at all shared it with him, but we are also entitled to be sceptical, working from the text of *The Politics* itself, of the presumption that Aristotle has accurately articulated a received opinion that is uncontentious, even among the class of hegemonic males whose interests he was patently promoting.

The working metaphors in Aristotle's vision emerge in *The Politics* as he discusses the *polis*. These are a presumption that everything has an end or *telos*, a best state to which it is tending, or which if attained marks its completion or perfection. This is really a way of inscribing functionality and purpose into the world, and of creating a hierarchy of best (and lesser) states of existence. Perfection is a powerful notion linked to goodness, itself a moralised notion ascribed to human action. How differing views of the good can be reconciled and regularised within the human community is, in a sense, the problem of the book. Nature is frequently invoked as the metaphorical regulator of human opinion, if only one can read what it says, understand what it does, and follow what it stipulates. There are vast problems of interpretation here (never mind philosophical issues), but what counts for me in sketching Aristotle's over-arching vision – as a vision – is his recourse to these metaphors for his more detailed judgements. A further important metaphor invoked by Aristotle is that of ruling, and indeed of the link between goodness and perfection, on the one hand, and a right to rule, on the other. Aristotle's vision is of developmental entities, emerging hierarchies, ruling entities, necessary subordination, perfection in form and goodness in completion. The challenge is to see what commonplace ideas and experiences, mentioned in the text, inspired the metaphorical discourses that drive the judgements in Aristotle's work, and to note carefully the patterns through which these metaphors are deployed, both to create boundary lines, and to distribute similarity and difference across them.

One of Aristotle's opening observations is that 'all men do all their acts with a view to achieving something which is, in their view, a good'.[13] This is not a very promising start, given that the passage itself references the notion that different 'men' have different views. There is thus not much uniformity, nor certainty involved in taking this as a reference point, given obvious presumptions (confirmed throughout the text) of human individuality and waywardness. In looking for a 'systematic view' (of the *polis*, its constituents, their relationships and its point of perfection), Aristotle unsurprisingly turns to a frame of reference that he construes as more stable, less subject to the vagaries of individual opinion, more universal and utterly unchangeable – 'things in the process of their growth':

> First of all, there must necessarily be a union or pairing of those who cannot exist without one another. Male and female must unite for the reproduction of the species – not from deliberate intention, but from natural impulse, which exists in animals generally as it also exists in plants, to leave behind them something of the same nature as themselves.[14]

This passage locates the dominant tropes of certainty in the universal ('animals' and 'plants'), in unintentional actions, in non-existence as un-unified parts of a whole, in an 'impulse' in individuals within a species to reproduce, and therefore to 'leave behind … something of the same nature'. Observation today tells us quite different things about plants and animals that make this picture far more ambiguous. The life/non-life and plant/animal boundary lines are now far from secure, and have in scientific terms impeded as well as facilitated research that scientists have valued. Also we know that reproduction is not necessarily sexual, and even when it is, it does not have to involve any 'union' of male and female. None the less current controversies over human reproductive technologies, bio-medical technologies involving human tissues associated with reproduction, animal reproductive and bio-medical technologies and genetic modification (wherever there are genes), have produced an explosion of arguments, legislation and policies. Some of the views and reasoning involved are not far removed, oftentimes, from Aristotle's 'observations'.[15]

In some cases this is because the religious or philosophical views involved are specifically derived from Aristotle in the first place. In others, it is because those involved are following a similar strategy of attempting to find certainty in a vision of universality, regularity and necessity mapped onto the world of animals and plants. In all these instances, the strategy is to deploy metaphors, as Aristotle did, to provide a foundation for judgement. For those metaphors to be intelligible to us, they must reflect features of our (idealised) world. It follows that those ascriptions of process and certainty to worlds outside the human are themselves always and already anthropomorphic. They are projections of what someone wants the world *to say* into the language of (apparent) description that in turn licences (the only) 'reasonable' judgements.[16] 'Plants' and 'animals' are thus made to tell us about universality, regularity and necessity, for our own good.

Aristotle is a particularly vivid example of this, and therefore helpful in depicting the general practice, because he incorporates such a consistent variety of metaphors into his 'mobile army',[17] and because he uses it to fight so many battles that his readers today have (rather shallowly) thought were won, or nearly so, in his own time. Those battles are famously the ones to do with slavery, women, barbarians (non-Greeks), tradespeople and 'citizens', or those who 'share in ruling and being ruled'. His vision is not only anthropomorphic but androcentric, and this is also revealing. To what extent are our visions of the human community, in its orderly, functional hierarchies of 'ruling and being ruled', similarly androcentric, that is, privileging of males (in some categories) and masculinities (in some conceptions)? And to what extent are these similarly founded on anthropomorphic inscriptions of certainty into 'nature'?

Distinctions and valuations

Turning from an 'impulse' to leave something behind (through reproduction), Aristotle directs his attention to 'preservation' in a unity, though one that is conceived rather differently. Male and female had come together, so he said, from 'natural impulse', an apparently egalitarian storyline tracking a unity between equals, or so it would seem, not least because the males and females involved seem to be animals and plants, rather than humans. In Aristotle's discussion, humans seem to require hierarchical relationships (that animals and plants do not, so it appears); he seems disinclined to argue here that male (non-human) animals are superior to, or rulers over, female ones in some sense. What happens in Aristotle's analysis of the *polis* is that he creates, in the beginning, a political anthropomorphisation of the human animal as *animal*, different from other animals, because of language:

> The reason why man is a being meant for political association, in a higher degree than bees or other gregarious animals can ever associate, is evident. Nature, according to our theory, makes nothing in vain; and man alone of the animals is furnished with the faculty of language.[18]

Ruling is associated by Aristotle with 'intelligence' and being ruled with 'bodily power': 'The element which is able … to exercise forethought, is naturally a ruling and master, element; the element which is able … to do what the other element plans, is a ruled element.'[19] Certainty about this is again located in 'nature', though in an ascription of functional purpose and economy of effort (rather than to any impulse-driven, unconscious processes in 'natural' creatures as such). Nature is anthropomorphised this time as a master toolmaker:

> Nature makes nothing in a spirit of stint, as smiths do when they make the Delphic knife to serve a number of purposes; she makes each separate thing for a separate end; and she does so because each instrument has the finest finish when it serves a single purpose and not a variety of purposes.[20]

Aristotle's 'nature' is invoked to provide certainty, and certainty is conceptualised variously as a purely physical process of plant reproduction; as an instinctual and therefore non-volitional process of animal reproduction; and as a skilled and intelligent human process of craftsmanship – all things on which one can rely as a matter of observational certainty, so it would seem. By naturalising those processes Aristotle renders them 'certain', and by rendering them 'certain', he naturalises them within the human social context. This makes them fixed points of meaning in any argument by analogy, and by extension in their practical incarnations as activities within the human community. Moral injunctions to leave 'natural' reproduction alone, and to value craftsman-like processes for their own sake, reflect this process of argument by metaphor that works both ways, however one fills in the categories. One finds the 'certainty' and naturalises it, because it is certain; where one found that certainty, is then 'natural', and so valued and respected as such.

Aristotle's opening enquiry in *The Politics* is to set the record straight about the essential differences in relationships of ruling and being ruled, and he proceeds in a way that provides a methodology of certainty. Having located intelligence as a value in the 'natural' world, and having argued that it is the 'ruling' part in hierarchies necessary for 'preservation', he has set his stage for the identification of those fit to be ruled: slaves, women and barbarians. Moreover this is a strong argument, that those beings are fit solely for that – remember the virtue of specialisation ascribed by Aristotle to the non-Delphic knife. Tracing the processes through which Aristotle's natural rulers are defined and characterised (whether they are ruling over fellow citizens, over wives and women, over slaves, over children and over barbarians) will trace out a concept of *hegemonic* masculinity, in which few men participate. To do that, Aristotle will have to identify to what sort of males this rulership can be ascribed, and in what qualities rulership 'naturally' consists. This will be quite an elaborate process, as there is quite a lot to learn about rulership as a masculine performance. That knowledge will be displayed through metaphorical similarities and dissimilarities between Aristotle's 'alpha-males' and other males who are ruled over, humans of other sorts, animals of various kinds and temperaments, and objects with various artificial and natural properties. The performance of a masculinity is thus a pastiche of metaphors, perilously close in this case to the 'slugs and snails and puppy dog tails' of the rhyme, though rather more targeted on a narrowly conceived group of males, rather than on 'little boys' in general.

Having established a 'natural' hierarchy of ruler over ruled, where the ruled are slaves, females and barbarians, Aristotle assembles his conception of human association in a kit-like way, from the simplest parts. These are male over female, and master over slave, calling this the household or family, and quoting Hesiod: 'First house, and wife, and ox to draw the plough', and then correcting the verse by noting that 'oxen serve the poor in lieu of household slaves'.[21] He also quotes another verse, saying 'Meet it is that barbarous peoples should be governed by the Greeks'. He thus completes his genetic account of (some) human development logically and historically from household to village to larger, monarchical assemblages including colonies. The dividing line between that stage and the *polis* seems to be both historical and qualitative: the *polis* emerges as a different form of association. Rulership in the *polis* is different from that of the monarchical rule of mastership within the household and over households in association as villages. Having attributed universality, regularity and necessity to nature, and then preservation, order and hierarchy in turn, Aristotle continues by ascribing a further value to 'nature': self-sufficiency, which he identifies as good and indeed the best. He thus prepares the way within his concept of nature for an object to fit in and exemplify it, in this case, the *polis* or Greek city-state. Not only does the *polis* represent the growth of the human community from mere existence to a state of self-sufficiency, that condition is itself the perfection of the idea and the process of human association, and the fulfilment of its 'nature'. 'Nature', on Aristotle's anthropomorphised and therefore value-laden account, itself identifies self-sufficiency with 'the best', and therefore naturalises such phenomena as realise this in practice, pre-eminently the *polis*.

It follows from this that some phenomena are 'other' to this judgemental structure, in particular barbarians who attempt or pretend to be heads of household (whereas they are slaves and only fit to obey commands, not to rule). Indeed since there are in barbarian society no 'natural' rulers (with the intelligence to rule), it follows that all are slaves, by nature. Aristotle's 'natural' rulers cannot be barbarians, females or slaves, and at this stage they occupy an implicitly defined category of ruling-class males. Maleness is evidently a necessary but not sufficient condition for rulership in a *polis*, and femaleness and barbarian-ness a conclusive disqualification.

Having attributed regularity, order, hierarchy, perfection and self-sufficiency to 'nature' as an inherent developmental and logical basis of valuation, Aristotle then reflects this back onto the human world as definitive criteria of value that others can find for themselves, if they have the philosophical intelligence to read 'nature' accurately. However, he also notes that 'nature' does not always realise its purposes nor do its work properly, a further anthropomorphisation, albeit one that ascribes to 'nature' qualities in humans that he really does not value.

'The female and the slave are naturally distinguished from one another', Aristotle notes with some firmness. The firmness, however, is located on the female side, which he evidently does not consider worth debating. The impression given is that the only distinction worth arguing over is the slave/free-'man' boundary. This is because at two points in *The Politics* Aristotle informs his readers that some writers (or thinkers) have or have had an opinion contrary to his carefully naturalised boundary lines (and, presumably, to his carefully anthropomorphised conception of 'nature' as well):

> There are others, however, who regard the control of slaves by a master as contrary to nature. In their view the distinction of master and slave is due to law or convention; there is no natural difference between them: the relation of master and slave is based on force, and being so based has no warrant in justice.[22]

Aristotle's initial refutation of this position is interesting, as it works by reducing the slave, metaphorically, to the status of an inanimate object, in the first (rather fleeting) instance, and then to the status of an animate object (controlling inanimate objects), in the second instance:

> We may make the assumption that property is part of the household ... we may conclude that each article of property is an instrument for the purpose of life; that property in general is the sum of such instruments [including slaves – TC]; that the slave is an animate article of property ...[23]

In both instances the usual boundary line, established by metaphor, between the human animal on the one hand, and non-living objects on the other hand, is re-crossed through metaphorical projection, in order to de-humanise slaves (beyond animals, into objects) and to render them indubitably 'property' (as property is paradigmatically objects). The 'other' in this discussion to the slave, whether as inanimate object or as animate object (controlling inanimate objects), is a fictional automaton,[24] a non-human object that, though not a slave, moves of itself, as if it were animate, and indeed in that way *like* a slave. This, of course, re-crosses the human/machine boundary line again through metaphorical projection, and in doing so re-crosses the fiction/reality boundary line as well by a feat of imagination:

> There is only one condition on which we can imagine managers not needing subordinates, and masters not needing slaves. This condition would be that each [inanimate – EB] instrument could do its own work, at the word of command or by intelligent anticipation, like the statues of Daedalus or the tripods made by Hephaestus … as if a shuttle should weave of itself, and a plectrum should do its own harp-playing.[25]

Even the idea that the slave is an animate object (that controls inanimate objects) is discarded, however, by withdrawing the slave from the sphere of production (oddly) and then drawing the definition tighter around the slave as a household article that serves people, rather than one that makes things. This article is said to belong to the master of the household as master. Masters of households, in this passage, are then conceptualised as in a realm of 'action', which is different in character from a realm of the commercial 'production' of objects. Property ownership is thus naturalised in mastership/rulership, and within 'nature' we now find a hierarchy of activities, namely household life (in which objects are *used* in accord with 'natural' purposes) over commercial life (in which objects are produced for non-immediate use, i.e. for trade and profit-making). This is how the ultimate value of self-sufficiency in the natural order (of which the *polis*, unique to some humans, is the fullest exemplification) is projected back into Aristotle's overall discussion of society. Self-sufficiency captures what goes on in an association of households and identifies this as the ultimate purpose and highest development of human association, which begins in the household. But the household also requires animate objects (slaves) and inanimate objects (e.g. garments and beds) to be in the sole possession of the master and therefore his 'natural' property. What is not required are fictional automata or other real instruments of commercial production, as that is not the activity of the household by nature, nor the kind of activity on which 'nature' places the highest value. Trade and profit-making are evidently 'other' to self-sufficiency.

The above convictions notwithstanding, Aristotle again attacks the view that 'all slavery is contrary to nature', arguing instead, once more, that 'there are … persons who are by nature such as are here defined [as slaves] … persons for whom slavery is the better and just condition'.[26] This time his tactic is to look at rulership in nature, rather than at a supposedly self-evident naturalisation of objects, namely slaves, themselves functioning within a naturalised phenomenon, the *polis*. This involves invoking a hierarchy of rulerships, determined by the kind of object ruled over: the lowest being inanimate objects; the next, animate objects or animals; the highest, rule 'over a man':

> [T]he rule which is exercised over the better sort of ruled elements is a better sort of rule – as, for example, rule exercised over a man is better than rule over an animal. The reason is that a function is a higher and better function when the elements which go to its discharge are higher and better elements … In *all* cases where there is a compound, constituted of more than one part but forming one common entity … a ruling element and a ruled can always be traced. This characteristic … is present in animate beings by virtue of the whole constitution of nature, inanimate as well as animate …

Aristotle's foray into inanimate compounds in nature that exemplify elements of rulership and being ruled (in order to discharge a function) is a rather half-hearted and haphazard mention of musical harmony, in which 'there is a sort of ruling principle'. While not animate, it might be intriguing to consider whether systems of musical harmony can be regarded as inanimate objects, or are rather perceptual constructions of the human mind instead. This might have rather dangerously diluted Aristotle's focus on 'observation' and objects, and thus invoked suspiciously Platonic realms of orderly logic and pure reason that cannot themselves be visually observed. Perhaps harmony was dropped as too distant from Aristotle's focus on preoccupations that seem literal and practical, indeed rooted in everyday life (of a certain very definite sort). This is where the stage is set for Aristotle's ruler to appear in the full garb of hegemonic masculinity.

Observing the body and baring the soul

Aristotle's last step in anthropomorphising nature is to inscribe there the concept of the soul or character. As is required by his method, he presumes that within nature there is an end or best condition, and a hierarchy downwards from that point to states of corruption. Moreover the problematic quality of indeterminacy and unpredictability re-emerges, in that 'nature' does not always achieve its best form or make manifest the distinctions that this requires. This is not to say that Aristotle's concept of nature is inconsistent within itself or in contradiction with his other observations of what it is said to be. Rather, this process of inscription, various as it is, shows how human qualities are made sacrosanct through strategies of naturalisation. Given the ease through which metaphors are shifted from a language of value to a language of fact, and the latter interred in 'nature' which supposedly presents objects for human study (rather than projections of human capacities), it seems that consistency and plausibility are movable feasts in the festivities of moralised redescription enjoyed by Aristotle and numerous others to our own day.

'We may content ourselves here', Aristotle says, 'saying that animate beings are the first [in the ascending scale of nature – EB] to be composed of soul and body, with the former naturally ruling and the latter naturally ruled'. The 'man who is in the best state both of body and soul, and in whom the rule of soul over body is accordingly evident', is clearly in the condition which 'nature intends'. He is not in a 'corrupt' state or 'bad condition', where the body rules the soul as the result of conditions that are evil and unnatural.[27] Aristotle's method here moves beyond an ascription of anthropomorphic features and values to 'nature' into an even more obvious circularity. He observes (in his prose) the 'authority of a master', both 'the sort exercised by a master over slaves' and 'the sort exercised by a statesman over fellow citizens'. He then projects this as a principle into 'nature', in order to read it out again as a principle operative in 'man's inner life', which cannot be so directly observed (according to his general trope that knowledge comes through visual observation).

> The soul rules the body with the sort of authority of a master: mind rules the appetite with the sort of authority of a statesman or a monarch. In this sphere … it is clearly natural and beneficial to the body that it should be ruled by the soul, and again it is natural and beneficial

to the affective part of the soul that it should be ruled by the mind and the rational part; whereas the equality of the two elements, or their reverse relation, is always detrimental.[28]

Circularly Aristotle then says that what 'holds good in man's inner life also holds good outside it', but follows this with further metaphors of similarity and difference, drawn from the animal world, as he observed it through his anthropomorphised conception of 'nature':

> [T]he same principle is true of the relation of man to animals as is true of the relation of his soul to his body. Tame animals have a better nature than wild, and it is better for all such animals that they should be ruled by man because they then get the benefit of preservation.

The naturalisation of domesticity in animals is licensed, apparently, by the naturalised value of 'preservation', though reading through Aristotle's anthropomorphisation of nature by metaphor, this outcome is no surprise. It happens to be opposite to most contemporary usage (surely 'wild' animals are more 'natural'?), yet our practice of taming, domesticating and ultimately humanising animals is rather more in line with Aristotle's naturalised values outlined here. Having read Darwin, why then do we 'save' species? The Darwinian inscription of metaphors into nature is far less laden with humanised and humanistic values, and far more mechanistic and far less 'caring' (cf. Aristotle's naturalised values of 'preservation', 'self-sufficiency' and 'perfection'). The battle over exactly which metaphors and values we inscribe into 'nature' continues through an important realm of contemporary politics in which, methodologically (as I have sketched it), Aristotle would feel entirely at home. His practice of inscribing values familiar from idealisations of everyday and 'practical' social relationships into 'nature' as a force for good in the universe features large in current environmental debate and policy-making, medical ethics and 'family' policies, even 'science' and what sort of research qualifies for funding.[29]

Aristotle could not apparently resist, at this point in *The Politics*, writing women in, just to make sure that a properly naturalised notion of rulers and ruled serves to nail this 'problem' down, too: 'Again, the relation of male to female is naturally that of the superior to the inferior – of the ruling to the ruled'. And further, this 'general principle must similarly hold good of all human beings generally', including barbarians at this point, just to make sure, once again, that the conclusion is driven home, and that home will be where those conclusions will be made agreeable through normalisation and discipline (or worse).

What then, for Aristotle, makes a 'ruling' male different from a slave or barbarian male? Note that there is not much difference between the two, merely that barbarians are not yet ruled by Greeks. Aristotle's initial stab at this is not very convincing (to him), precisely because it seems to rely on qualities that are not directly observable:

> A man is thus by nature a slave if he is capable of becoming (and this is the reason why he also actually becomes) the property of another, and if he participates in reason to the extent of apprehending it in another, though destitute of it himself.

Here we arrive at another boundary-crossing metaphorical attempt to explain the slave, this time in terms of 'tame animals' (rather than as animate property):

> Herein he [the slave] differs from animals, which do not apprehend reason, but simply obey their instincts. But the use which is made of the slave diverges but little from the use made of tame animals; both he and they supply their owner with bodily help in meeting his daily requirements.[30]

Aristotle's conclusion is suitably sweeping:

> We may thus conclude that all men who differ from others as much as the body differs from the soul, or an animal from a man (and this is the case with all whose function is bodily service, and who produce their best when they supply such service) – all such are by nature slaves, and it is better for them … to be ruled by a master.[31]

Physical differences, though, are what interest Aristotle, as he expects 'nature' to manifest its 'intention' in this visible way, making observation easy and certainty visual. Alas this does not always happen, and indeed in some cases, the exact opposite occurs. If 'nature's intention were realized – if men different from one another in bodily form as much as the statues of the gods [differ from the human figure – EB]', then 'we should all agree that the inferior class ought to be slaves to the superior'. Sadly, as Aristotle remarks, 'it is not as easy to see the beauty of the soul as it is to see that of the body'.[32] Rather than dwell on the all-to-obvious ironies of this situation, methodologically, I propose to focus instead on exactly what Aristotle did think was visible in his 'rulers by nature' and in the 'inferiors' over which he rules:

> But it is nature's intention also to erect a physical difference between the body of the freeman and that of the slave, giving the latter strength for the menial duties of life, but making the former upright in carriage and (though useless for physical labour) useful for the various purposes of civic life – a life which tends, as it develops, to be divided into military service and the occupations of peace.[33]

While hardly exhaustive as a characterisation of hegemonic masculinity, Aristotle's idealisation is certainly a start, and instantly recognisable today, where the alpha-male image is pervasively signalled.[34] This is despite our contemporary gestures towards inclusivity of race/ethnicity, gender and sexual orientation and other categories laid out (and battled over) in policies of non-discrimination, whether in military or in civilian life. Where masculinised values rule, there is hegemonic masculinity. Succeeding chapters in Aristotle's Book I fill out the picture, as he saw it, and he saw that it was good.

Aristotle observes hegemonic masculinity 'by nature' in masters (of households) and in statesmen (who share in ruling and being ruled). They are 'superior in *goodness*', and this is an endowment (not the product of education or training), conferred 'just as man is born of man' [sic], and animal of animal'. The master, he continues, 'must simply know how to command what the slave must know how to do. This is why those who are in a position to escape from being troubled by it delegate the management of slaves to a steward, and spend on politics or philosophy the time they are thus able to save.'[35] He then discusses the 'natural' acquisition of wealth for subsistence and introduces the conception of a limit or 'bound' that is fixed to resources acquired for the household. The 'other' to this is an unnatural, unbounded acquisition of wealth through monetary exchange, which is merely quantitative and is therefore potentially unlimited. This activity of 'production' is then carefully bracketed off from the activities ('action') of the master of the household, which Aristotle likens to a form of hunting. This is explained as an activity that garners subsistence by making 'war' on wild animals, and on 'human beings who are intended by nature to be ruled by others and refuse to obey that intention'.[36] Aristotle's picture is very much the ideal of the non-commercial, moneyed 'leisure' class, 'naturally' given by birth to ruling over inferiors, to non-commercial 'hobby' forms of 'self-sufficiency' in their households-writ-large, and to activities of cultural patronage:

> The natural form, therefore, of the art of acquisition is always, and in all cases, acquisition from fruits and animals. That art, as we have said, has two forms: one which is connected with retail trade, and another which is connected with the management of the household. Of these two forms, the latter is necessary and laudable; the former is a method of exchange which is justly censured, because the gain in which it results is not naturally made [from plants and animals – EB], but is made at the expense of other men.

Inferior masculinities come into view here: 'The trade of the petty usurer … is hated most, and with most reason: it makes a profit from currency itself, instead of making it from the process [i.e. of exchange – EB] which currency was meant to serve.'[37] Further:

> A general account has now been given of the various forms of acquisition: to consider them minutely, and in detail, might be useful for practical purposes; but to dwell long upon them would be in poor taste. Suffice it to say that the occupations which require most skill are those in which there is least room for chance; the meanest are those in which most use is made of physical strength; the least noble are those in which there is least need for the exercise of goodness.[38]

Filling out the picture, Aristotle sketches the behaviour of his ruling males in realms of authority beyond the control of slaves, namely paternal authority over children and marital authority over wives. 'The relation of the male to the female is permanently that in which the statesman [temporarily – EB] stands to his fellow citizens.' Although between the statesman and citizens there is over time an interchange of ruling and being ruled, at any one time rulers are awarded a difference in terms of outward forms of respect and modes of address. Husband over wife reflects a relationship in which the male is permanently in the rulership position. Aristotle at this point makes brief reference to the claim by Socrates in *The Republic* that temperance, fortitude and justice are the same in a woman as in a man, and unsurprisingly flatly denies this. With respect to children, the male parent is in a position of authority both in virtue of the affection to which he is entitled and by right of his seniority. His position is thus in the nature of 'royal authority'. The ruler, by contrast with slaves, women and children, 'must possess moral goodness in its full and perfect form ..., because his function ... demands a master-artificer ... reason'.[39]

Male-order metaphors

Aristotle has produced a vision of nature that already reflects the very image and constituent values of the hegemonic masculinity that that concept of nature is said to contain and validate. The crucial social distinctions amongst humans (hierarchically categorised), animals (tame and wild), instruments (animate and inanimate), and objects (for subsistence as opposed to trade) are the primary things Aristotle is most worried about, and the areas where he feels the thrust of contrary, critical views most keenly. Despite the evident difficulties with his methodology of observation, and his attribution to 'nature' of powers that are meant to generate the goodness and perfection of any and all entities, Aristotle sticks relentlessly to his promotion and validation of rule within the household, and over the *polis* (as households in association), by an hereditary elite of men. What distinguishes them is their fully developed reason (rather untested as to observation) and a claim that in physical terms – and in terms of effortless expertise and leisured values – there *ought to be*, by nature, visible physical distinctions between this class and the class of male slaves and barbarians. Woman, of course, is already distinct (with no possibility of ambiguity or confusion); 'nature' never fails, so it seems, to mark sexual difference as 'woman', and therefore gender inferiority, with 100 per cent success. The boundaries and gradations between men, on the other hand, are subject to observational difficulties, reversals between bodily appearance and composition of the soul, and corruption far beneath even those inferiorities that are part of Aristotle's natural hierarchies of 'goodness', depending on the kind of creature and the purpose for which it was created.

This might be all somewhat quaint were it not for the persistence of Aristotelian modes of thought, erecting and protecting boundary lines and hierarchies with respect to modes of life and forms of value.

Moreover the persistence of unselfconscious attributions of purpose and value to 'nature' needs careful examination, given that the process through which metaphors are deployed to do this is seldom exposed for what it is: a deployment of linguistic forces to persuade and convince, rather than — as is pretended — a reliable description of what has been discovered 'in nature' to be true. All our metaphors are anthropomorphic — they could not be otherwise, as we could make no sense of them if they reflected some other form of life. All of our descriptions are as metaphorical as they are linguistic; neither fact nor nature nor truth can break out of language. Certainty, especially when naturalised in the eternal verities, hierarchies and values of 'nature', has been immensely attractive and also immensely damaging as a political force. The production of visions that do not naturalise values, and do not rely on naturalised certainties to persuade, is the challenge of the postmodern age.

Notes

1 See Chapter 6 for comment on Hobbes's critique of 'the schools' and specifically of Aristotelianism (in his own burlesque version), pp. 132–3, 137.
2 Plato, *The Republic*, 471d–541a; Ferrari, pp. 173–251; cf. Waterfield, pp. 190–276.
3 Aristotle, *The Politics*, 1260b–1269a; Barker, pp. 39–73; cf. Everson, pp. 20–39.
4 Aristotle, *The Politics* 1252a; Barker, pp. 1–2; cf. Everson, pp. 1–2.
5 See the discussion of women, rulership and *The Republic* above, pp. 27–32.
6 See below, pp. 43–5.
7 Plato, *The Republic*, 369d–376c; Ferrari, pp. 51–60; cf. Waterfield, pp. 59–69.
8 See below, pp. 51–2.
9 Plato, *The Republic*, 373a–376c; Ferrari, pp. 55–60; cf. Waterfield, pp. 65–9.
10 Plato, *The Republic*, 459d–461e; Ferrari, pp. 157–60; cf. Waterfield, pp. 173–6.
11 Plato, *The Republic*, 415a–d; Ferrari, p. 108; cf. Waterfield, p. 119.
12 Thomas S. Kuhn, *The Structure of Scientific Revolutions*, 3rd edn (Chicago, IL and London: University of Chicago Press, 1996), pp. 10–65, 144–59.
13 Aristotle, *The Politics* 1252a; Barker, p. 1; cf. Everson, p. 1.

14 Aristotle, *The Politics* 1252a–b; Barker, p. 1–3; cf. Everson, pp. 1–3.
15 See, for example, H. Tristram Engelhardt, Jr., *The Foundations of Bioethics*, 2nd edn (New York and Oxford: Oxford University Press, 1996), pp. 32–101; Christopher Megone, 'Potentiality and persons: an Aristotelian perspective', in Mark G. Kuczewski and Ronald Polansky eds, *Bioethics: ancient themes in contemporary issues* (Cambridge, MA: MIT Press, 2000), pp. 155–77; David Heyd, *Genethics: moral issues in the creation of people* (Berkeley, CA: University of California Press, 1992), pp. 1–17, 210–28.
16 Richard Rorty, 'The contingency of language', in *Contingency, Irony and Solidarity* (Cambridge: Cambridge University Press, 1989, repr. 1995), pp. 3–22.
17 'What then is truth? A mobile army of metaphors, metonyms, and anthropomorphisms—in short, a sum of human relations, which have been inhanced, transposed, and embellished poetically and rhetorically, and which after long use seem firm, canonical, and obligatory ...'; Friedrich Nietzsche, *The Viking Portable Nietzsche*, trans. Walter Kaufman (New York: Viking, 1968), pp. 46–7.
18 Aristotle, *The Politics*, 1252b–1253a; Barker, pp. 5–6; cf. Everson, pp. 2–4.
19 Aristotle, *The Politics*, 1252a–b; Barker, p. 3; cf. Everson, p. 2.
20 Aristotle, *The Politics*, 1252a–b; Barker, p. 3; cf. Everson, p. 2.
21 Aristotle, *The Politics*, 1252a–b; Barker, p. 4; cf. Everson, p. 2.
22 Aristotle, *The Politics*, 1253b; Barker, p. 9; cf. Everson, p. 5.
23 Aristotle, *The Politics*, 1253b; Barker, pp. 9–10; cf. Everson, pp. 5–6.
24 See the discussion of Hobbes's rather different use of the automaton example and metaphor, below pp. 142.
25 Aristotle, *The Politics*, 1253b; Barker, p. 10 ['EB' marks an editorial insertion]; cf. Everson, pp. 5–6.
26 Aristotle, *The Politics*, 1253b–1254a; Barker, p. 11; cf. Everson, p. 6.
27 Aristotle, *The Politics*, 1253b–1254a; Barker, p. 12; cf. Everson, pp. 6–7.
28 Aristotle, *The Politics*, 1254a–1254b; Barker, p. 13; cf. Everson, pp. 6–7.
29 See, for example, Michael Watson and David Sharpe, 'Green beliefs and religion', in Andrew Dobson and Paul Lucardie, eds, *The Politics of Nature: explorations in green political theory* (London and New York: Routledge, 1993, repr. 1995), pp. 210–28; Robert E. Goodin, *Green Political Theory* (Cambridge: Polity Press, 1992), pp. 26–77; Tim Hayward, *Political Theory and Ecological Values* (Cambridge: Polity Press, 1998), pp. 21–41; and especially John M. Meyer, *Political Nature: environmentalism and the interpretation of western thought* (Cambridge, MA and London: MIT Press, 2001), pp. 1–10, 89–118.
30 Aristotle, *The Politics*, 1254a–1254b; Barker, p. 13; cf. Everson, p. 7.
31 Aristotle, *The Politics*, 1254a–1254b; Barker, p. 13; cf. Everson, p. 7.
32 Aristotle, *The Politics*, 1254a–1254b; Barker, p. 14; cf. Everson, p. 7.

33 Aristotle, *The Politics*, 1254a–1254b; Barker, pp. 13–14; cf. Everson, p. 7.
34 For a discussion of 'hierarchies of citizenship' in the context of gender and sexuality, see David T. Evans, *Sexual Citizenship: the material construction of sexualities* (London: Routledge, 1993), pp. 1–9. and in particular on the special status of militarised masculinities within contemporary hierarchies of value, see R. Claire Snyder, *Citizen-Soldiers and Manly Warriors* (Lanham, MD: Rowman & Littlefield, 1999).
35 Aristotle, *The Politics*, 1254b–1255a; Barker, pp. 15-16; cf. Everson, p. 9.
36 Aristotle, *The Politics*, 1254b–1256a; Barker, pp. 19-21; cf. Everson, pp. 9–12.
37 Aristotle, *The Politics*, 1257b–1258a; Barker, pp. 28-9; cf. Everson, pp. 13–14.
38 Aristotle, *The Politics*, 1258a–b; Barker, p. 30; cf. Everson, pp. 14-16.
39 Aristotle, *The Politics*, 1259b–1260a; Barker, pp. 35–6; cf. Everson, pp. 17–20.

CHAPTER THREE

Jesus: masculinity and the 'son of man'

Unholy orders

Jesus is very problematic. He was problematic, even to himself.[1] As a figure in the political theory canon, he is problematic in almost every way. His place there is not at all certain. When he does appear, it is usually as prologue to the Christianity through which all political thought of the European middle ages was mediated. Occasionally he appears as a kind of inverse theorist, someone with an anti-political vision, compared with the usual definitions and models derived from Greco-Roman and contractarian writers. While he sometimes commented on contemporary Jewish and Roman politics, his messages were oblique, equivocal, puzzling and unsystematic. His kingdom was said by him to be of the next world and to be his father's, but this is utopianism at two removes. Altogether his sayings are but fragments, and hardly enough to fit him into the classic works of the genre.

The most direct function that can be assigned to Jesus, in this context, is that of author of a number of sayings, widely quoted and revered, that function in the political theory of others. This, too, is problematic. We do not have good evidence, either that Jesus did exist or that he didn't, in the usual way that authors do. The texts in which his sayings feature were clearly put together by other writers, transmitted through a largely unknown set of hands (or mouths), and then collected and edited in ways on which we have some testimony from church councils, but hardly a complete account. From what we can surmise, we are left with many questions as to the editorial criteria for inclusion and exclusion of materials about which we have but sketchy speculations, and mostly we are in the dark as to how accurately the source materials (whatever they were) were sifted and collated. It seems unlikely that the men (and women?) involved in the process had standards similar to those of modern textual scholarship in mind, and indeed their efforts have been largely mythologised as faith-driven and god-inspired activities undertaken by the 'fathers' of the church, which is perhaps not entirely inaccurate.

This has left us with considerable curiosity as to the contents of some of the accounts discarded along the way to the early Christian councils. Twentieth-century discoveries of rather similar materials (e.g. the Dead Sea scrolls)[2] have suggested that perhaps Jesus was one of many such preachers, or maybe a composite figure, or (very likely) both. Altogether from what we know and surmise, it is rather difficult to get the feel of the religious life and political projects of the early first century in Roman-occupied Palestine anyway. Or rather, it is difficult to make this imaginative engagement if one's perspective derives in the usual way from the transmission of classical (i.e. Greek and Roman) texts into the values and preoccupations of modern 'western' commercial culture and political life. These sit rather uneasily with those of the gospels and other biblical texts; witness the enormous efforts made since the dark ages to reconcile the classical and biblical outlooks!

It may be that retro-translation of Jesus' teachings from the gospels in demotic Greek back into a presumed Aramaic will pass the computer tests of consistency in expression that serve now to establish authorship. If they do, the best that can be said for this is that the gospel authors will have given us a lively dramatic figure with a more empirical claim to authenticity than Plato's character Socrates.[3] *The Republic* is too obviously a dramatic construct to give much credence to the idea that Socrates is a verbatim reproduction of the gadfly-philosopher saying just those things on just that occasion; indeed the interpretive tradition is rather the opposite, that Socrates is a mouthpiece for Plato, who makes him say what he wants him to say, in a situation where he never was. Thucydides, at least, tells us that in his dramatic reconstructions he sometimes departed from verbatim recollections.

> With reference to the speeches in this history, some were delivered before the war began, others while it was going on; some I heard myself, others I got from various quarters; it was in all cases difficult to carry

them word for word in one's memory, so my habit has been to make the speakers say what was in my opinion demanded of them by the various occasions, of course adhering as closely as possible to the general sense of what they really said.[4]

Supposing, then, that Jesus' teachings were at some early point remembered and recorded as such (and were really those of one man), it still must be the case that other writers have contextualised them in the (various) New Testament narratives that make up the familiar gospel story. There are, of course, famous interpretive problems involved in interpreting the four books of the gospels left to us, namely which sources served which writers, which presumed sources were common, which materials from these sources are thought to be of earliest origin (and why), which variant of similar stories qualifies as more authentic (and why, and what that might mean), and what one can learn from comparing and contrasting the narrative strategies and arrangement of incidents amongst the four 'books' as we have them. There are further problems with the Gospel of John, due to the supposed leakage of Greek (or 'Eastern'?) philosophical ideas into the text, and what relationship this might bear to the (presumably) Aramaic-speaking Jesus (and what teachings he might have experienced that his 'recorders' might not have known about or understood).[5]

Whether Jesus as a political theorist would survive the excision of the storyline that surrounds his sayings[6] seems rather unlikely, as intelligibility generally demands of us that we supply some authorial characterisation and contemporary contextualisation around a presumed or known audience. The stories in the gospels fill in the audience for these teachings on occasion, and we do get some suggestions, slightly on the model of *The Republic*, what their reactions were and what difference Jesus' teaching and preaching mode of activity – not just the words of his 'teachings' – made on them, at the time, and at certain points in the text, on their lives, though this involves us with the all-too-knowing narrator(s) who 'voice' the gospel stories for us. To what extent ought we to be looking at the political theory of the gospel-narrator(s) (rather than the four canonical 'authors') as they construct Jesus, his social and political interactions and thus the meaning of his words when he speaks them?

The textual Jesus has rather undercut his own case, anyway, too often commenting of his own teaching and action that it has just fulfilled a prophecy. This is bound to undermine confidence in his political enterprise and in what his teachings must mean. Can they have serious perlocutionary force if they are really being said to confirm some transhistorical and supernatural venture? Evidently, unlike most theory, Jesus' words seem to have an illocutionary status – speaking them performs a role in a divine plan, just when they are spoken, and things happen within that plan as a result. Other theorists in the canon do not perform their theory as a theodicy.

Perhaps social contract theorists have intended the contractual terms given in their texts to be illocutionary formulae such that contracting parties would genuinely create the intended political relationships and structures just when they actually recited the words. However, what we know of contractualism in early modern times (and later) suggests that those writers in the canon did not intend their texts to function in this way, but rather more as an *ex post facto* 'as if' justification for obligations already in place. Still, the retro-prophetic and illocutionary qualities of Jesus' sayings need not disqualify them as theory, when they seem to cover relevant issues, nor prevent some qualified attention to the gospel contextualisations that tell us what Jesus was doing in this-worldly terms. After all, whoever pictured the situation and filled in the audience seems to have had a vivid appreciation of forms of life that look very plausible for the early first century AD, and indeed there is some fairly direct corroboration elsewhere for the kinds of events that occur (e.g. Roman trials, Jewish politics, itinerant preaching). In so far as we have a political situation characterised, and views offered, some of which come from a self-conscious teacher, we are somewhere in the realm of canonical political theory. There are, however, yet further difficulties.

The gospels have a narrative, but there is evidence of more than one narrator (leaving aside any questions of the authorship which created the narrators). Moreover, none of the narrators is made visible in the text, and worse, none really seems reliable. A reliable narrator, visible in the text, is like Hobbes, who put his name to *Leviathan*, and who maintains a clear authorial voice throughout. Or like Thucydides, who famously makes himself visible in the text, expounding a methodology of critical scepticism:

> And with reference to the narrative of events, far from permitting myself to derive it from the first source that came to hand, I did not

even trust my own impressions, but it rests partly on what I saw myself, partly on what others saw for me, the accuracy of the report being always tried by the most severe and detailed tests possible. My conclusions have cost me some labour from the want of coincidence between accounts of the same occurrences by different eye-witnesses, arising sometimes from imperfect memory, sometimes from undue partiality for one side or the other.[7]

I have argued that *The Republic* has no reliable narrator and no resident authorial voice,[8] but that it is no less packed with political theory for that, given what the visible characters say and do. Aristotle is a little wobbly in this respect, possibly arriving in written form via lecture notes or recollections, but none the less we seem to have a reliable narrator coinciding with the author. He presents some problems of consistency, but these could have been with himself in the first place, and not the fault of students or editors (we will probably never know). Jesus is really far more difficult, in that the gospel authors have given us narrator(s) who derive their testimony from the Old Testament, and so – as D.F. Strauss meticulously revealed – they undermine their credibility as historians or eyewitnesses.[9] Leaving aside supernatural events, and internal contradictions, I note that so much in the stories is so obviously invested with hindsight and significance by narrators that they are all rather beyond what reliable testimony can stand. While eyewitness accounts inevitably acquire a 'knowing' cast as they are passed down amongst people who already understand how the story is supposed to end, and therefore what the (real) significance of any remark or teaching actually is, the New Testament narratives are so invested with symbolic portentousness that even the most vividly ordinary little details – that might otherwise lend credence to a transmitted account of someone's real-life experience – seem suspect. They seem artfully there to create an illusion of immediacy and therefore veracity as the tale is unfolded by the narrator(s), including what Jesus says, in order to give the scene its point and to make the drama progress.

Worse, yet, a gospel narrator knows Jesus' innermost thoughts and exactly what is in his mind at certain points, and what he says when he is obviously alone,[10] very much in the manner of the omniscient authorial voice of the modern novel. Thucydides, by contrast, is very sparing on this kind of thing, obviously recognising that such psychologising is more in the mode of fictional constructions. Hence he avoids speculations (such as states of mind in others) that would harm his reputation as a trustworthy recorder of events and ideas. The gospel narrator(s) venture occasionally into inner dramas which function to humanise Jesus, who of course is also amply furnished with supernatural powers, so that we see both sides of a dual nature. This is an ambiguous and troubling conundrum, possibly accounting for some of the success of Christianity as a 'mystery' religion that uniquely incorporates an intensely human character into an enigmatic godhead. Certainly there were various attempts along the line to clarify this, and notable compromise wordings (in prescribed and standardised creeds and catechisms) that kept the problem on the table. Disagreement is not necessarily bad for proselytisation.

It is not surprising that the gospel story of Jesus has adapted well to the screen (and perhaps that other great works of philosophy and political theory have not made it in this medium). It is itself almost a screenplay already. The narrative unfolds through vivid vignettes and powerful scenes, very sparely drawn yet incorporating economical drama, concise dialogue and a strong leading role (though not, as argued below, a conventional 'leading man'). There is a wide cast of characters from all walks of life, and an over-arching political drama of uneasy power-sharing between the Jewish and Roman political communities. The regional and local geographies are clearly set and indicatively sketched, down to very particular houses, palaces, roads, hilltops and so on. And it makes an excellent musical, witness Handel's *Messiah* (rather reliant, though, on the Old Testament/New Testament analogical overlaps) and Bach's passions (in which an Evangelist-narrator appears to tell us the story – quite an interpretive breakthrough). These latter have recently been semi-staged, realising the dramatic action portrayed in the music and text. Of course passion plays have a long history and a politics, too, most recently in whether the Pharisees and Sadducees are judgementally portrayed, and what lessons concerning contemporary Judaism and Zionism are perhaps purveyed.[11] For comparison, *The Republic* opens with a trip down the road to Piraeus, but in cinematic, dramaturgical and political terms, it really doesn't compete, lively as it is. Other theorists are less showy in terms of how their publications and careers interacted with their texts. Thomas More's *Utopia* is possibly a comparator here, as he created a narrator and left us puzzled about an authorial view. The work has a satirical sting that could be exploited in a film or play, but little drama to speak of (except as a traveller's tale). Perhaps it could do as a musical, on the model of Bernstein's *Candide*. However, there doesn't seem much direct connection between the theoretical content of the work and the historical More's journey to the scaffold, so unsurprisingly it makes no serious running in *A Man for All Seasons*.

Certainly there is *some* connection, following out the gospel story, between what Jesus said and how he ended up crucified. I leave aside the ontological issue concerning political theorists who rise from the dead and continue to speak. Our problem is that we really don't know if Jesus existed and met that particular end (whichever one it was), and that if he did, whether he said exactly those things in that way as events took their course. If we knew that all those things took place, we might take Jesus more seriously as a political philosopher. Alternatively, if he is fictional, and if we don't have an author immersed in some identifiable context from which the narrated fiction arises, and to which it speaks, we are left rather high and dry. What is the relationship between the gospel author(s), the textual narrator(s) and the Jesus(es?) who speak the sayings? Normally commentators on political theory try to sort this kind of thing out before recounting and evaluating the 'thoughts' or 'doctrines' of the 'theorist', or at least they should. We are never going to get there with Jesus, or even as close as we can come with some of our more problematic author/narrator/text combinations (cf. *The Republic* and *Utopia*). Still, political theory is a broad church, and perhaps there is room there for the ever-problematic 'son of man'.

An overt involvement of political theory with religion, or even a religious mission, has been no disqualification for the canon. While modern liberal theorists have (perhaps rather idealistically) presumed that religion can be organised politically as a 'private' matter, and indeed must be protected there as such, most theorists have generally given some recognition and lukewarm endorsement to 'civic religions' that incorporate and promote values of stability and solidarity. This is because they help to create and maintain the orderly community that the theorists recommend. Some political theorists have been notably anti-Christian (e.g. Machiavelli, blaming Christian values for martial weakness in contemporary Italy, and praising instead classical cults of blood sacrifice and warlike fervour).[12] Others have been anti-Church (e.g. Hobbes, blaming 'unpleasing priests' for dissension and civil war).[13] Two in particular have been pro-atheist (Marx and Engels, flatly rejecting the supernatural and spiritual as intellectually unsustainable and politically oppressive modes of thought and activity).[14]

Whether we are looking at the gospel narrator(s) or at Jesus himself, there is clearly a religious politics at issue, and not just a politics of religion. This need not disqualify these texts and sayings as political theory, since we cope well with Augustine of Hippo and Thomas Aquinas in the canon, though few modern commentators take their status as saints on board in recounting and interpreting their work for our times. None the less larger issues concerned with the human subjects of political thought, and with appropriate ontologies and epistemologies, are handled within the political theory framework, even when religious beliefs and values are involved. Indeed there is no reason why the canonical concepts and issues have to be limited to a (supposedly) non-religious view of the cosmos. What we expect, though, is an account of the cosmos, and the role of the divine within it, expounded by a human, citing texts which are accounts based on revelations to others or deductions from some argument concerning the nature of being, consciousness, death etc. that counts as a religious outlook.

Hegel is a case in point, as there is clearly a supra-human *Geist* built into his conceptualisation of the human experience (as a part of the realisation of this *geistliche* manifestation of meaning in the universe). While this is not precisely religious (or even perhaps spiritual), it is certainly a philosophy constructed on an analogy with religious ideas, particularly a highly transmuted version of the Christian doctrine of the incarnation. A text written by a human citing revelations from personal experience of the divine as a matter of direct communication would be an interesting test case, though not one with which political theorists have tangled as yet. Notably Hobbes advised extreme scepticism concerning the claims of such persons to have experienced in their own ears the voice of God.[15] Jesus is in a slightly different position.

In the gospels there is clearly an element of the divine in Jesus, since he is self-defined and self-proclaimed (on some occasions, and albeit somewhat covertly) as the son of God. Quite what this means (and doesn't mean) has been the subject of a number of well-known debates, heresies and schisms over the years. In considering Jesus as a political theorist, and the gospels as canonical texts, however, I am going to rule the question of divinity out of order. For present purposes Jesus will be a man whose various and ambiguous claims to divinity are highly relevant to his political context, but not so to the business of examining him as a political theorist in the way that others in the canon are treated. For that purpose, his evident status as a man (in the sense of male) will be relevant as well, and so in the discussion which follows, he joins the other subjects of study in the present volume. What can the gender lens, turned on the masculinity of Jesus, tell us about his politics as he pursued it and about his theorisation of power-relations in society?

Ecce Vir

In the gospels we learn quite a lot about Jesus as a man, just a little about him as a boy, and perhaps rather too much about him as a baby (from the gospels of Matthew and Luke – the gospels of Mark and John notably lack the nativity material). As an infant, Jesus is circumcised,[16] and as a boy (in the sole story that made it into the canonical texts) he appears as precocious and self-willed, teaching his elders in the temple, and thus already embarked on a career of transgression and disruption. At this stage, though, his male audience of teachers in the temple, and his family audience of astonished parents (who had been looking for him for three days …), seem comparatively undisturbed by this event, and the narrator reassures us that after this enigmatically excused lapse ('to be in my [real] father's house'), he went home to be obedient to his earthly parents. Of his actual teachings at that point, we unfortunately learn nothing.[17]

After baptism (by the eponymous John) and temptation (by the devil), Jesus emerges as a man resolute on a mission … though to do what? The first indications are that he tells people to repent of their sins, and that he heals the sick. Appearing at Nazareth, he makes a good impression until he himself taunts the crowd that he will not perform miracles there (quoting a rather confused and confusing proverb) and that he will be rejected in his hometown (which he was, rather dramatically):

> All the people in the synagogue were furious when they heard this. They got up, drove him out of the town, and took him to the brow of the hill on which the town was built, in order to throw him down the cliff.[18]

Clearly, though, Jesus had considerable presence, and presence of mind, as he simply walked through the angry crowd and proceeded along his way. What emerges from these accounts of his early ministry is that his teaching (generally in synagogues, though not always, and sometimes to generalised mixed gatherings) was succinctly prophetic ('The kingdom of God is near. Repent and believe the good news!'[19]) and miraculously curative:

> That evening after sunset the people brought to Jesus all the sick and demon-possessed. The whole town [Capernaum] gathered at the door, and Jesus healed many who had various diseases. He also drove out many demons …[20]

What really brings out the crowds is the prospect of healing. This (seems to) attest to a social practice and popular need unfulfilled elsewhere, and indeed persistent in (tele)evangelism and mass pilgrimage today. Reading the gospels as drama, and viewing them in the mind's eye as cinema, the overwhelmingly prevalent and persistent image is that of crowds gathering, bringing out their sick, desperate for a cure. In masculinity terms, Jesus is following on well-trodden ground, judging from the testimony of the gospels, and what we know and can surmise about itinerant preachers and healers. He has intellectual authority and notable charisma; he is kind and caring about the sick, though not indiscriminately so. They seem important as part of his vocation, rather than as suffering individuals (with some notable exceptions, where his feelings become involved).[21] He does not charge for his services, nor appear to have gainful employment. As a traveller he partakes of traditional hospitality, and as a preacher, he gets respect (provided he fulfils expectations on his performance, both as teacher and as healer). Given the subordinated character of his community in Roman-occupied Palestine, and his family's evident non-connection with the career-track teachers in the temple and synagogues, he is successful in his slot. Alternatively, as a young man he could perhaps have gone down the road of collaboration with the Romans, something which their imperial policies generally encouraged, but at this stage in the text the Romanised rulers of the area do not appear directly (though Caesar Augustus himself makes a very distant appearance early on in the nativity pageants).[22]

In political theory terms there is little so far of interest. Two things wind the tension up and turn the discussion more towards those issues, such that it becomes more plausible and interesting to read Jesus into this particular canon. One is the emergence of political tensions between Romanised rulers, the Jewish religious establishment and Jesus' activities, especially where crowds are involved. The other is Jesus' rather unsettling practices with regard to the normal masculinity that teachers and healers as respectable males were expected to follow. He rather persistently and deliberately transgressed boundaries of gender, and gendered boundaries of race, religion and class, that put his own status as a masculine ideal at stake. As the denouement arrives when he is (said to be) in his early thirties, he departs from the masculinity script entirely by becoming a willing victim, complicit in his own torture and demise, self-absorbed in an 'other world' beyond the family and the other relationships through which masculinity is normally enacted.

In departing from 'normal' scripts of masculinity Jesus has been interpreted, particularly visually, as somewhat feminised, or at least 'softened' into an alternative masculinity of suffering and victimhood, more than a little self-inflicted. The theodicy of the gospels and the divinity of resurrection have worked to normalise this image as something peculiar to Jesus and 'not of this world', anyway. Putting Jesus' aberrant masculinity back into the world of real-life activities, which is in essence how I am reading the gospel narratives here, creates a rather different impression. Is Jesus an eccentric or a model? What kind of man is the 'son of man', as the story unfolds, and what is he saying, through words and deeds about this? What sort of politics does this kind of man do, and what sort of general recommendations (to men about their masculinity) would follow from what he says and does? What would politics look like, in relation to women, and in relation to society generally, if men were like Jesus?

The challenge here is to explore a variant of masculinity that is not in some way hegemonic over femininities, as well as over subordinate masculinities. I am not saying that Jesus achieved that, or that it is unequivocally desirable, or even that it is a logical possibility. My precise point is that it is hard to envisage such a thing, and most certainly it is not in the logic of the language. Hence the enterprise itself would be highly theoretical and most probably off in the realm of science fiction (or traveller's utopian fantasy), were it not for the suggestive and puzzling qualities exhibited by someone, namely Jesus, whose life-story is very well known and researched. Unfortunately, the attention paid to Jesus as a man operates on a binary with Jesus as 'son of God' and party to the godhead trinity, rather than on a binary with women, and with men whose masculinities are significantly different from his. What follows is therefore a dual project: who is Jesus in gender terms? and on that basis, what kind of political theory can we make of his words and deeds as they are narrated to us in the gospels?

A politics of gender

Jesus' gender politics is not just transgressive within himself, as a performer of a reinterpreted masculinity. He also transgresses boundaries and whole institutions that are constitutive of gender itself. Strikingly he takes men away from their families, or at least we may presume that the fishermen and other apostles were fishing to support family members, possibly wives and children, before they departed 'to follow' Jesus. Quite what this says, in particular and in general, is difficult to say, and no doubt male desertions (or apparent desertions) were (and are) not that difficult to find, particularly when pursued for goals that are individualistically defined, and pursued in the 'public' world outside the home. Jesus even makes this explicit, about himself and about others. After all, he had himself left his birth family behind, whereas the general, and certainly masculine, norm would presumably have been for him to help support his kinfolk as a family unit:

> As they were walking along the road, a man said to him, 'I will follow you wherever you go'
> Jesus replied, 'Foxes have holes and birds of the air have nests, but the Son of Man has no place to lay his head.'
> He said to another man, 'Follow me.'
> But the man replied, 'Lord first let me go and bury my father.'
> Jesus said to him, 'Let the dead bury their own dead, but you go and proclaim the kingdom of God.'
> Still another said, 'I will follow you, Lord; but first let me go back and say good-by to my family.'
> Jesus replied, 'No one who puts his hand to the plow and looks back is fit for service in the kingdom of God.'[23]

In much the same spirit Jesus advised seventy-two followers to set out to teach and heal, making it clear that this is a kind of work for which they will be paid in kind ('eating and drinking whatever they give you').[24] Yet given the borderline here between services rendered and freely given hospitality, this seems a little disingenuous. The story of Martha and Mary[25] rather confirms Jesus' resolute disengagement with the monetary, barter or domestic economies. Most startlingly he sums it all up with an attack on the gendered character of society, and the self-worth of the individual. These are parameters within which even the most rudimentary political theory – at least so far in our conception of the genre – would have to operate:

> Large crowds were travelling with Jesus, and turning to them he said: 'If anyone comes to me and does not hate his father and mother, his wife and children, his brothers and sisters – yes, even his own life – he cannot be my disciple'.[26]

Following out this topsy-turvy scheme, Jesus also inverted the place of children in the gender order of respect:

> Jesus called the children to him and said, 'Let the little children come to me, and do not hinder them, for the kingdom of God belongs to such as these. I tell you the truth, anyone who will not receive the kingdom of God like a little child will never enter it'.[27]

Interestingly in the parable of the rich man (who is told to sell all he has and give to the poor), Peter interrupts to confirm, 'We have left all we had to follow you!' and Jesus persists with his confirmation that following him has required a complete departure from the gender and economic order: 'no one who has left home or wife or brothers or parents or children for the sake of the kingdom of God will fail to receive many times as much [of what? – TC] in this age and, in the age to come, eternal life'.[28] In a subsequent passage a rejection of marriage altogether (for those who are considered worthy of taking part ... in the resurrection from the dead) actually silences the Sadducees. Unsurprisingly after that 'no one dared to ask him any more questions'.[29] Given the terrifying unreality of Jesus' answer, in terms of the gender order (or any conceivable gender order), it is again unsurprising that no further questions were pressed (in the narrative, as we have it). Very disturbingly Jesus even denies the relationships of the gender order, and economic order, right to the faces of his mother and brothers:

> Then Jesus' mother and brothers arrived. Standing outside, they sent someone in to call him. A crowd was sitting around him, and they told him, 'Your mother and brothers are outside looking for you.'
> 'Who are my mother and my brothers?' he asked.
> Then he look at those seated in a circle around him and said, 'Here are my mother and my brothers! Whoever does God's will is my brother and sister and mother.'[30]

Perhaps this is all very figurative but the sheer repetition (even allowing for overlaps in the gospel accounts) is striking. Jesus as a man, and the men whom he calls 'to follow' him, are preaching and living transgressors of the dominant gender and economic orders, not just teachers and healers who respect the dominant order, or at least do not overtly antagonise it. Matters get even more transgressive when we look at the moral teaching, in the light not just of conventional norms of right and wrong, but of conventional norms of masculinity within the gendered order. Those norms are apparently generic to humanity but in practice masculinised, as feminist analysis has shown, with respect to women. That is, they presume male actors behaving in characteristically masculine ways, with 'woman' as adjunct or exception to the norm of malestream assumptions concerning agency and responsibility. Jesus' teaching, as it has come down to us in the texts, unsurprisingly does not seem to question this, and indeed, given the nature of conventional language (whether his or the language of his supposed recorders), this is not surprising. It is mildly surprising, though, that he does not follow the more conventional practice, easily witnessed in the Torah and in his encounters with the teachers of the synagogues, that adds to apparently generic moral requirements various special requirements for women. Either Jesus is addressing men only, despite the presence of women (and his textual encounters with them in reported conversations), or he is genuinely generic in his address to humanity, or he is simply unaware of any 'problem' there may be with women that might be said to challenge a generic view. Given his evident disdain for conventional gender relationships, and his focus on some 'world beyond this one', it seems likely that he simply had a generic vision in which women and men, in terms of denominated sexual differences, reproductive circumstances and life-cycle issues, simply did not exist. How then do Jesus' moral teachings mesh with his (un? non?)masculinity?

Jesus' inversions of the gender and economic orders clearly have moral implications, at least with respect to the lives he (is said to have) affected, when he called men 'to follow' him, foresaking the relationships that they (and he) were already in. It is somewhat unclear, in terms of the injunction to the rich man to sell all and give to the poor, whether this is a moral prescription to some within the parameters of subsistence production, or an economic injunction to all to foresake market relationships and economic efforts entirely (and thus to live as hunter-gatherers?). Beyond that, though, Jesus taught a morality of inverted masculinity, judged against the gendered presumptions of conventional moralities to that date:

> Blessed are you who are poor ... Blessed are you who hunger now ... Blessed are you who weep now ... Blessed are you when men hate you, when they exclude you and insult you and reject your name as evil, because of the Son of Man ... But woe to you who are rich ... Woe to you who are well fed ... Woe to you who laugh now ... Woe to you when all men speak well of you.[31]

An even more explicit upending of traditional masculinised norms comes with this passage:

> But I tell you who hear me: Love your enemies, do good to those who hate you, bless those who curse you, pray for those who mistreat you. If someone strikes you on one cheek, turn to him the other also. If someone takes your cloak, do not stop him from taking your tunic. Give to everyone who asks you, and if anyone takes what belongs to you, do not demand it back. Do to others as you would have them do to you ... But love your enemies, do good to them, and lend to them without expecting to get anything back ... Be merciful ... Do not judge ... Do not condemn ... Forgive ...[32]

It is hard to imagine a more thorough inversion of conventional masculinised values, albeit values sometimes covertly (or hypocritically) practised beneath a pro-forma preaching of the opposite. From Jesus' persistently transgressive behaviour, and his persistent rebukes of those practising conventional moralities (e.g. Sadducees and rich men), it is evident that he is genuinely different in what he does and what he says, and therefore, presumably, in what his teachings meant at the time (following the supposition that this, or something like it, actually happened). It would follow that his teachings would mean something transgressive in later eras (given the widespread presumption that his teachings would have some meaning to be appropriately transferred to other situations).

This reading of Jesus' moral (and indeed religious) teaching as inversionary may align it with some feminist (and gay) moralities that invoke values revisionary of, or opposite to, conventional masculinist presumptions and practices.[33] This seems a valid enough strategy as far as it goes for readers today, but one which does not quite pursue the issue here, which is whether this might count as an alternative masculinity. Any recognisable alternative to conventional hegemonic masculinity works to de-naturalise and de-universalise this pervasive and (arguably) damaging construct – hegemonic masculinity. Indeed this particular alternative masculinity as practised by Jesus might have something to recommend it. If men behaved this way, and if it were masculinity in a form that inverted any notion of hegemony, the world would be somewhat different, to put it mildly.

It is worth noting that the only Christian communities (that we know of) which seem to have taken the inversion of the gender order seriously, and the abolition of sexual relations, marriage and reproduction altogether, were run by women, or at least inspired by a female founder (Mother Ann of the Shakers). Interestingly the gender-order of sexual difference persisted there precisely to ensure that proper segregation was enforced so that sexual relations and reproduction did not occur. Perhaps there could have been a more obviously androgynous regime in terms of economic and social relationships, but these communities seem to have fallen back on gender segregation, rather than to trust that androgyny could be a matter of persuasion, rather than constraint.

The textual evidence suggests that Jesus' new moral order was rather like this, in that he seems to have stuck to his all-male group. Given the number of other barriers that he transgressed, and his somewhat transgressive relationships with women (the Canaanite woman and Mary Magdalene, for instance),[34] there seems little reason to presume that he could not have transgressed further and had female followers and disciples, at least ones that were recognised more overtly. Women are said merely to be among his followers. Of course, his (holy?) ghost-writers and editors may have excised anything more deliberately inclusive and egalitarian, and there is some evidence suggesting that transgressions of this kind were discarded as apocrypha. Still, as with sorting and sifting generally, in the interests of censorship, plenty of transgressions are left in. However, Jesus' new masculinity seems to me more focused on inverting conventional values exemplified in the hegemonic masculinities of his milieu, rather than on addressing female concerns, issues and aspirations. This may seem interpretively unimaginative on my part, and insensitive to the symbolic and metaphorical realms of transference and subversion. But then if we go down that road, and make Jesus' transgressions other-worldly, we lose the focus on what could possibly be some of the everyday realities of life (vividly evoked in the gospel texts) and perhaps rather easily overlooked as mundane and quotidian, given the theological framing of the narrative and interpretive tradition.

A politics of disruption

Jesus' activities were highly disruptive in political terms, as the gospel story is narrated, though apparently not deliberately so, according to his self-effacing political style. This was somewhat disingenuous, given his self-propelled collision course with the two political establishments of the time and place. It is this political drama, and the playout of the triangle of tension between the principals (Jews of the religious establishment, rulers of the Roman establishment, and Jesus and his followers … of no apparent establishment) which mark out the points in the gospels when political theory starts to emerge in what Jesus says.

As presented in the gospels Jesus seems deliberately concerned to be disruptive, and indeed the (subsequent) deduction that his was a ministry for the world (rather than just for the Jews) derives from this pattern. This begins (in Luke's account) with his banqueting with Levi the tax collector and his colleagues, which is reported to have annoyed the Pharisees and other teachers of the law who regarded such 'sinners' as unsuitable company. Jesus further irritated them by defending banqueting as part of his religious experience, rather than just the fasting and praying which they piously endorsed (for him).[35]

The Roman world makes a curiously non-disruptive appearance with the healing of the centurion's (Jewish) servant, though the fear of multiple disruptions is palatable. The centurion wisely sends messengers to Jesus, rather than manifesting himself in the company of Jews as such, or possibly in the company of one Jewish sect rather than another, thus keeping the appearance of highly politicised social boundaries intact. His message, though, demonstrates such firm belief in the preacher's capacity to heal that Jesus exclaims: 'I tell you, I have not found such great faith even in Israel',[36] surely a recipe for further dissension and strife if ever there was one.

Stunningly Jesus forgives the transgressions (unspecified) of a 'sinful woman' in the house of a scandalised Pharisee and his other guests, crossing several boundaries at once.[37] This strategy extended even to an incident in which Jesus refused to wash in their company, leading 'the Pharisees and the teachers of the law ... to oppose him fiercely and to besiege him with questions, waiting to catch him in something he might say'.[38] Of course, the gospel writer may be the one glorying in the transgressive frisson that Jesus generates, thus giving the Pharisees (and Sadducees, and other teachers) a come-uppance that is one of the strongest and most consistent political obsessions of the texts. None the less this merely underlines the extent to which a highly charged political picture is painted here.

Teaching in the temple in Jerusalem (as an adult) Jesus replies to the question 'by what authority' are you doing these things?' with a question of his own: 'Tell me, John's baptism – was it from heaven or from men?' The chief priests realised their dilemma – if from heaven, they would have to believe him; if from men, 'all the people will stone us'.[39] The large crowds that Jesus drew were thus presumed to have beliefs of their own, and to be uncontrollable and violent. In that concern the politics of the Jews and the Romans coincided exactly.

After that a plot is evidently hatched to hand Jesus over to the Roman governor by making him blaspheme, as it were, in the political sphere. This would happen by getting him to treat the Romans with the contempt that the Pharisees (etc.) felt that he had openly displayed towards their authority in the religious sphere. Jesus' reply does not really answer the question whether taxes should be paid to Caesar. Rather the identification of the coin as (somehow) Caesar's property and therefore due for return is really a clever *non-sequitur*. Evidently Jesus' *gravitas* prevented supplementaries, or the gospel story ceases there, having made its point. Someone who rejected the worlds of gender and economics as thoroughly as did Jesus, so it follows, would have little to say about the specifics of the Roman political order in terms of political obligation, civil disobedience and a right to rebel.

The merchants and money-changers in the temple did not get off so lightly, as Jesus disrupted their activities very forcefully and violently, yet evidently this was a politically safe thing to do.[40] When arrested by the officers of the temple guard (on rather unspecific grounds of religious disruption), by contrast, Jesus made an overtly political reference (rather than the usual reference to his authority to teach): 'Am I leading a rebellion, that you have come with swords and clubs?'[41] Of course, from the perspective of the religious authorities Jesus was as good as leading a rebellion, not merely in virtue of his insubordination and contempt, but because he was surrounded by such volatile crowds:

> Then the chief priests and the elders of the people assembled in the palace of the high priest ... and they plotted to arrest Jesus in some sly way and kill him. 'But not during the Feast,' they said, 'or there may be a riot among the people'.[42]

The tale unfolds from this point with a ring of political (though not perhaps factual) truth, in that the chief priests make their accusations to Pilate, who discovers that Jesus belongs in another jurisdiction, and sends him to Herod (conveniently visiting in Jerusalem at the time).[43] Herod has his fun with Jesus and rather inexplicably is reported to have become friends with Pilate as a result of the odd referral of this prisoner ('before this they had been enemies'). Pilate seems to have accepted Jesus back, but then eventually gets fed up and gives in to sheer pressure, ordering yet another crucifixion. What is clear from this political tale is that Jesus was a rather uncertain quantity. Teaching and healing might just be tolerable to the Jewish and Roman establishments, but what terrified them was large crowds with no clear leader. Jesus artfully avoided appearing as a leader, either in a religious or governmental sense, or rather as a rebel in both. The overall dramaturgy is that of sending out followers to do the same as he did (which they do in the Acts of the Apostles) and retiring to his 'father's house' via a messy and miraculous process of engineered self-sacrifice and resurrected mystery. The political theory is thin on the ground, especially given that the 'render unto Caesar what is Caesar's remark' is a trick answer to a trick question made in safety nowhere near the presence of the Romans. It is difficult to build too much on that brief rejoinder, though many have tried.

The injunctions to help the poor and the miracles that fed some thousands are perhaps more to the point. It is possible to construct Jesus as a critic of class-divided and exploitative societies, and indeed a critic of overly harsh and gender-biased systems of 'justice' (e.g. he stops the stoning of the woman 'taken in adultery').[44] However, it has to be said that in Jesus' teaching the notion of crime has virtually disappeared as well as the notion of punishment (e.g. turn the other cheek, allow others to take one's things, forgive others no matter what happens and so on). What replaces it is a pervasive accusation of sin, but this is extremely unspecific: why exactly are tax-collectors sinners? because they are rich? dishonest? working for the Roman state? any state? What about the woman who had led a 'sinful life'? what exactly was that? did he think it was really sinful? What is wrong with the merchants and money-changers in the temple? are they all right elsewhere? were the chief priests getting a rake-off? were the mercantile practices of these traders merely making noise? It is rather hard to know.

Politics and paradise

Jesus (as we are told in the gospels) did not set out to make his kingdom of this world, for the Jews or anybody else, or at least he had the sense not to say so in Roman-occupied Palestine. It may be that his focus on the 'next world' was merely a blind, and that the clue to his political theory lies in his disruptive activities and exemplary judgements. He practises a performative politics of gender and economic transgression, mixing constantly with the 'wrong' people, challenging received moral wisdom as a matter of principle, and inverting it in a vision of self-denial and self-sacrifice that is hard to generalise into a social system. The nearly de-gendered quality of individual experience, which Jesus seems to propound and to practise, marks some genuine limit to theorisations of human nature and society. Even Hobbesian man has natural lust and fear of death, and indeed is therefore a man. Jesus' version of masculinity is so reversed that it inverts the 'man's world', which frames our understanding of politics as such, and leaves us wondering how humans could live if they followed his teaching and example.

Jesus thus joins those in political theory who are critical of authority, and therefore of the state, on grounds that they oppress rather than liberate the individual. He differs from most in identifying what in fact oppresses individuals and how they might be liberated, as his answers seem to be religious ones: bearing the guilt of unrepented sin seems to be a critical oppression (though sin is itself rather poorly specified), and following his model on earth and thereby reaching heaven seems to be the kind of liberation that he has in mind (though I have trampled here on his presumably intended ambiguities). There is no particular reason why this view should not convince some people, or indeed many millions, as it has certainly done over the centuries. The job for political theory has largely been to contain this kind of utopia within more worldly bounds, and to pay lip-service on occasion to its ideals whilst creating just the kind of institutions that Jesus sought to disrupt: economic, religious and gender orders, suitably legitimated in one way or another. Jesus also joins those in political theory whose contribution seems to be wholly critical and negative, in that the positive tenets and overall solutions are only hinted at, and never outlined in detail. This is a theoretical stance recently celebrated as irony, frustrating the reader and provoking unsystematic action.[45] The political theory of Jesus, 'son of man', is not necessarily a bad contribution to this tradition and perhaps a tribute to the idea, at least, of a performative politics of subversion.

Notes

1. *Mark* 14:36; 15:33.
2. Still being slowly deciphered ... some say, deliberately so.
3. Note the current cinematic project to film *The Passion of Christ* in the 'original' Aramaic proposed and undertaken by Mel Gibson.
4. Thucydides, *The History of the Peloponnesian War*, trans. Richard Crawley (New York: Dutton, 1950), pp. 14–15.
5. The film *Life of Brian* portrays and satirises some of these problems, viz. reports from the back of a crowd that a preacher has said, 'Blessed are the cheesemakers', and a subsequent interpretive gloss from another 'witness' as to what this might mean.
6. The edition of the Bible I am using (the New International) has printed Jesus' words as they appear in the gospel texts very conveniently in red.
7. Thucydides, *History of the Peloponnesian War*, p. 15.
8. See pp. 15–16 above.
9. David Friedrich Strauss, *The Life of Jesus Critically Examined* (London: SCM Press, 1973).
10. *Matthew* 26:36–46.
11. This has been a continuing issue at passion play performances.

12 Niccolò Machiavelli, *The Discourses*, ed. Bernard Crick, trans. Leslie J. Walker, S.J. (Harmondsworth: Penguin, 1976), I.12, pp. 142–6.
13 Thomas Hobbes, *Leviathan*, ed. C.B. Macpherson (Harmondsworth: Penguin, 1968, repr. 1985), ch. 12, pp. 181–3.
14 Karl Marx and Friedrich Engels, *Manifesto of the Communist Party*, in *Karl Marx, Later Political Writings*, ed. and trans. Terrell Carver (Cambridge: Cambridge University Press, 1996), pp. 18, 21–2.
15 Hobbes, *Leviathan*, ch. 2, pp. 92–3.
16 *Luke* 2:21–39.
17 *Luke* 2:41–52.
18 *Luke* 4:28–30.
19 *Mark* 1:15.
20 *Mark* 1:32–34.
21 'Jesus loved Martha and her sister [Mary] and Lazarus. Yet when he heard that Lazarus was sick, he stayed where he was two more days'; John 11:4–6.
22 *Luke* 2:1.
23 *Luke* 9:57–62.
24 *Luke* 10:5.
25 *Luke* 10:38–41.
26 *Luke* 14:25–27.
27 *Luke* 18:15–17.
28 *Luke* 18:28–29.
29 *Luke* 20: 35–40.
30 *Mark* 3:31–35.
31 *Luke* 6: 20–26.
32 *Luke* 6: 27–37.
33 See, for example, Joan C. Tronto, *Moral Boundaries: a political argument for an ethic of care* (London: Routledge, 1993); Mark Blasius, *Gay and Lesbian Politics: sexuality and the emergence of a new ethic* (Philadelphia: Temple University Press, 1994).
34 *Matthew* 15:21–28; Luke 8:2.
35 *Luke* 5:27–32.
36 *Luke* 7:1–10.
37 *Luke* 7:36–50.
38 *Luke* 11:37–54.
39 *Luke* 20:1–8.
40 *Matthew* 21:12–13; *Luke* 19:45–46.
41 *Luke* 22:52–53.
42 *Matthew* 26:3–5.
43 Matthew, Mark and John do not record the Herod episode.
44 *John* 8:1–11.
45 Seery, *Political Returns*, pp. 250–62.

CHAPTER FOUR

Augustine: confessing like a man

Knowing too much

Political theorists like their theorists. They like these men, though everyone has favourites (and *bêtes noires*), and lately there are women, too (Christine di Pisan, Aphra Benn, Mary Astell, Olympe de Gouge, Mary Wollstonecraft, and so on – though not many).[1] Texts without authors are very puzzling, and difficult to warm up to, as they lack the human face (generally pictured on the book cover or inside, even if utterly anachronistic, e.g. busts or paintings of Plato or Aristotle). Even the apparently authorless gospels have divine inspiration, if not fully fleshed human authorship to appeal to, or failing that, they at least have a strong central character who speaks to us in the first person, and gives us that sense of character and immediacy behind the thoughts, such as they are.[2] Most political theorists are better informed about the 'biographical context' of their thinker-of-the-day in a lecture course (or rather the lowest common denominator of the biographical tradition, for the most part) than they are about the establishment of the text they are reading, or recommending their students to read (though there are towering scholarly exceptions in the profession, of course). It would seem to follow that political theorists would be happier the more contextual material there is about an author: the more contemporary memoirs and eyewitness testimony, letters, autobiographical writings, early biographical accounts, juvenilia, family and school papers etc. there are, surely the better it is. Jesus, his gospel-writing authors and God himself (whatever his role in making, inspiring or inhabiting the text) all have doubtful existences, and would seem to be the odd case out. Still, the textual narrative of the gospels is itself strongly biographical in form and content, so effectively we have there in terms of authorial hermeneutics a one-stop shop.

Augustine (AD 354–430) is the exception that proves the rule. We know far too much about the man, even far more than we want to know about him *as a man*. It is bad enough writing 117 books (extant) over his lifetime, and figuring in correspondence with other towering intellects of the epoch and fellow saints (or famous heretics), he is also the author of a massive work about himself that tells us far more than we should ever want to know about anyone, even perhaps ourselves.[3] *The Confessions* is a work of such staggering complexity, unsurpassed originality (Proust is the only other name that crops up in comparison these days) and unfathomable ambiguities and apparent (or real?) contradictions, that nothing sensibly summarising about Augustine can really be stated.[4] Perhaps Hegel would have been in this league if he had turned his mind to himself, and his pen to self-revelation, rather than his intellectual ambitions to everything else. Augustine's *City of God* (to pick an obvious choice from the 116 other books) thus has *too much author* for us to cope with.

What theorists are often looking for, other than such human warmth as they feel they need to 'humanise' their readings and analyses, is a 'fit' between the person's life-world, politics and their world of ideas, as recorded in the books or manuscripts left to us. It is helpful in this regard if an intelligible trajectory through clear periodisations can be established for us, preferably one laid down quite soon after the author's death (or occasionally) before, and ideally by some trusted, scribe-like and apparently unproblematic friend or disciple (Engels comes to mind, and Augustine's Possidius).[5] Failing that, some harmless eccentric will do (e.g. John Aubrey on Hobbes). Worst of all is getting such a bad reputation in or near your own time that all biographies must begin by repeating it and (thus self-contradictorily) trying to expunge it in favour of something much more nuanced and interesting (e.g. 'the Machiavel' and Machiavelli). Augustine had a number of highly political roles and episodes in his life, well documented by sources other than himself, and again we know far too much. For all the urge to simplify, no one has successfully pinned him down to some politics of practice to fit what he seems to say in terms that count to later readers as political theory.

Political theorists like their theorists to be serious about politics in a theoretical way, that is, the higher order issues about human life: why society? why a state? what is justice? who decides? how do we know? when to use force? There is a faith here that answers to these questions in the abstract (even if by implication from detailed examples) will be useful, and that peace, order and prosperity (at some level) will flow from getting this right. Paul Weithman sets the stage:

> Augustine never devoted a book or a treatise to the central questions of what we now call 'political philosophy'. Unlike Aristotle, he did not attempt serially to address them and to draw out the institutional implications of his answers. Unlike Thomas Hobbes, he did not elaborate a philosophical theory of politics, if by that is meant a synoptic treatment of those central questions which relies on theoretical devices contrived for the purpose ... it is questionable whether Augustine thought that political philosophy has a subject-matter which should be sharply distinguished from the subject-matters of other areas of philosophy or of political enquiry ... It is possible to recover a distinctive set of political views from Augustine's texts ... a loose-jointed and heavily theological body of political thought ... It does not fit comfortably into any one of the disciplinary categories now standardly associated with the study of politics.[6]

Moreover some sense that the author was at least ready to practice what he preached is reassuring when political theorists get ready to present and evaluate an author (drafting some laws or constitutions is helpful here, e.g. Plato, Rousseau). Problematically Augustine does not measure up to this in quite the right way. While deeply involved in practical politics (right down to the level of violent disputes, and legal claims and counter-claims), and in applications of principled reasoning (when it is right to torture, or to authorise forced conversion), Augustine's practice does not seem to follow from some architectural consistencies in a political theory that we can trace with assurance, and then re-assemble from his writings and remarks (which we attempt with all due sympathy for a busy man who did not have time to put it all together 'properly' for us).[7] If only his *Confessions* had revealed him to be a doctrinaire and predictable Platonist, crypto-Manicheaen, Catholic (but not Roman), Neo-Platonist, pupil of Plotinus, persecutor of Pelagians and Donatists (never mind pagans), Biblical fundamentalist, anti-zealot ... or whatever. Sadly he has too many thoughtful and complicated things to say about so many aspects of so many controversies and views that we are left staggered by the subtleties of feeling, never mind intellect and erudition, that his surviving work displays, and in the end we are gripped only by simple notions of 'pessimism' concerning the inherent 'sinfulness of man'.[8]

Weithman is again symptomatic:

> Political theory and political philosophy articulate norms by which actual societies are to be judged ... Where their practitioners part company with Augustine is in their view that political activity can be made or shown to be a rational undertaking ... By contrast, what seems to interest Augustine about politics is what it shows about the divine and psychological forces which govern human life but which human reason cannot fully penetrate or control ... He thereby promises a corrective to political theories which exaggerate the role that reason can or should play in ordering political life.[9]

For political theorists these are interesting themes, but not in themselves analytical and practical, at least in principle. The most detailed commentaries on Augustine's (detailed) commentaries on The Fall of Man arrive at no cut-and-dried conclusions concerning Original Sin, never mind any account of human nature such that politics is necessary, possible and valuable enough even as a craftsman-like activity to make theory really worthwhile.[10] Political theorists do sometimes reflect on the place of their own ruminations in the political world and the greater order of things, and in these moments they do not generally over-estimate themselves. Indeed for a while in the late 1950s they famously declared their subject dead (it rose again). Occasionally someone of real political significance is nearly promoted to the canon: Lenin comes to mind (Locke worked at the Board of Trade for a while, but that is hardly in the same league). Doubtless had Lenin lived longer and prospered more (in some ideologically defensible sense), he would today be more widely read (though again, he really wrote too much, though virtually nothing about himself). On the whole, though, political theorists like their thinkers to be pretty much unsullied by failure, or at least not seriously implicated (e.g. Plato), and martyrdom, with all due regret, is one way to keep the output limited (e.g. Luxemburg). Minor scandal and dubious associations are not so bad (no one is perfect, and we all have to live in the real world): Hobbes and Locke would nowadays (in Chicago and Los Angeles, anyway) have to declare their interests in companies benefiting from slavery. Rousseau's effusions on women and education are difficult to read and evaluate today, even in terms of how one would feel about him in his own time. We often seem to think that 'contextually' we can do this, and make further judgements how we would feel about him today, as if he were telekinetically available for opinion pages and talk shows. Leaving these difficulties aside, though, his views are seriously compromised and effectively confused for us by the biographical 'news' that he abandoned his five children to the foundling hospital. This train of events seems to have confused him, as well. Still, we remain here in the territory of 'warts and all', which is generally familiar ground for biography and introspection. Augustine is way beyond any 'warts', and way above our introspections. Even on memory, consciousness and time, Proust looks a real slouch by comparison. Augustine did not seem to spend that many days in bed (in quite that way, anyway), and quasi-monastic episodes to the contrary (a retreat from being an academic, administrator and bishop), his lifestyle circumstances were never ground down to brief appearances at parties and neurasthenic retreat into a cork-lined room. It is even suggested that he created the categories of biography itself through which we then try to view him.[11]

At this point the reader may well wonder why Augustine appears in the political theory canon at all, and why political theorists consider him one of theirs (though hardly exclusively – we're good at interdisciplinary sharing).[12] To follow through on that thought in more specific terms I turn to two contemporary political theorists, writing on Augustine, and putting their own answers to these questions – Jean Bethke Elshtain and William Connolly. This will, of course, expose a view as to what there is of Augustine that contemporary theorists are likely to find interesting (even if they do not completely agree about this, or about any Elshtain or Connolly interpretation along the line). Given that we have too many of Augustine's books, and know far too much about him (and given that even the classicists are still grappling with the myriad allusions of his late-Roman rhetorical style and scholarly erudition), how do a pair of contemporary political theorists approach him? What texts and issues do they fix on? And which ones do they skate lightly over, or even seem to miss? This chapter, then, is a meditation, not on Augustine's political theory, but on what political theorists have made of Augustine, on what they want their theorists to be like, and on what does and does not give someone an authorial presence in our imaginations.

True confessions/sex in the city

Jean Elshtain's freshly personal account puts us right in the thick of the political theory world, looking back to a time when, as an ill-prepared and over-stretched graduate student, she turned up to lecture on Augustine at 8.00 a.m. one cold morning in the north-eastern US.[13] Looking over her lecture notes from 1972 (what filing! not many of us are up to that), she confesses to getting him wrong on a big issue (God and the nature of evil) and so apologises to her students now (wherever they are), also noting that at an early morning class, perhaps not that many were really awake. She also confesses to using truncated texts and having little Latin, and thus not aiming to contribute to the recondite world of Augustinian scholarship (which is indeed formidable, given the modern languages involved, never mind the ancient ones). She also hints at religious feelings and near-conversions in her own life, and generally (and no doubt self-consciously) gets into the confessional mode for which her theorist-of-the-day was so famous. That is, she is going to speak truths to us, particularly uncomfortable ones, even ones that acknowledge her own guilt … and then feel better for it, as will we, if we take to heart this improving example. Moreover, public confession has a sermonising quality to it: here is an example of truthfulness, and of timeless wisdom gained therefrom. Confessing in the first person and in the present tense, so many years after the event, lends a window-like quality to the exercise. Surely we are looking straight into the soul, as who could have better access than the person confessing? Given that unforced confession must be truthful, and that the person confessing tells tales against themselves, what scepticism could there be about this? Sincerity, commitment to truth, self-knowledge, and didacticism are a potent mix. Those confessing in this way will have an audience, as it completes the reflexive circle – we look inwards at ourselves so we can look outwards at others, so we can know them better, so we can look inwards with more knowledge, etc., etc.[14] What then does Elshtain find in Augustine's 'loose-jointed' thoughts on things that she takes to be of relevance to political theorists today, and to today's politics?

Elshtain focuses on '*the self*', something with which political theorists have been particularly (and possibly overly) concerned, ever since 'their man' Rousseau posthumously published his own Augustinian (but scandalous) *Confessions* in 1782. Having written a little book on *The Social Contract* (1762) (itself a rewrite of the second of Locke's *Two Treatises of Civil Government* (1689) – and that itself a rejoinder to Hobbes's *Leviathan* (1651). among other things), Rousseau has experienced little difficulty in maintaining his place in the canon. Add in Hegel's (phenomenal) *Phenomenology of Mind* (1807), a novelisation of 'the self' as self-consciousness, developing quasi-phylogenically and crypto-historically into a modern, rational 'self', and the stage is set for considerable philosophical interest. But what is the connection with politics?

Elshtain uses Augustine as a 'self' of evident complexity and ambiguity as an ally against views of 'identity', that is 'identity politics', an organising principle such as race/ethnicity, gender, sexual orientation, and so on. In her view this is a naïve politics of 'absolutizing difference', assertions of sameness not just between individuals (and of correspondingly absolute differences against other 'groups'), but also of self-consistency 'all the way down' and of uniformity in what others must be made to recognise. Elshtain is against arrogance and narcissism, and finds in Augustine a substantive and methodological ally: 'The self judges, acts, wills, and nills, but it can never attain perfection ... Hence, Augustine's ease at spelling out a hermeneutic theory of polysemy and multiple interpretations.'[15]

Augustine is thus an exemplar, and the *modus operandi* seems fair enough: find an unsystematic but engaging thinker, collect the thoughts that fit the message, and thus the man is made to speak to us. We gain authority and respect through associations of this kind, and we like nothing better than to hear someone else so famous stick up for our views. It has been said that the advantage of dialogue with the dead is that they take criticism so well.[16] It should also be said that they make wonderful friends and stalwart allies. Machiavelli's own little memoir tells us how much better he feels when he is in his study, in dialogue with the (dead) ancients, and putting his contemporaries to right.[17] These activities give us a sense of engagement, but it has to be said that there is also the appearance of a certain evasion and displacement. On that note, however, I have to say that I suspect that Elshtain and many other political theorists have somewhat unsung areas of more direct engagement in the political present that are only dimly reflected in their scholarly output.

As Elshtain says, there are so many Augustines:

> the pessimistic Augustine … the pluralist Augustine; the romantic Augustine; the reactionary Augustine; the sexist Augustine; the anti-sexist Augustine; even a sort of proto-socialist Augustine. It is altogether too easy to slice off one chunk of Augustine and turn that piece into the *real* Augustine or the only Augustine worth salvaging.[18]

Elshtain, however, is fighting on more than one front, against 'thin' forms of liberalism, as well as against 'identity'-centred politics. Augustine proves useful for taking a swipe at liberal political theory, and at liberals, in terms of their presentation of the human 'self'. This is a famously schematic conception, defended as truthfully abstract and therefore universally applicable, 'a free-standing individual' connected to 'the state' in 'a series of reciprocal rights and obligations'.[19] Elshtain's Augustine (intriguingly accompanied by a shadowy Wittgenstein, who reportedly kept a copy of Augustine's *Confessions* on his Cambridge bookshelf) functions here as a substantive and methodological subversive: he can be made to dispute the whole liberal enterprise, with its focus on rationality and perfectionism, and to undercut its reductionist and triumphalist methodologies. Augustine thus 'complexifies our understanding', and like Wittgenstein, he humbles the very philosophers themselves before the performative truths (truths *because* performed) of ordinary language.[20] This is stimulating stuff, though the very Augustinian Rousseau has already enacted his own somewhat similar, and nearly as pessimistic critique of liberal thought and liberal 'man'. In Rousseau's works this happens with irony and satire, and he at least had the advantage of knowing all too well the material he was criticising, which Augustine frankly did not. And with Rousseau whatever difficulties we have with his thought (and persona), theological obsessions and religious erudition do not figure amongst them.

Augustine scores, though, when we get to the problem of evil. There is no better ally in political theory for those wanting to make us quake in the knowledge of human viciousness. Elshtain scores here, too, with perceptive considerations of Camus and Arendt, and considerable reportage of the 'western' evils which they wished to impress on their 'western' readers. Neither was much loved in their own time for the pains they took, accused as they were of disloyalty to various interests and ideologies that claimed them. Elshtain arrives here at her Augustine, a corrective not just to liberal optimism, but rather the expositor of a '*via negativa*' that is important and truthful in itself:

> Augustine displays the negative of ideology by articulating a canny and scrupulous attunement to the here and now with its very real limits. There are affirmations that flow from his negation of positive philosophy. Augustine creates a complex moral map that offers space for loyalty and love and care, as well as for a chastened form of civic virtue … Human affairs … are murky and bound to remain so. Earthly time is not subject to a progressivist teleology or reading … change, yes, but continuing transformation toward some preformed ideal, no.[21]

Given the unpopularity of this message ('downer' and 'bummer' come to mind), the strength of liberal views about reason and rationality (pandering to our 'feel-good' side), and the sell-out character of 'conservative' political philosophies (to moneyed interests, masquerading as 'traditions'), it is small wonder that Elshtain looks for allies. In Augustine she has one with an eponymous majesty (intellectually he is certainly 'august'), and a certain world-weariness from late Antiquity (and about a ramshackle and dangerous 'empire' to boot), that today's readers should find compelling, even eerie. While she nods in the direction of Augustine's famous battles with sexual desire, and his (in)famous conversion to Christian asceticism and celibacy, Elshtain is not that much interested in this familiar, 'biographical' ground. Augustine is marked in her account as unusual for his interest in love, specifically his metaphorical invocation of fatherly kites who watch over their young in the nest, and for further metaphors celebrating fecundity, birth and motherhood, which she says should make up for any apparently anti-female comments elsewhere. Surely, then, he neither felt estranged from women in his real life (his forsaking of sexual relations with them to the contrary) nor in his theoretical outlook (given his empathy with the *feelings* of motherhood and evocations of natality).[22] Quite what kind of *man* this makes him, though, is a question that Elshtain does not pose.

William Connolly finds another Augustine, indeed one that is 'other' to his (militantly) non-Christian ideal – Nietzsche. What he finds stimulating in Augustine are the existential struggles (while leaving most of the conclusions aside), and the way that such struggles 'still infuse the culture of predominantly Christian regimes'. This allows him to question just how secular Western 'secularism' actually is, and thus to pose a kind of cultural struggle that mirrors the Augustinian one – except the other way round, towards deconversion, and a 'pluralizing religiosity'. Like Elshtain, Connolly dislikes the 'thin, intellectualist conceptions of public life advanced by secularists' (he mentions Bertrand Russell and John Rawls here), and identifies instead with an 'abundance of being' as his highest existential faith, one that values Augustine's reading of memory and practice of confession, his engagement with 'love or *caritas*', and even a respect for, and deep interest in, mystical experience. What Connolly wants to expunge from Augustine, and from societies that still mirror this (even in their supposed secularism), is the theism (decidedly not Elshtain's project).[23] Nietzsche intoned that God is dead, and that, for Connolly, is that. Even more importantly, Connolly identifies an 'Augustinian Temptation'. This is the

> temptation to translate a series of alternative faiths that deviate from the intrinsic order you confess into instances of blasphemy, heresy, evil, infidelism, or nihilism … That is the danger your faith poses to others.[24]

Connolly thus has a programme to hand:

> One objective of this study is to plumb the existential sources of the demand for an intrinsic moral order; another is to reduce the intensity of universalizing that demand by showing how the ethical life can be sustained without it.[25]

And he has a goal in view:

> … a world where multiple ethical sources achieve a modicum of public legitimacy in and across regimes … a vision of deep pluralism that coincides neatly with neither theological universalism nor secular models of private diversity and public deliberation.[26]

Connolly thus frames his work around a political dynamic, encapsulated in the tempting imperative to bolster one's beliefs with moralising that privileges an in-group and their beliefs and thus demonises out-groups as deviants. While Augustine is hardly the world's worst example of this, Connolly takes him to be an influential one, precisely because there are so many things about the man that are admirable, and indeed widely admired. Perforce he is a saint! As Connolly says, his book is not about Augustine the man, and what can be done today to make him speak to us the things we want to hear (and to make others hear), or to make him disclose to us his participation in flawed ideas and intolerant practices (so we can learn from his bad example). Rather Augustine is a kind of starting place for delving into the turmoils of still-Christianised but somewhat-secularised societies that want to be atheistic, but not quite yet.[27]

This is an interesting turnaround. Rather than our theorist-of-the-day as man-of-his-times, we have the times-of-our-day as man-of-his-theory. Connolly thus makes an abstract though normatively charged distinction between morality (both 'orders' of command and 'orders' of design) and an ethic, which draws on neither variant of morality as it 'strives to inform human conduct'. Augustine, Connolly says:

> straddles both determinations of *order* (as command and design); he reads history and myth through the lens of this conception; he offers authoritative prescriptions on the basis of these readings, and he strives to maintain congruence between both dimensions within this ...[28]

True to the scheme of the argument, Connolly argues:

> Augustine himself both inspires a conception of moral order still exerting a powerful influence over modern life and exemplifies the attractions and difficulties such a conception runs into. A Christian god is the single moral source for Augustine. This god is both a commander and a designer. We receive the god's commands through scripture.[29]

Connolly then summarises Augustine's mission:

> But since these words [of god] are clouded by translation from the god to humans and from humans in one culture to those in others, these commands have to be subjected to interpretation. We receive glimpses of its *design* through scripture and through a common experience of harmonies in the world (within the self and outside the self). But since the overall design is beyond human powers of comprehension, we are limited in our attempts to fathom its character. When these two resources are combined, however, Augustine is confident they suffice to give us excellent guidance how to think and behave on earth.[30]

For Connolly, though, Augustine is not simply a bigot, and Nietzsche no 'Overman' hero. They have qualities in common that Connolly finds admirable and is happy for them, in their different ways, to recommend. (There's a picture here of one of those Shavian dialogues in a hell of philosophical contestation where these rather contrived debates-through-the-ages get a life of their own, once the immortals get to grips with each other properly, shade-to-shade):

> Whereas Augustine draws attention to the moral significance of memory, forgetting, sensuality, mystery, paradox, the uncanny, reverence, and awakening, Nietzsche redefines and relocates these same modalities. By comparison to, say, the dead leaves of utilitarianism, proceduralism, or contractualism, Augustine and Nietzsche share a lot. At those points where they converge before sliding off in divergent directions, they mark oversights and superficialities in doctrines that pretend to dispense with these dimensions of ethical life.[31]

Sucks, then, to Hobbes, Locke, Rousseau and Rawls. We like our theorists in teams, choosing up sides, sporting their colours, working together in alliances.

Connolly's discussion then gets seriously to grips with Augustine, but in a way that sets him on one side as a person. The *Confessions*, in Connolly's treatment, are no longer a window on Augustine's tortured soul. The confessional mode is itself analysed as something on which Augustine is not a final authority, and for Connolly the conversion story no longer has a happy ending, either personally or politically. This entails some interesting excursions not into Augustine as a man, but into manliness in Augustine's prose and in his dramaturgy. Augustine thus becomes a discursive object, albeit one constructed by himself, but available textually to others. None the less, the self doing the constructing is never really there for Connolly and cannot be, not because the man is dead, but because that is not the point anyway. The friendly chumminess we sometimes cultivate with our theorists vanishes here as Connolly considers a textual surface. This enables him to queer up Augustine quite considerably without taking any flak from those who would be alarmed or offended at such suggestions about 'their man'. Connolly is also insulated against more restrained methodological scepticism concerning what can be attributed to the subjectivity and sexuality of someone so distant from us and so determinedly masculine and heterosexual (or so Augustine tells us himself).

Connolly disputes the Augustinian idea that confession (of guilt, of desire, of willfulness) drew him closer to God; rather in Connolly's view these words, repeatedly interspersed with biblical repetitions, *produce* 'the god he worships' and engender a self 'prepared to kneel before this production'. Augustine presents a voyage of discovery (of divinity) that entails a turning aside from worldly and bodily temptations; Connolly presents a discourse that constructs Augustine as 'a sly or self-deceptive master whose will to power over others is advanced through the illusion of subservience'. What sounds like a confession to God is actually a way to define God, the God of order and of commandment (the interpretation of which flows through his obedient servant, Augustine). Connolly's re-reading of this as projection and performative repetition positions Augustine as only slyly submissive, and longing instead to command in God's name. Moreover it re-positions his discourse of healing and wholeness as the result of successful conversion, in which the 'divided will' finds 'unity, consistency, harmony' when 'infused with grace' and therefore obedience. All of this becomes a 'circle of self-aggrandizing fictions'.[32]

Even more startlingly (given the intense realism that the *Confessions* constructs for its readers) Connolly makes Augustine's mother Monica into a 'shadowy' figure. The outlines of the familiar story are rehearsed: she prays for her son, she dismisses Augustine's concubine, she and Augustine glimpse eternity together after his conversion. For Connolly all this excitement in vivid characterisation and family drama evaporates, because textually, in his analysis, she *is* Augustine. Or rather, as a character who is already converted, she represents a goal, and as a woman-character, she represents submissiveness. Connolly suggests that Augustine had more than two wills; he had two voices, and that Monica (in the text) is the feminine one, enabling him to enact 'the traditional code of a devout woman with respect to this god'. She is

> the dominant voice through which Augustine confesses to his god. She provides the model through which Augustine forms his relation to divinity – the model he imitates in confessing to this masculine, mysterious, powerful god. Augustine becomes an artful, traditional, subordinate woman ...[33]

Connolly knows that psychoanalytically inclined readers can make what they will of this, if they are interested in Augustine as a person. Connolly is not, but his textual hermeneutics paradoxically makes Augustine far more interesting as a *character* than conventional biographies manage to make him as a *person*, even when they are informed with psychoanalysis and concentrate, even more than Augustine himself does, on sex.[34]

The upshot is that Augustine, by (apparently) confessing to his god (but as a woman), actually 'folds a benevolence into its omnipotence and grace into its willfulness'. Connolly writes very critically of 'gender-duality' (clearly applicable to Augustine's god, as well as to Augustine himself), and indeed Augustine has a counterpart masculine voice of his own in 'official letters to authorities, members, converts, opponents, and heretics of his church'.[35] Connolly views this as an Augustinian institutionalisation of confession, which effectively re-runs the conversion narrative, but puts Augustine himself in the god-position, to whom the anxious converts turn in submissive obedience and continual re-confession. Augustine's rules for and advice on convent life, as well as his famous letter to Ecdicia (on how to obey her husband, and never disturb him with sinful rebelliousness) are prime targets for exegesis.[36] Note that in this analysis the focus of commentary has shifted away from the (supposedly) personal struggles of the hyper-masculine Augustine to tame his 'flesh', towards more ambiguous conceptions of gender and sexuality, and more overtly political accounts of his confession and conversion, ultimately writ very large upon the communities where he lived, and succeeding churches and civilisations.

My guy

There are clearly elements in Connolly's work for a much queerer reading of Augustine than historical and psychoanalytical methodologies have allowed for, or even as suggested by his own rather tentative remarks on gender pluralism.[37] This would open out the text considerably (by following along with the metaphors, authorial voicing and dramaturgy), and would allow a richer reading of how the text may have functioned historically (along with the hagiography accorded to its author), and how it could function in the present, as we re-read it in line with current issues and obsessions.

However, we are always going to be interested in the author as a person, however bravely we kill the author stone dead, and a queered-up Augustine will have to be ready for this, and we for him. In this reading we are not going to take him so much at his own word, and his own self-characterisations so much at face value. Reading him this way may also possibly expand our notions of sex, gender and sexuality – as if they needed any further stimulus, given the collision of sexuality and commodification that the modern marketplace displays.[38] In time, this kind of creativity in reading will react politically in public policy, and in commercial technologies of the body and 'lifestyle', as Foucauldians have resolutely demonstrated.

In that light I propose to look back over Connolly's account, rich as it is, and to take up some further testimony highlighted by Augustine's major biographer, Peter Brown. My aim is to consider the question 'what is a man' that Augustine, in effect, poses in his *Confessions*, and to offer political theorists a new light on a much-loved icon, not because we have new texts, but because the gender lens through which we now view those texts, has altered. Sexualities are today much more important in tracing the way that gender works, as a power structure, and in tracing how numerous (supposed) binaries and hierarchies are constructed conceptually and recognised politically, whether celebrated or persecuted. Stable identities are now *vieux jeux*, never mind confessional or therapeutic quests 'to discover' them, as their performative and hence unstable construction has been demonstrated.[39] This should have a practical effect on conventional constructions of man/woman and masculine/feminine, and indeed through all kinds of technologies and campaigns this is becoming more and more apparent. It may seem odd to connect Augustine's (apparently straight) confessions[40] with a world of trans-sexual and trans-gender politics, and moreover one in which parenthood and marriage are increasingly redefined in gender terms (and are thus re-defining gender). None the less, as anyone who has followed Connolly's analysis should certainly see, Augustine's text does give himself a feminine voice, as well as a masculine one, given that Monica is a fictive construction (and not in the narrative a 'photo' of his real mother, whatever she was like).

That is just the beginning. Augustine presents himself not only as feminine but as submissive, and at one with his dominant and commanding god. Surely there is a dom/sub and even S&M reading here.[41] Given that this occurs with his (otherwise) masculine persona in feminine drag, we have a further element of sexual fantasy. Given that he is dragged up as his mother, we are in a queer world indeed. Alternatively Augustine's frankly sensuous and nearly sexual invocations of the god he loves are easily read as same-sex desire; it would be scandalous in his own terms to feminise the object of his (religious) love, and the passages in question are rather more like his evocations of same-sex friendship earlier in the *Confessions*. Compare this passage:

> I love you, Lord, with no doubtful mind but with absolute certainty. You pierced my heart with your word, and I fell in love with you … I do love a kind of light, a kind of voice, a certain fragrance, a food and an embrace, when I love my God … I am clasped in a union from which no satiety can tear me away.⁴²

With this one:

> I had a friend who shared my interests and was exceedingly dear to me … He was not then [in boyhood] such a friend to me as he was to become later, though even at the later time of which I speak our union fell short of true friendship, because friendship is genuine only when you bind fast together people who cleave to you … I did love him very tenderly, though, and similarity of outlook lent warmth to our relationship … You [God] took him from this life after barely a year's friendship, a friendship sweeter to me than any sweetness I had known in all my life … Black grief closed over my heart and wherever I looked I saw only death … My eyes sought him everywhere, but he was missing; I hated all things because they held him not, and could no more say to me, 'Look, here he comes!' as they had been wont to do in his lifetime when he had been away.⁴³

Of course it no more matters whether Augustine did anything in the line of same-sex sexuality, or even felt like doing it. It has come out (for us) in his text, and that is for us, who he is. More conventional psychoanalytic readings may worry away at the moment of ecstasy that he (says he) experienced with Monica, his mother; but this is to presume that the text is a window on that incident (and that memory is truthful about it). After that, the usual questions about his 'real' desires will arise. Even with real people in real psychoanalysis, these are notoriously unanswerable and resistantly metaphorical conundrums. In a more textual reading, on the other hand, we are free to see the evident beauty and freedom of this construction! If Augustine had said he was his mother ... but in a dream, we would probably have little problem with it biographically, or psychoanalytically (though in different ways). In textual terms, however, saying that it was a dream *does not make any difference*.

It is hard now to read the conversion narrative as other than analogous with a coming-out narrative.[44] The tortured gay self struggles with social impositions that force an unwelcome sexuality on the mind and body. There is a division to be healed when a 'whole' identity, deeply personal and openly public, is confessed, and therefore found, and joyfully gained. Mentors who have been there already are important, and the convert turns away from previous practice without regret. This is the modern version of self-satisfying personal change. Augustine, though, seems to have had an ascetic drive to piety, rather than the erotic drive we would assume today. Frustration comes for Augustine when worldly matters (such as women, marriage, sexual desire) disrupt the urge to piety and religious 'wholeness'; he attains that eventually through confession and a mystical transmutation of sensual experience. This reading disrupts the usual (modern) one of erotic sex-drive; Augustine no longer conquers erotic desire through heroic religiosity, and displaces it (successfully?) in the pious life. Rather he was never erotic at all, but looking all the time for a religious experience (against which bodily desire was but a symbolic distraction, even if the pleasures he recounts were real). Alternatively perhaps his desires were indeed highly erotic, but not heterosexual; perhaps women as objects of sexual desire were deeply disturbing both physically and intellectually (hence all the struggles, and the need to find all pleasures there, somehow). Perhaps the conversion was away from all these disquieting difficulties to a homosocial life of 'intense male friendships' (where a shadowy and somehow more satisfying eroticism was the mode of enjoyment). These are possibilities raised, though not conceptualised as such, by Peter Brown in his essay on Augustine in a survey volume on the body and society. This erudite and riveting work does not, however, articulate the conceptions of sex, gender and sexuality according to which the discussion proceeds and the historical materials assembled and analysed. In examining this essay, though, Brown's criteria will emerge, and form a useful contrast with the more protean forms of queer theory articulated above.

Brown surveys Augustine under the historical rubric of sexuality and society, but more specifically, his is a study of sexual renunciation across the early Christian world. His task is to render intelligible the struggles of 'real men and women', such as they can be known to us through texts. Invoking Foucault (and suggesting that acquaintance with his ideas came personally), Brown avers that he has no wish to 'sink into the cozy, even arch, familiarity with which a modern person often feels entitled to approach the sexual concerns of men and women in a distant age'. Quoting Foucault, he suggests that we need this radical 'otherness' to make sure that we continue thinking and reflecting, and not just re-inscribing ourselves in familiar and all-too-comfortable terms.[45] Augustine, he says, 'is the only one' of the writers of the Early Church, 'whose past sexual activity is known to us'. The reason, Brown says, is frankly political: Augustine was trying to address, and to form, 'a distinctive group' – 'Catholics of ascetic experience'. Noting that Augustine wrote the *Confessions* in about 397, Brown thus has little difficulty making the narrative there (of events that allegedly took place around 386) into a crafted exhortation to follow the example of one who had successfully converted an 'active sex life' into an intensely liberating and satisfying (not to mention professionally successful) religious commitment.[46]

If that were all to his testimony, though, Augustine would be just another saint-in-stained-glass or icon-on-the-altar. While treating the text fairly unproblematically as a window on experience (albeit one constructed retrospectively in order to exhort), Brown factors the remainder of the autobiographical detail into a realm of quirkily personal 'idiosyncrasy', and thus looks through the language yet again, rather than at it.[47] This is not to tax him with some methodological flaw. Rather my point is that whichever methodology one chooses (text-as-window-on-experience or text-as-surface-of-metaphor), the result is much the same. Augustine's story of himself as a man offers rather more than an inexplicable conversion from heterosexual masculinity to celibate Catholicism. Again, my point is not that he was bent or kinky in some further ways, or that he wrote texts that say as much; rather that his intense rhetoric of self-revelation ought to prompt us to consider more seriously the inadequacy of the sex, sexuality and gender categories that we use as a baseline, from which idiosyncrasies and 'queerness' are said to deviate, and out of which (these days) Freudian heteronormativity arises.[48]

Brown's take on Augustine is that he had strong sexual needs (for 'a woman' – evidently this is what heterosexuality is), a similarly intense 'longing for clear, unproblematic relationships', and rather unfortunately, sociological circumstances such that he could not be other than dysfunctional given these desires:

> He belonged to a small but influential class of young males whose sexual arrangements reflected only too faithfully the marginality of their social position. Marriage was out of the question for him. Those who wrote and preached for more settled persons – for landed aristocrats or for less ambitious townsfolk – might think that sexuality could be rendered magnificently unproblematic, by linking it to early marriage, and by limiting sexual experience to the solemn duties of reproduction performed in the marriage bed. Such high-minded mystifications did not apply to boys who intended to live by their wits.[49]

Brown's conclusion is stark, but unsensationalised: 'Augustine had few options. Intense male friendships and the less public pleasures of life with a concubine were the best he could expect.' This of course raises issues as to what heterosexuality is, exactly, because there certainly seems to be more at issue here than desire for the opposite sex as such (appropriately qualified by age and other factors, of course). 'Woman' in that society (as in any society) is constructed against some masculinised norm, which Brown sees as working against the unity that (again) he sees Augustine desiring. Augustine's own words on 'intense male friendships' are Brown's cue, both to the sociology and to the psychology:

> To talk and laugh. To do each other kindnesses. To read pleasant books together; to pass from lightest joking to talk of deepest things, and back again. To differ without rancor, as a man might differ with himself ... these, and such like things, proceeding from our hearts as we gave affection and received it back, and shown by face, by voice, by eyes, and by a thousand pleasing ways, kindled a flame which fused our very souls together, and, of many, made us one.[50]

To get Augustine to his (self-announced) goal, Brown adds another 'idiosyncrasy': 'Augustine had been an *auditor*, a 'hearer' or catechumen of the church of Mani since 373':

> For Augustine, the Manichaean auditor, sexuality and society were antithetical. Only in a 'true church,' composed of the continent Elect, would a true society be found ... Intercourse, and especially intercourse undertaken to produce children, collaborated with the headlong expansion of the Kingdom of Darkness ...[51]

Brown then takes the story forward to Milan, the prospect of a career and an advantageous marriage proposed by Monica, the result of which is that Augustine's concubine is dismissed, and his emotional life is in ruins. What emerges is more of a career choice than sexual renunciation or even religious conversion (appearances and testimony to the contrary). If no marriage, then no brilliant career; if concubine here or gone, then no career, either:

> In a few months, in the summer of 386, the sudden touch of a strange new capacity for spiritual delight destroyed forever Augustine's hankering for a conventional future as a married man and a successful courtier ... He gained access to some of the works of Plotinus and Porphyry in Latin translation.[52]

Add to that, Brown says, in August 386, 'Augustine came to know, for the first time, of the ascetic movement'. The conversion of Saint Anthony and tales of the desert settlements in Egypt 'were crucial in bringing about his own decision'. Rather against the reading of the text as a self-absorbed confessional, this was, 'a group decision'. His (male) friends, it seems, had an ideal shared life of intellectual friendship in mind, with no girls allowed (the plot of *Love's Labour's Lost* comes to mind here ...):

> The collective decision taken in August 386, in Milan, pointed directly toward the little monastery that Augustine would found five years later, on becoming a priest in Hippo ... This monastery, and the single-hearted interpersonal bonds fostered within it by continence and poverty, remained the calm eye of the storm for the remaining forty years of Augustine's life as a Catholic bishop.[53]

Brown then generalises on these idiosyncrasies: 'Compared with Jerome, and even with Ambrose, Augustine moved in a monochrome, all-male world.'[54] The rest of Brown's survey draws out the implications of Augustine's career choice, when he went 'ascetic' and returned to Africa. It is clear from this discussion that Augustine's elaborately articulated positions on Church controversies, and his lengthy disquisition on Genesis and the Fall, for instance, were all ways of tracing out his renunciation of married love, in favour of a spirituality of continence. What does not emerge in Augustine's text, but does in Brown's, is the homosocial Church as an alternative life (remembering here, that marriage in late Roman society was evidently part of a career, not an adjunct). While it is easy enough to picture male heterosexual desire, and it is within comprehension to picture its renunciation, the line that Brown takes on strictly continent sexual relations amongst the men of the Church seems to falter at Augustine's own descriptions of the intensities of 'union' that he had in mind. It also falters at Augustine's vision of the total union that Adam and Eve would have had in Eden, according to Augustine's account, had they not fallen first into the necessarily imperfect character of human bodies and relationships.[55] Is that vision of perfect union actually anything to do with heterosexuality? Or with sexuality of another kind? Brown writes:

> He [Augustine] presented sexual intercourse [between Adam and Eve in Paradise] as secondary to friendship. In Paradise, Adam and Eve had been what he himself had once so dearly wished to be. Friendship, and not sexual desire, had set the pace of their relations ... Augustine was adamant that Eve had used no sexual attraction to lure Adam to eat the fatal fruit: he had eaten with her *amicali benevolentia*, 'out of the good nature of a friend' ... It was necessary that Adam should have had a woman for a friend – even though, Augustine admitted, in a manner that recalls his early student days, a woman's company was plainly less stimulating than a man's ...[56]

Again, the point is not Augustine's feelings, but the pliability of the supposed line between the chaste and the erotic, and in particular, the disciplinary forces (then and now) that define the homosocial as the chaste. But is it?

Brown traces the arguments of Augustine's critics, who strove to find a role for married sexuality that glorified God (and was not irredeemably tainted with the Fall, sin, shame and death), as opposed to Augustine's line, which was that married couples would be better off spiritually living chastely, if they could manage it. Julian of Eclanum, Brown writes:

> had to go on to demonstrate [*contra* Augustine] that, in strict theory, sexual desire did not have to be renounced at all. It was in no way corrupted. It was both irrational and impious to suggest that the sexual urge, as now used in married intercourse, was in any way different from that which God had first place in Adam and Eve.[57]

The extent to which sexuality in those debates became an indelible metaphor for theological distinctions, rather than a lived experience for real people in the first instance, seems extraordinary. Julian wrote, not to save sexuality as such from taint, but to valorise the human will and experience as positive, against gloomy doctrines, such as Augustine's, that so much that is inherent in the human will and in human experiences reflected 'an abiding, unhealed fissure in the soul' (even impotence!).[58] But then sexual renunciation was Augustine's lived experience, or at least the lived experience he confessed to, and to which he 'converted'. Whether this lived experience was that of renunciation, or indulgence, however, the influence of the male group in the Augustinian narrative is pertinent: he just changed groups (of men) when he went from Milan to North Africa. Feminists who have argued that sexuality is constructed from a masculine perspective have a distinct point; and the same is true of the non-sexual perspective, with perhaps some very occasional feminine exceptions.

Conclusions

Whether autobiographically, historically or textually, Augustine's *Confessions* have told us too much. Or rather what he has given us has stimulated us to deploy different ways to revitalise him and his thoughts, and will doubtless continue to do so. As an author in the political theory canon he stands alone, representing through 'excess' the futility of getting an author pinned down atop his text, other than with considerable violence (or good fortune with the historical record, i.e. in rare cases where hardly anything is known). *As a man* Augustine can be made to disrupt conventional notions of masculinity, heterosexuality and gender difference. This is all to the good, but it is rather sad that the opportunities have not been taken. Does he have a 'feminine side'? a 'gay side'? a 'kinky side'? What could those things possibly mean? Surely he could be a saint for all seasons, if we let him.

On the whole we'd like our theorists to be less interesting, their texts less self-revelatory, their metaphors less transgressive. We would like them less provocatively homosocial in their habits. If they can't be married (Hobbes and Locke were bachelors), they should at least be straight-acting.[59] If they are (all) like that, then we can keep our usual boundaries and categories in place, and can then reimpose them unselfconsciously in theoretical work and scholarly commentary.

Most theorists pose no problem. But Augustine, who famously tells us too much, has a gadfly role here. He is the queer one out.

Notes

1. Political theorists now have an official set of texts to turn to, clearly marking out a canon (in bright blue livery). The 'Cambridge Texts in the History of Political Thought' is an epochal scholarly and professional achievement, though one on which 'closure' was recently visited (at approximately 102 volumes).
2. See pp. 59, 63 above.
3. See Henry Chadwick, *Augustine* (Oxford: Oxford University Press, 1986); Jean Bethke Elshtain, *Augustine and the Limits of Politics* (Notre Dame, IN: University of Notre Dame Press, 1995), p. 3.
4. Elshtain, *Augustine*, p. 5. Peter Brown refers to *The Confessions* as 'disturbingly uncategorizable'; *Augustine of Hippo: a biography*, new edn (Berkeley, CA: University of California Press, 2000), p. 487.
5. Brown, *Augustine of Hippo*, pp. 441–2, 498.
6. Paul Weithman, 'Augustine's political philosophy', in Eleonore Stump and Norman Kretzmann, eds, *The Cambridge Companion to Augustine* (New York: Cambridge University Press), p. 234; see also Elshtain, *Augustine*, p. 22.
7. Chadwick, *Augustine*, pp. 75–86.
8. Peter Brown suggests that in a comparative context against certain contemporaries Augustine should be read as 'erring on the side of optimism'; *Augustine of Hippo*, p. 510.
9. Weithman, 'Augustine's political philosophy', pp. 248–9; see also Elshtain's spoof-filleting of the *City of God* as 'Augustine Lite'; Elshtain, *Augustine*, pp. 19–20.
10. Chadwick, *Augustine*, p. 87–95; Elshtain, *Augustine*, pp. 44–5.
11. Brown, *Augustine of Hippo*, p. 503.
12. We are also good at interdisciplinary debates. Locke's political theory of human nature in his *Two Treatises of Government* famously does not fit philosophically with his *Essay on Human Understanding*, published the same year (1689).
13. Elshtain, *Augustine*, pp. xi–xii, 20–2.
14. Michel Foucault identifies confession as a dominant discourse of modern society; Philip Barker, *Foucault: a critical introduction* (Cambridge: Polity Press, 1994), p. 97.
15. Elshtain, *Augustine*, pp. 15–16.
16. John E. Seery, *Political Theory for Mortals: shades of justice, images of death* (Ithaca, NY: Cornell University Press, 1996), p. 6.

17 Niccolò Machiavelli, Letter to Francesco Vettori, 10 December 1513, in *The Prince*, ed. Quentin Skinner and Russell Price (Cambridge: Cambridge University Press, 1994), p. 93.
18 Elshtain, *Augustine*, p. 24.
19 Elshtain, *Augustine*, p. 25.
20 Elshtain, *Augustine*, pp. 24–34.
21 Elshtain, *Augustine*, p. 91.
22 Elshtain, *Augustine*, pp. 44–7.
23 William Connolly, *The Augustinian Imperative: a reflection on the politics of morality*, new edn (Lanham MD: Rowman & Littlefield, 2002), pp. xvii–xxiv.
24 Connolly, *Augustinian Imperative*, pp. xviii–xix.
25 Connolly, *Augustinian Imperative*, pp. xviii–xix.
26 Connolly, *Augustinian Imperative*, pp. xviii–xix.
27 Connolly, *Augustinian Imperative*, pp. xxvii–xxviii.
28 Connolly, *Augustinian Imperative*, pp. 34–5, 38–9.
29 Connolly, *Augustinian Imperative*, p. 39.
30 Connolly, *Augustinian Imperative*, p. 39.
31 Connolly, *Augustinian Imperative*, p. xxxi.
32 Connolly, *Augustinian Imperative*, pp. 43–55, 65.
33 Connolly, *Augustinian Imperative*, pp. 57–60.
34 Connolly, *Augustinian Imperative*, pp. 55–61.
35 Connolly, *Augustinian Imperative*, pp. 15–23, 59, 66–7.
36 Connolly, *Augustinian Imperative*, pp. 68–74. See also Peter Brown's meditations on newly discovered letters and sermons of Augustine that show his pastoral and episcopal persona in a somewhat different light; 'New Evidence', in *Augustine of Hippo*, pp. 441–73.
37 Connolly, *Augustinian Imperative*, pp. 19–20, 23–30. See also Alan Sinfield, *Cultural Politics, Queer Reading* (London: Routledge, 1994); Steven Seidman, *Queer Theory/Sociology* (Cambridge, MA: Blackwell, 1996).
38 See David T. Evans, *Sexual Citizenship: the material construction of sexualities* (London: Routledge, 1993), pp. 36–64.
39 See Judith Butler, *Gender Trouble: feminism and the subversion of identity* (Routledge: 1993), pp. 16–25. Connolly points out the anxieties inherent in the performative repetition of confession; *Augustinian Imperative*, pp. 86–7.
40 Confessing today that you do not want straight sex at all, and incidentally deplore sex of any other kind, would be an unexpected sort of confession from a 'straight man'.
41 The theme of submission in relation to 'ruling and being ruled' in political theory is imaginatively explored by Elizabeth Wingrove in

Rousseau's Republican Romance (Princeton, NJ: Princeton University Press, 2000).

42 Augustine, *The Confessions*, trans. Maria Boulding (Hyde Park, NY: New City Press, 1997), Book X, §6.8, pp. 241-2; cf. Elshtain, *Augustine*, pp. 5–6.

43 Augustine, *Confessions*, Book IV, §§4.7–9, pp. 96–8; cf. Elshtain, *Augustine*, p. 4. There are pre-echoes here of Proust's narrator and the sexually ambiguous Albertine, and of the overtly homosexual characters Charlus and Jupien, and many other post-nineteenth-century text that define (male) homosexual identity; see Jeffrey Weeks, *Sex, Politics and Society: the regulation of sexuality since 1800*, 2nd edn (London: Longman, 1989) and Jonathan Ned Katz, *The Invention of Heterosexuality* (New York: Dutton, 1995).

44 I am indebted to John Seery for this suggestion. See Jeffrey Weeks, *Coming Out: homosexual politics in Britain from the nineteenth century to the present*, rev. edn (London: Quartet, 1990); Tim Edwards, *Erotics and Politics: gay male sexuality, masculinity and feminism* (London: Routledge, 1994); Mark Blasius, *Gay and Lesbian Politics: sexuality and the emergence of a new ethic* (Philadelphia, PA: Temple University Press, 1994).

45 Peter Brown, *The Body and Society: men, women and sexual renunciation in early Christianity* (New York: Columbia University Press, 1988), pp. xiii, xvii–xviii.

46 Brown, *Body and Society*, pp. 387–9.

47 Brown, *Body and Society*, p. 388.

48 For important contemporary attempts to open up the categories of gender, sex and sexuality, see Butler, *Gender Trouble*, and Joan Wallach Scott, *Gender and the Politics of History*, rev. edn (New York: Columbia University Press, 1999).

49 Brown, *Body and Society*, pp. 389–90.

50 Augustine, *Confessions*, quoted in Brown, *Body and Society*, p. 389.

51 Brown, *Body and Society*, p. 391.

52 Brown, *Body and Society*, p. 394.

53 Brown, *Body and Society*, p. 395.

54 Brown, *Body and Society*, p. 396.

55 Brown, *Augustine of Hippo*, p. 501.

56 Brown, *Body and Society*, p. 402.

57 Brown, *Body and Society*, p. 412.

58 Brown, *Body and Society*, pp. 471–18.

59 But not too straight-acting; Rousseau went too far with this! For biographical detail and discussion, see Robert Wokler, *Rousseau* (Oxford: Oxford University Press, 1995).

CHAPTER FIVE

Machiavelli: discourses on masculinities

Versions of *virtù*

Machiavelli without masculinity would not amount to much. This is the theorist famous for saying that 'Fortune is a woman, and the man who wants to hold her down must beat and bully her'. Unsurprisingly he is also famous for erecting as his ideal the prince who exemplifies *virtù*, the quintessence of alpha-masculinity.[1] A chapter in this book on Machiavelli could well be extremely short, or possibly pointless. Surely the link between the man, his conceptualisation of masculinity and his political theory is there already, and any commentary merely reinscribes the obvious. On this line of reasoning it would also seem obvious that feminists would have little to learn from reading Machiavelli that they had not already come to understand, the hard way, from elsewhere. Yet feminists have famously re-read Machiavelli very tellingly, and used the gender lens to good effect by turning it on his work.[2] Perhaps the trick is that Machiavelli is a theorist whose discourse is so obviously gendered, and one for whom gender plays such an obvious role in structuring politics and political thought, that his work repays handsome dividends in this area.

I am going to follow that line of thinking, and explore masculinities (plural) in Machiavelli, not to reinforce a binary line of difference over and against the feminine, but rather to do something different. This will be to complicate his picture of masculinity by pluralising it, and in particular by finding subordinate or disavowed masculinities, against which his notion of *virtù* and other manly ideals for rulers, is made to shine.[3] For Machiavelli politics was 'man's world', but there were a fascinating array of character-types and examples of manhood in that world, good and bad, on his own definition thereof. His exemplars of *virtù* had liberal numbers of 'others' in contrary apposition, whose character traits and recorded performances never reach the top. It is not difficult to see that something is necessarily defined by what it is not, as well as by what it is, and in that way a ruler with *virtù* must have numerous comparators. They show us what *virtù* is not, and what happens when it is lacking. Indeed that would seem to be Machiavelli's principal preoccupation as he comments evaluatively on rulers and ruled. If Machiavelli is the theorist for the masculinised realities of the age, then he is also the theorist for the masculinities that do not measure up.

One of the interesting things about Machiavelli's theorising is the extent to which his overtly gendered discourse (about an alpha-male, an exemplar of hegemonic masculinity) is relentlessly that of warriordom and cunning. The images and metaphors are very much those of a late-Renaissance set of ideals, themselves projected back into the classical past of Greek and Roman histories, where Machiavelli looked for origins and ideals.[4] Other writers have more nuanced and domesticated versions of masculinity to recommend, all context dependent, and all familiar contexts: husband, father, son, patriarch. In most accounts those exemplars mark important ways that the political community is secured and reproduced. By focusing on statecraft, however, Machiavelli's theory backgrounds those traditional concerns, and makes his ruler engage urgently and professionally with a limited range of public issues, virtually all of which are those of security for ruler and state.[5] Working against a methodology of generic abstraction, Machiavelli explores the world of *virtù* (and its opposite numbers) in as much detail as he likes, without the need to keep to a general account of the human situation, and to make it work as an outcome of fundamental relationships, anchored in men as generically human (so we are told) and subordinating women (when they come into view). What Machiavelli's work lacks in analytical comprehensiveness and universality, it makes up in variety and surprises. He encourages his readers to draw 'practical lessons', but these are unlikely to be very general and will certainly be anything but abstract.[6]

Many men, gendered as men, and acting in character, are never going to be candidates for exemplifying *virtù*, which after all requires supportive context ('birth', resources, 'good fortune') as well as personal determination and intelligence. These sub-alpha-males are the unsung 'anti-heroes' of Machiavelli's discourses on masculinities, to whom I now turn. If Machiavelli has the reputation of being the man's theorist, then it is a short step to being the theorist of men more diversely, precisely to make his point through effective contrasts. The 'also-rans', in this way, will have considerable interest for us, not least because to portray the world of the political as '*men's* world' will mark an advance on the simplistic idea that 'it's a man's world', which tends to suggest that there is only one kind of man. Over and against women, the world belongs to Machiavelli's men, and over and against many of those, if they are lucky and have fortune on their sides, their world belongs to the man of *virtù*. Or at least in Machiavelli's view, when we are dealing with principalities, it ought to. Part of *virtù*, then, is manipulating non-alpha-males, and that process is therefore critical to understanding *virtù*, and indeed to practising it. As a theorist of the ways that different masculinities interact, Machiavelli is in a class of his own, more attuned than anyone else to the hierarchies within masculinities that make the (man's) world go round.

Making 'man' a complex category

Machiavelli is a theorist of both strong dichotomies and subtle gradations. The strong dichotomies are famously as follows: conventional moral standards aspiring to 'goodness' for its own sake vs. a willingness to do evil when necessary for self-preservation and the preservation of the state; a rejection of idealism and the 'imaginary' in favour of a cynical 'realism' directed towards obvious kinds of rewards and securities; a sharp line between classical models and lessons at the expense of Christian ideals and practices; and a strongly binary view of gender dividing the masculine from the feminine, of which the former is clearly the hierarchical superior. However, methodological attention to finely drawn gradations, rather than sharply drawn binaries, elicits a further range of meaning from his text.

Deployment of the gender lens within that hermeneutic perspective reveals complex studies of similarity and difference within the masculinised concepts of value and interest that form, for Machiavelli, the known political world. The gender lens is just as suited to this kind of analysis as it is to re-ascribing the masculine/feminine or male/female binary to the concepts through which we know what we do in politics, and most everything else. The cast of characters in this masculinised world is of much more than conventionally sociological and commonsensical significance: ruler or prince; citizen-soldiers, mercenaries and auxiliary troops; nobles, priests and common people; men who are physically strong vs. those who are physically weak; those of mental agility and those with no wit; assertive men and men who merely await events; men of courage and those who are cowards; men who take risks and those who are risk-averse; those who flatter and those expressing disdain; men who anticipate change and those who have no foresight. Applying the gender lens in this way means that we forego here in this analysis the conventional translation of Machiavelli's gendered language of masculinities into the (apparently) de-gendered liberal terms of personhood that we are used to, and for which there are some notable feminist defences, as well as landmark critiques.[7]

Thus it is all too easy and conventional to interpret Machiavelli's lessons and exhortations as in principle (that is, in terms of *our* principles) gender-neutral in the sense that men or women could fulfil them (e.g. be a wise if not 'liberal' ruler; be a good soldier even though female; be a good citizen whatever your sex). This is not a great mistake, but rather a limitation on what can be gained from careful attention to Machiavelli's writing, and through that to his world. Following the kind of analysis that I am undertaking, the reader will be left with the question, how much less (or perhaps more?) masculinised is the present-day world by comparison with Machiavelli's, and what might one want to do about this? Whatever one's perspective on politics and on gender, there is merit in following through on the analysis of *virtù* and its 'others', as Machiavelli artfully arranges his examples through his extraordinarily vivid language. The result will be something like the wide-screen technicolor epic, a kaleidoscope of masculine activities, attitudes, poses and costumes – from plumed conquerors through grubby soldiers-of-fortune to preening narcissists and other-worldly priests.

Conventional readings of Machiavelli, as with most commentaries in political theory, tend toward a hermeneutic reductionism, forcing a distinction between the literal and the metaphorical, where the literal coincides with the methodological perspective of the commentator's lens. That is, 'realism' will emerge from Machiavelli if one register of his language is privileged as literal and the rest devalued or ignored as merely colourful metaphor. While 'fortune is a woman ...' may seem in itself to be a powerful metaphor, in an overly literal but gendered reading, 'woman' will be a literal victim, and Machiavelli's alpha-male will be first and foremost a rapist, or at least complicit with a hyper-masculinised politics of the public and private. It all depends on where you locate the literal, and therefore where you think the metaphorical begins. What I am aiming for is a wider net for metaphor, and less reductionism towards a 'literal'. While my reading of Machiavelli is anchored in an apparently literal concept of maleness (through which he envisioned his masculinised world of 'public man'), I am asking the reader to cut loose from the gender binary and its insistence on sexual difference. Instead I am advising readers to look through a range of Machiavelli's metaphors at what he says about men as men, the more to illuminate what he might be saying to anyone, living in a gendered and still masculinised world, about how masculinities are performed. These masculinities enact gradations of esteem, and important political consequences follow from this.[8]

Once tendencies are revealed conceptually through analysis, they can be resisted, and it is to that aim that my analytical consideration of masculinities in Machiavelli's *Prince* is dedicated. My contention is that a complex and graded construction of masculinities is integral to Machiavelli's text, and that those characterisations and gradations are to be established from his language, precisely because he (and his translators) have put them there. Moreover that vision of the complexities of man's world is not merely a reflection (through Machiavelli's intellect) of the masculine manners and mores of his time, but has also been a considerable factor in the broad construction of modern masculinities themselves in all their post-Renaissance varieties.[9] While not precisely defending this point with examples, I therefore merely suggest that readers move from my text to their world and get a feel for the social practices and genealogies involved. This requires imaginative effort, but then in political theory, that is one of the things we are aiming for.

There is a certain unity and force in *The Prince* that makes it an attractive text for this kind of analysis, though an extension of the project to the *Discourses* (on the first ten books of Livy's *History of Rome*) and to other texts is certainly possible and to be encouraged. The similarities between, as it were, Machiavelli's twin treatises, one on principalities and the other on republics, have been well researched, as well as their inevitable areas of difference. As most readers of Machiavelli begin with *The Prince*, and because it well illustrates the method and the payoff, I (reluctantly!) confine my attention to the more famous, and notoriously infamous, little book, unpublished as it was in Machiavelli's lifetime. Written (in 1513) for just one man (Lorenzo the Magnificent), there is a further interpretive difficulty in maintaining a perspective that does not relentlessly centre 'the prince' as alpha-male to the exclusion of other masculine subject positions. These are the 'others' that help to define the prince and to teach him the lessons that Machiavelli draws through his apparatus of research amongst the classical historians (and occasionally the Old Testament). Without these 'others' there would be no 'world of men' within which the prince must learn to operate, and with that in mind I shall begin with Machiavelli's view of the common man, otherwise conceptualised (in a crudely gendered, excluding and misogynistic way) as 'the people'.

It is important to note that amongst 'the people' women are mere objects: 'their women', Machiavelli says, referring to men of all kinds as a group who are masculinised through their presumptive heterosexuality as well as other primary lusts. Female 'princes', e.g. the Countess of Forlì, appear in Machiavelli's analysis in precisely the way that one would expect: as a masculinised figure, visible as a person or indeed as a woman, only through that narrow window of conceptualisation. Unsurprisingly Machiavelli is complicit with the misogynistic masculinity of his time, and given that his focus is on successful rulership (and followership, admittedly at a low level of consciousness and participation), this would necessarily follow. From the feminist point of view, even Machiavelli's disdained 'effeminate' men have little to recommend them,[10] though in a more adventurous way, his conceptualisations of power and authority may perhaps achieve some resurrection in feminist politics. That would require a suitable adjustment of not just the gender lens, but of feminism itself towards statecraft, which might (or might not) be reinvented or reinterpreted in a feminised world or a world beyond gender (two rather distinct goals, both rehearsed within feminism itself).[11] With those qualifications in mind, I lead the reader into Machiavelli's masculinised world, and world of masculinities, would-be Virgil to your Dante.

Arma virumque cano ...

Machiavelli's concept of 'the people' in *The Prince* is clearly coincident with his concept of the common man. What demarcates the common from the uncommon man is 'birth', ironic now as a marker, given that Machiavelli has so little interest in the womanly aspects of this, or even the manly ones, beyond the famous metaphor of rape rehearsed above. A treatise on statecraft written for a prince, it may be argued, is not of course a full treatise on the state, giving overt consideration to crucial matters of reproduction (of the state, through inter-generational renewal of its citizens), and detailing the values of family life and the role of the state in promoting them (few political theorists wish to leave the male citizenry to their own devices in these matters and the female inhabitants to theirs).[12]

Machiavelli's concept of statecraft in *The Prince* is unusually narrow in its focus – how to get power and keep it – but the work is none the worse for that. On his chosen subject, there is no one better. That focus, however, reinforces the masculinised character of the enterprise, and makes it less and less likely than anything female or coded feminine is likely to emerge. It also narrows the extent to which anything like (male) participation in (anything like) politics is likely to emerge, either, other than in the 'power games' between competitive rivals, which are the stuff of Machiavelli's discussion. Those power games are really the preserve of the nobles, or the ennobled, who are also marked as such by 'birth', save the other way round from the common man. In Machiavelli's world, the rare ennoblement of a commoner re-enacts the originary moment in noble families, inaugurating a cycle of birth that then marks succeeding generations, thus transcending an obvious contradiction. So powerful in Machiavelli's world was the birth mark, and so important was it politically, that he chronicles instances where allegations of 'low birth' were used to political effect. In the context of *The Prince* this is, of course, yet another warning of the kind of thing that – if applicable – a ruler would have to watch out for and guard against:

> [The Roman Emperor Maximin] was not long in power, because two things caused him to be hated and despised: one was his base birth (he had once been a shepherd in Thrace, everyone knew it, and it was much held against him); the other was his delay in entering Rome at the beginning of his reign to take possession of the royal throne.[13]

There is also more than a suggestion in Machiavelli's text that the lower the birth, the worse the qualities, and the further off the prince will be from the *virtù* (and way off the *gloria*) that he so much admires, however successful the prince may be in gaining and holding power:

> Agathocles the Sicilian became prince of Syracuse, not simply from the rank of a private citizen, but from a base and abject position in life. Born the son of a potter, he led a life of complete iniquity at every stage of his career; yet he joined to his villainies such power of mind and body that after enlisting in the army he rose through the ranks to become military governor of Syracuse ... Yet it certainly cannot be called 'virtue' to murder his fellow citizens, betray his friends, to be devoid of truth, pity, or religion: a man may get power by means like these, but not glory.[14]

Machiavelli's two examples of a rise from private citizenry to princely power (Agathocles and Oliverotto de Fermo) contrast the ancient world with the modern, though as his evident method is to link the two as source material for his illustrative lessons in successful statecraft, there is a certain conventional formalism at work in the choice of subject matter. Oliverotto de Fermo came from a rather better family than Agathocles, and indeed behaved in a rather better way, though one still replete with scandalous but highly successful mass murder and concomitant terror.[15] These two were rulers who came to power through crime and cruelty; other private citizens might be chosen by 'the people' or by the nobles; and some might come to power through good luck and the arms of others. At this point Machiavelli's birth marking of private citizens or commoners to set them apart from the nobility shades into a view about family transmission of skills, resources and experience, though in a crucially interesting and masculinised way. The (male) nobility are raised to arms, and have early experience of command and combat, which the (male) private citizenry do not:

> When simple good luck raises private citizens to the rank of prince, they have little trouble in rising, but plenty in holding their positions ... Men of this sort depend entirely on the good will and good fortune of those who raised them up ... The new rulers do not know how to hold what they have been given, and they could not do it if they did know. They don't know because, unless they are men of great shrewdness and vigor, they cannot be expected to have the knack of command after

living all their lives as private citizens. And they cannot, because they have no troops of their own, which are devoted to them and trustworthy.[16]

The surest way to success in rising from private citizen to prince, as Machiavelli explains, is to begin as a soldier, like Franceso Sforza, who 'raised himself from private citizen to duke of Milan; his successors, who tried to avoid the hardships of warfare, became private citizens after being dukes'.[17] Machiavelli's 'community of men', bifurcated by 'birth', is also bifurcated by arms:

> Between a man with arms and a man without them there is no proportion at all. It is not reasonable to expect an armed man to obey one who is unarmed, nor an unarmed man to be safe among armed servants; because, what with the contempt of the former and the mistrust of the latter, there's no living together.[18]

Moreover Machiavelli recommends arming 'the people' (i.e. common men, at least some of them) as a way of creating the kind of male and masculinised 'community' through which a successful principality is run and secured, both from conspiracy within and attack from without. That 'community', of course, is a sharply graded pyramid of competitive hierarchy, with the prince at the pinnacle, but then that is the presupposition of Machiavelli's whole enterprise in *The Prince* in the first place. As a representation of the structures of hegemonic masculinity, both real and symbolic, it is hard to do better than Machiavelli's pithy account. Arms maketh the man, and indeed the men:

> There never was a new prince who disarmed his subjects; on the contrary, when he found them without weapons, he always armed them. The reason is that when you arm them, their arms become yours; those who were suspect become your faithful supporters, and those who were faithful before continue so, and from merely being your subjects become your partisans. Naturally, you can't arm all your subjects, but when those whom you've armed are well treated, you can consider yourself safer from the others.[19]

It is useful to disconnect these discussions from the generic 'person' and to see them in a masculinised context, since they make much more sense there contextually, and *pari passu* in contemporary terms. Violence, competition and sport are not exactly out of date today, nor at all remote from politics (and indeed from ideas about what politics *is*), either in gangland Los Angeles, in occupied Baghdad or in the White House:

> Therefore the prince should never turn his mind from the study of war; in times of peace he should think about it even more than in wartime. He can do this in two ways, by training the body and training the mind. As for physical training, apart from keeping his troops well disciplined and exercised, he should do a great deal of hunting, and thus harden his body to strenuous exercise, meanwhile learning to read the terrain.[20]

Machiavelli thus traces an alpha-masculinity unfamiliar to us only in its emphasis on 'birth' (though modern analogues in 'race'/ethnicity and class are easily constructed). One of the aims of the men's history literature has been to make obvious and problematic what has been assumed and normalised in the utterly familiar and overwhelmingly uniform connections we observe between men, masculinisation, sports and armies.[21] These are processes, not natural events; men are not born, they are made, most famously through 'basic training' and 'boot camp', but less obviously through compulsory sports (and sports-talk). Machiavelli alludes to the 'sport of kings', and his comments fracture the usual framing of the connection, namely that 'sport' must be leisure and therefore of little significance. Looked at from a power perspective, 'sport' has an important place very central to the way that statecraft is still conceived and implemented through the symbolic and practical efforts of men, operating in man's world.

Unsurprisingly there is in Machiavelli's *Prince* an 'other' to this account of princely rulership properly rooted in arms-bearing and security considerations learned most readily amongst the nobility:

> ... it is clear that when princes have thought more about the refinements of life than about war, they have lost their positions ... being defenceless makes you contemptible. This is one of the disgraces from which a prince must guard himself ...[22]

Also unsurprisingly this 'other' is brutally marked by Machiavelli in gender terms:

> And here it should be noted that hatred may be earned by doing good just as much as by doing evil ... let us now consider [the Roman

Emperor] Alexander, who was such a good man that, among his other praises, this one is recorded: that in the fourteen years of his reign, no man was ever put to death by his orders without trial. Yet, being considered effeminate and under his mother's thumb, he fell into contempt, the army conspired against him, and murdered him ... as the armies were disgusted by the effeminacy of Alexander, after his death they elected Maximin emperor.[23]

Possibly Maximin's low birth as a shepherd was a 'manly' antidote to the 'womanly' conduct of the despised Alexander.

Within the environment of man's world, however, there are realms of trust and restraint, obligation and forgiveness. These are also established constituents of the homosocial environment, an uneasy mix of competition and deception, on the one hand, and co-operation and truth-telling, on the other.[24] Any student of rational-choice theory can easily see the characteristic patterns of individualised 'games' of strategic interaction for individual gain, and any gender-sensitive critic of this self-described 'game theory' of human interaction can easily spot the masculinised presumptions through which such generic claims about 'humanity' are made. Co-operation can arise on a basis of trust, even though the risks are obvious; co-operation can easily unwind back to the chaos of open conflict, once the fragile basis of trust is shattered. Machiavelli summarises the whole scenario:

> Those [men] you [the prince] select for special favor [by arming them] will think themselves obliged to you, and the others will forgive you, judging that men deserve special rewards when they assume special risks and obligations. But when you disarm them, you begin to alienate them; you advertise your mistrust of them, which may come from your suspecting them of cowardice or treachery; both these insinuations will raise hatred against you.

'Otherness' itself has a scale, and at the opposite end from effeminacy, we find the mercenaries. For Machiavelli these are men who are masculinised beyond the realm of calculated risks, trusting co-operation and mutual security. Successful masculinisation occupies a space between effeminacy and refinement (as Machiavelli puts it), but stops short of relentless criminality and mindless violence. These are the characteristics that he attributes to a portion of common men and common soldiers, categories that overlap. Princely commanders are good rulers who use cruelty and other 'immoral' behaviour wisely and sparingly to secure themselves and their principalities. Mercenaries and criminals are *lumpen* males who endanger everyone unnecessarily, including themselves, and ultimately care for nothing beyond their bare existence. Machiavelli's scorn for rulers who employ them is well known; what is less remarked is his portrayal of a masculinity of the criminal classes:

> Any man who founds his state on mercenaries can never be safe or secure, because they are disunited, ambitious, undisciplined, and untrustworthy – bold fellows among their friends, but cowardly in the face of the enemy; they have no fear of God, nor loyalty to men ... The reason is that they have no other passions or incentives to hold the field, except their desire for a bit of money, and that is not enough to make them die for you. They are all eagerness to be your soldiers as long as you're not waging war; when war breaks out, they either turn tail or disappear.[26]

Those that are not cowardly are untrustworthy or incompetent:

> To demonstrate further the ill effect of these troops, let me say that either mercenary leaders are skilled soldiers, or they are not; if they are, they cannot be trusted, because they will always be trying to increase their own authority, either by attacking you, their employer, or by oppressing people with whom you have no quarrel. But if your mercenary is not a brave leader, he will ruin you with his incompetence.[27]

Mercenaries are individuals, forming companies after hire; auxiliaries, also derided by Machiavelli as 'useless', are troops already formed into companies for hire *en bloc*. His advice is characteristically mordant and sarcastic:

> Anyone who wants to make dead sure of not winning, then, had better make use of armies like these, since they are much more dangerous than mercenaries. In these you get your ruin ready-made; they come to you a compact body, all trained to obey somebody else ... when you have mercenaries, their cowardice is most dangerous to you; when you have auxiliaries, it is their courage you must fear.[28]

The Machiavellian finale to this discussion is his claim that the ruin of Italy was caused by the employment of mercenary armies, and by the absence of a prince – on the model Philip of Macedon – who would 'go to war in his own person, and assume the captain's post'.[29]

While this is familiar territory to commentators on *The Prince*, who focus on Machiavelli's advice, my eye here is on the 'others' to his recipe for success, and why – in gendered terms – they are 'other':

> As these examples have all brought me to the consideration of Italy, which for many years has been controlled by mercenary armies, I would like to look into the backgrounds, so that when we have seen the origin and progress of this warfare, we can take steps to change it … Many of the big cities took arms against their nobles who previously, with the help of the [Holy Roman] emperor [Maximilian I], had kept them [the private citizenry] under [control]. The Church favored these risings as a way of increasing its temporal power; and thus private citizens became princes in many cities. Thus almost all Italy came into the hands of the Church and of a few republics; and since neither priests nor ordinary citizens know much about military matters, they began to hire foreigners … [T]he result … has been that Italy has been overrun by Charles [VIII, of France], sacked by Louis [XII, of France], raped by Ferdinand [II, of Spain], and disgraced by the Swiss [who appeared independently in 1512 and compelled the French to retreat].[30]

Machiavelli plainly has the prince and his nobility in mind as his alpha-males, acculturated to arms and command, interested in power, but for a common purpose, focused on security rather than morality, steeled in peacetime by the hunt, determined in wartime to win. Private citizens are not in his view experienced enough to do the job, no matter how dedicated they are to their cities. They simply want not to be oppressed, and thus they have no stomach for the iron domination, strategic cruelty and personal leadership that he thinks are crucial to maintaining such stability as there is within his community of men at arms. About the Church and its priests, Machiavelli is notoriously scathing. Clearly they have a culture of non-manliness in relation to women, non-violence in relation to politics, non-patriotism in their alternative power structure, and non-*virtù* in their 'saviour' who is utterly out of tune with the classical religions (and Old Testament politics) that Machiavelli commends. Most crucially the Church and its priests threaten the ideals of masculinity that are the axis on which Machiavelli's advice always turns. Suffice it to say that Machiavelli praises only popes who father sons (Alexander VI) and who lead their armies personally into battle (Julius II):

> ... [T]he temporal power of the pope was little respected in Italy. Then Alexander VI [father of Cesare Borgia] was raised to the papacy, and he showed, more than any other pope that ever was, how much can be done in that office with money and arms ... [A]nd after his death ... Pope Julius [II] followed, and he ... found handy ways of accumulating money, that before Alexander had never been used. Julius not only followed his predecessor but pushed beyond him; he planned to take Bologna, crush the Venetians, and drive the French out of Italy. In fact he accomplished all these things ...[31]

Notably one marker that does not appear particularly relevant for Machiavelli is that of 'infidel', as he considers Turkish government, soldiery and history on a par with that of Christian countries. While what he says is qualified and critical, his even-handedness in these discussions is surely inflammatory, anti-Church and anti-Christian. Moreover the geo-politics of the time was necessarily fraught with paranoia, as the Turks were embarked on westward expansion, having conquered Greece some 150 years earlier. By Machiavelli's time they were well established in eastern Europe, and indeed the crucial Venetian victory at the Battle of Lepanto was only forty years ahead in 1571. However, in the context of the evident Turkish threat and ingrained demonisations of 'the infidel', Machiavelli tells a tale of bad leadership, mercenary armies, and casual enslavement, involving Turks and Christians, in tones that are much like any other historical episode he recounts:

> The emperor of Constantinople, in order to put down his neighbors, brought into Greece an army of ten thousand Turks [in 1353]; when the war was over, they refused to leave, and thus began the enslavement of Greece by the infidels.[32]

Given his confirmed predilections about security and soldiery, the sultan's realm would be bound to attract Machiavelli's approbation. His analysis, though, focuses on the strengths and weaknesses of their state structure. The prince there, as it were, rules without a nobility:

> The whole monarchy of Turkey is governed by a single master; everyone else is his servant ...The problem in gaining control of Turkey is that you cannot hope to be invited in by the district rulers, or to make use of a palace revolt in gaining a foothold ... since they are all the slaves of their master and obliged to him ... Hence, anyone who attacks the

> Turks may expect to find them completely united, and had better count on his own strength rather than any internal disorders. But once they are thoroughly beaten and crushed so their army cannot reform, there is nothing more to fear except the family of the prince; once his line is extinct, there is no other danger, since nobody else [e.g. barons, nobility] has any standing with the people …[33]

His comments on their religion would have been interesting. One can guess how they would run. Notably he reserves the term 'barbarian' with all due scorn for the European and of course Christian invaders of Italy.[34]

Overall, then, the line between common men and the nobility is marked by 'birth' (and lines of ennoblement coincident with this ambiguous criterion) and by an overwhelming division of interests, rooted in the culture of arms that generally coincides with the nobility and princedom:

> … you [the prince] cannot satisfy the nobles honestly and without harming others, but you certainly can satisfy the people. In fact, the aim of the common people is more honest than that of the nobles, since the nobles want to oppress others, while the people simply want not to be oppressed … The worst thing a prince can expect from a hostile population is that they will abandon him; but hostile nobles may not only abandon him, but attack him directly.[35]

The world of men that the prince confronts is thus bifurcated by different institutionalisations of masculine experience such that the two realms must figure differently in the prince's calculations. Indeed, the primary factor here is the culture of arms (or inexperience of it), through which two kinds of masculinity are crucially interpreted and differently utilised in princely politics.

Common man

There is some case for attributing to Machiavelli a generic masculinity common to all men. In commentary that does not sharply divide the apparently de-gendered 'man' from the overtly gendered men that Machiavelli presents, this point is somewhat lost. While there may be reasons for thinking that he has correctly described 'human nature' and thus offered a concept universally applicable to women (or at least a concept generally applicable to all humanity, subject to exceptions), this represents a further (and highly debateable) point. Thus far I have argued that Machiavelli characterises his apparently sociological divisions (commoners, private citizens, nobles, princes, priests, popes, etc. – all male) in terms of differentiated (and colourful) masculinities. Here I suggest that he offers a singular, baseline masculinity rather different from that of the alpha-male masculinity represented in the best of his princely exemplars. Common denominator masculinity is a fairly low form, just capable of betterment into the warrior-prince mode that Machiavelli praises, but also prone to debasement into the criminal, mercenary masculinity that he excoriates. Effeminacy and refinement, on the one hand, and other-worldliness and self-abasement, on the other, represent masculinities even further from the ideal, as both reject the soldiering skills that Machiavelli values above all else in politics. On that fundamental point he addresses his prince:

> The chief foundations on which all states rest, whether they are new, old, or mixed, are good laws and good arms. And since there cannot be good laws where there are not good arms, and where there are good arms there are bound to be good laws, I shall set aside the topic of laws and talk about arms.[36]

Generic masculinity for Machiavelli is not a pretty picture; few feminists would want any of these attributes generically attributed to women. It is even a shock to consider these qualities as generic to masculinised humans, particularly males. This is Machiavelli's famous cynicism, expecting the worst of humanity, or in my use of the gender lens, of men as men:

> ... it is the nature of people [sic] to be fickle; to persuade them of something is easy, but to make them stand fast in that conviction is hard. Hence things must be arranged so that when they no longer believe they can be compelled to believe by force.[37]

While the advice to rulers is familiar, my focus here is on the ruled, and why – in Machiavelli's view – they need rulers of that kind, using those methods:

> If Moses, Cyrus, Theseus, and Romulus had had no weapons, they could never have imposed their institutions on their peoples [sic] for so long.

> In our own times, there is the example of Fra Girolamo Savonarola [who] had no way of keeping the backsliders in line or of converting the doubters.[38]

And in a similar vein Machiavelli portrays the (male) citizenry as overwhelmingly unreliable even in defence of their own state:

> At crucial moments a prince always finds himself short of trustworthy men. This is why a prince should never count on what he sees in times of quiet, when the citizens find the state useful to them, and everyone pushes forward, making big promises and professing readiness to die for the prince – as long as death is far away; but when times are tough, when the state really needs its citizens, few are to be found.[39]

Common man is easily deceived:

> … those princes have accomplished most who paid little heed to keeping their promises, but who knew how craftily to manipulate the minds of men … Thus a prudent prince cannot and should not keep his word when to do so would go against his interest, or when the reasons that made him pledge it no longer apply. Doubtless if all men were good, this rule would be bad; but since they are a sad lot, and keep no faith with you, you in your turn are under no obligation to keep it with them … you [the prince] must be a great liar and hypocrite. Men are so simple of mind, and so much dominated by their immediate needs, that a deceitful man will always find plenty who are ready to be deceived.[40]

Thrillingly Machiavelli's example here is Pope Alexander VI, who 'never did anything else, never had another thought, except to deceive men, and he always found fresh material to work on'. Continuing this unqualified praise, Machiavelli wrote:

> Never was there a man more convincing in his assertions, who sealed his promises with more solemn oaths, and who observed them less. Yet his deceptions were always successful, because he knew exactly how to manage this sort of business.[41]

To get away with this, though, the credulity of common man must be widespread and desperate, and the level of foresight and intelligence very low: 'For it is a general rule about men, that they are ungrateful, fickle, liars and deceivers, fearful of danger and greedy for gain.'[42]

Summing up, Machiavelli advises that common man is at his best when he has the sense to imitate a good example, and indeed he himself recommends the very greatest:

> Men almost always prefer to walk in paths marked out by others and pattern their actions through imitation. Even if he cannot follow other people's paths in every respect, or attain to the merit of his originals, a prudent man should always follow the footsteps of the great and imitate those who have been supreme.[43]

But at worst common man is insolent and self-destructive.

Uncommon man

By contrast, what makes Machiavelli's princely exemplars alpha-males? Here again the answer is fairly unflattering, even to an ego imbued with hegemonic masculinity. What is interesting at this juncture is Machiavelli's unusual recourse to a human/animal boundary line played out in metaphor. While Machiavelli's 'the lion' and 'the fox' are famous in commentaries throughout political theory, the prior distinction between the human and animal is less remarked upon, probably because his concept of the 'human' interests him so little. His discussion as a whole is dismissive of the 'human frame of reference, probably because he sees it as a gesture at the divine – which he considers to be useless or worse. In open contradiction with rhetorical convention he identifies the human with a world of ideals that wise, masculinised (and generally male) rulers will regard with a wily and animal-like instrumentality:

> It is good [for the prince] to appear merciful, truthful, humane, sincere, and religious; it is good to be so in reality. But you must keep your mind so disposed that, in case of need, you can turn to the exact contrary. This has to be understood: a prince … cannot possibly exercise all those virtues for which men are called 'good'. To preserve the state, he often has to do things against his word, against charity, against humanity, against religion. Thus he has to have a mind ready to shift as the winds of fortune and the varying circumstances of life may dictate. And as I said above, he should not depart from the good if he can hold to it, but he should be ready to enter on evil if he has to.[45]

Conversely Machiavelli subliminally identifies ideals of 'humanity' with the Church, its teachings and its concern for the divine. His princely reader(s) will already know his opinion of the Church's role in contemporary politics, and they will also be familiar with the discord he establishes between political practicalities and the conventional moral teaching of Christianity. His comments that he dare not venture into such territory but instead will leave it to God's representatives on earth are clearly tongue-in-cheek, and frankly cheeky:

> These [ecclesiastical states], then, are the only safe and happy governments. But since they are ruled by a heavenly providence to which human reason cannot reach, I shall say nothing of them. Instituted as they are by God, and sustained by him, it would be a rash and imprudent man who ventured to discuss them.[46]

While Machiavelli seems to recommend 'moral' behaviour some of the time, admittedly when it works to the interests of the prince (and his state), his meditations on the 'mind' that makes those choices delivers nothing that would please anyone with conventional moral views. The self-interested, suspicious and security-minded 'mind' that chooses a moral outlook is clearly no moral mind – in Machiavelli's view, never mind our post-Kantian views on conscience and the moral outlook. This is not just because Machiavelli's 'mind' does not choose moral goodness for its own sake (a classical idea rehearsed in *The Republic*, so not anachronistic here), but because this 'mind's' prior agenda as a 'chooser' is so at odds with the singularity and consistency that Christian (or Christian-derived) moral philosophies require. From that perspective, the 'you' that is behind your choice whether to be moral or not is a rather 'thin' sort of 'you', as all it does is choose, and to be moral, it already has to be at one with its choice. Machiavelli's 'you' that he advises the prince to learn and internalise is rather different, since it is dedicated to survival (not self-sacrifice), self-interest (not the interests of others) and an inegalitarian view of other men as weak, deceptive, credulous and fickle. Chiron the Centaur, in that respect, is the model teacher, rather than the model alpha-male. He embodies two natures, the human and the animal, and is thus an obvious object lesson, not in how to be, but in which two choices are available:

> You [the prince] should consider then, that there are two ways of fighting, one with laws and the other with force. The first is properly a human method, the second belongs to beasts. But as the first method does not always suffice, you sometimes have to turn to the second. Thus a prince must know how to make good use of both the beast and the man ... a prince must know how to use both these two natures, and that one without the other has no lasting effect.[47]

Machiavelli's alpha-male is thus neither half-human, half-animal, nor fully human nor fully animal. Intriguingly metaphors fail here. Whatever the alpha-male prince is, his mind has at its disposal an understanding of the (lesser) male world such that laws (which animals do not have) may sometimes be appropriate, and at other times, force (which Machiavelli takes to be inconsistent with the human ideal, hence an attribute of 'the beast'). Existentially the prince is in a category of his own, well out of any morality of egalitarian sacrifice, and always attuned to brutality. Brutality is the 'other' to the human (but useless and self-destructive) moral ideal. What tempers force is not morality but cold calculation.

Moreover, when the alpha-male prince needs to be 'of the beast' and use force in ways contrary to conventional morality, he has a choice of animals:

> Since a prince must know how to use the character of beasts, he should pick for imitation the fox and the lion. As the lion cannot protect himself from traps, and the fox cannot defend himself from wolves, you have to be a fox in order to be wary of traps, and a lion to overawe the wolves.[48]

Machiavelli's princely star in this regard was the Roman Emperor Severus, 'a most ferocious lion and a very clever fox'. He used ruthless force, though short of cruelty, and wily foresight, picking his enemies off one by one: 'he was feared and respected by all, and his army did not hate him'.[49]

Metaphors have failed Machiavelli in snappily characterising his alpha-male prince. The ideal ruler is not a fox or a lion, metaphorically speaking, and certainly not literally. Nor is he half-human/half-animal, nor fully human (i.e. male) as others are, in the character of the common man described above: weak, deceptive, credulous and fickle. This princely creature is above it all, in some sense, a flexible consciousness choosing instrumentally to fulfil a goal, unbounded by either the strictures of morality that supposedly define the human (but in practice lead individuals and states to destruction) or by the unimaginative and repetitive nature of animals, who do not really choose. Moreover, animals in the literal sense are not really the model. Are foxes really wily? Or do we just think that they look and act that way? Lions are not kings of anything; princes should not spend their time watching them for lessons. Lions *stand for* brutality and forcefulness, which clearly needs intelligent direction; foxes *stand for* a calculating intelligence. Common man, in Machiavelli's view, is not all that bright. Princely man, the ultimate alpha-male, has got brains, and is not afraid to use them. He understands the symbolism already inscribed in the animal metaphors that Machiavelli uses to remind him of his specific, this-worldly concerns, and to reinforce his contempt for Christian views of 'the human' that evoke other-worldly moralities.

Man's world

This discussion of Machiavelli's *The Prince*, surely one of the most notorious yet readable little books ever circulated, has attempted to set any degendered readings of 'man' and 'humanity' that might seem to inhere in the text well over to one side. Another reading of *The Prince* can weigh up those questions. Instead, I have striven to take gender seriously by analysing the gendered character of Machiavelli's thought in great detail, not by detailing its marginalisation, exclusion and brutalisation of the feminine (which has already been done), but by exploring similar issues through the lens of multiple masculinities. This rearranges the voicing of Machiavelli's text, in that he as author speaks to the prince, and we as readers/eavesdroppers tend to listen in. By turning the social hierarchy, within an overtly and relentlessly masculinised perspective, bottoms up, I have tried to interest the reader in the low-life aspects of male society as such.

This is rather apart from the text's own view, which is that they – the lesser males – are all problems for the prince. Rather they are now problems for us (inclusively), in so far as statecraft still crucially revolves around the powers, prerogatives and privileges of armed men and their masculinised leaders, who must strive to protect their own position (as 'nobility', however this position is achieved these days). In Machiavellian fashion we can expect them to deceive the unarmed private citizenry, and to cope as Machiavelli advises with the temptations of mercenaries and auxiliaries, not to mention masculinised criminality (such as is found in the drug trade, sex trade, arms trade, etc.). Machiavelli's low opinion of 'common man' does not help anyone who wants to make a case for democracy, but then perhaps his princely scenario (and his reservations about republican regimes with respect to arms culture) are salutary warnings for those who take the higher, non-masculinised ideals of 'humanity' more seriously than he does. Democracies have mixed feelings and mixed institutions relating to leadership, military establishments, conscription and militarised values in wartime, peacetime or any point in between. Those values are decidedly masculinised in the Machiavellian mode, and they cannot be successfully reformed unless and until their gendered qualities are thoroughly explored, evaluated and remade. Alternatively if those values merely need revising to include women, gays, racial/ethnic and religious minorities, or whomever, then this at least detaches the masculinisation from the stereotypical 'noble' male body, however 'birth'-marked with the familiar identifiers of hegemony and prejudice.[50]

These are tough questions, posed – in effect – by a tough author. If the world is to be less tough, then masculinisation through the hegemonic alpha-male and his culture of arms and force will have to be different, or non-existent. If there is to be rule by laws and rights, then the 'minds' that do the choosing to make them operative and secure will have to be rather different from the 'mind' that Machiavelli advises the prince to adopt, namely the one that has sometimes to be immoral, deceptive and cruel in order to prevent greater harm. For that to be the case, the greater harm would have to recede. At present great harm still resides in the princely geo-politics that the masculinised mind constructs, and which continuous 'conflict' makes visible. The masculinised 'mind' constructs these arms races and armed encounters through presuming, and reinforcing, the denigrated masculinities that are 'other' to it, and against which it appears necessary and effective.[51] Masculinities that are 'other' to it are sometimes portrayed as feminised, a universal 'other' to masculinised domination. Whether there is a way of conceiving gender as a set of less destructive binary and hierarchical power-relations remains to be seen. It may be, on the other hand, that gender as a set of binary and hierarchical powers simply is – always and already – necessarily destructive. This is an alternative, and even more daunting, possibility.

The resolution to this dilemma is not in Machiavelli, nor as yet in anyone's political theory, but it is possible that with Machiavelli we have a good guide to what the answer is not.

Notes

1 Niccolò Machiavelli, *The Prince*, ch. XXV; trans. and ed. Robert M. Adams (New York: Norton, 1977; hereafter 'Adams'), p. 72; cf. *The Prince*, ed. Skinner and Price (hereafter 'Skinner'), p. 87.
2 Hannah Fenichel Pitkin, *Fortune is a Woman: gender and politics in the thought of Niccolò Machiavelli*, new edn (Chicago, IL: Chicago University Press, 1999) is the classic study.
3 R.W. Connell, *Masculinities* (Cambridge: Polity Press, 1995), pp. 76–81.
4 See Quentin Skinner, *The Foundations of Modern Political Thought*, vol. 1: *The Renaissance* (Cambridge: Cambridge University Press, 1978).
5 The public/private and domestic/international distinctions, and the concept of security as deployed in traditional statecraft, have all been extensively critiqued within the feminist tradition. While commending this critique to readers, I am rather exploring Machiavelli's own terms further to expose the interesting and important nuances of man's world.
6 Machiavelli, *Discourses*, Preface to Book 1, p. 99.
7 Zillah Eisenstein, *The Radical Future of Liberal Feminism* (Boston, MA: Northeastern University Press, 1986); Carole Pateman, *The Sexual Contract* (Cambridge: Polity Press, 1988); Terrell Carver, '"Public man" and the critique of masculinities', *Political Theory* 24 (1996), pp. 673–86.
8 Evans, *Sexual Citizenship*, pp. 5–6.
9 Charlotte Hooper, *Manly States: masculinities, international relations, and gender politics* (New York and Chichester: Columbia University Press, 2001), pp. 2-6.
10 In recommending to gay men an anti-militaristic and anti-military politics, Peter Tatchell also recommends them to feminists, commenting 'a little effeminacy harms noone [sic]'; *We Don't Want to March Straight: masculinity, queers and the military* (London: Cassell, 1995), p. 14.
11 See Kathleen B. Jones, *Compassionate Authority: democracy and the representation of women* (London: Routledge, 1993); Judith Grant, *Fundamental Feminism: contesting the core concepts of feminist theory* (London: Routledge, 1993).
12 See Jacqueline Stevens, *Reproducing the State* (Princeton, NJ: Princeton University Press, 1999).
13 Machiavelli, *The Prince*, ch. XIX; Adams, pp. 57–8; cf. Skinner, p. 70.
14 Machiavelli, *The Prince*, ch. VIII; Adams, pp. 25–6; cf. Skinner, pp. 30–1.

15 Machiavelli, *The Prince*, ch. VIII; Adams, pp. 26–7; cf. Skinner, pp. 32–3.
16 Machiavelli, *The Prince*, ch. VII; Adams, p. 19; cf. Skinner, pp. 22–3.
17 Machiavelli, *The Prince*, ch. XIV; Adams, p. 42; cf. Skinner, p. 52.
18 Machiavelli, *The Prince*, ch. XIV; Adams, p. 42; cf. Skinner, p. 52.
19 Machiavelli, *The Prince*, ch. XX; Adams, pp. 59–60; cf. Skinner, p. 72.
20 Machiavelli, *The Prince*, ch. XIV; Adams, pp. 42; cf. Skinner, pp. 52–3.
21 For an overview, see Harry Brod (ed.), *The Making of Masculinities: the new men's studies* (Winchester, MA: Allen & Unwin, 1987).
22 Machiavelli, *The Prince*, ch. XIV; Adams, p. 42; cf. Skinner, p. 52.
23 Machiavelli, *The Prince*, ch. XIX; Adams, pp. 55, 58; cf. Skinner, pp. 68, 70.
24 Jeff Hearn, *Men in the Public Eye: the construction and deconstruction of public men and public patriarchies* (London: Routledge, 1992); Connell, *Masculinities*, pp. 164–81.
25 Machiavelli, *The Prince*, ch. XX; Adams, p. 60; cf. Skinner, p. 72.
26 Machiavelli, *The Prince*, ch. XII; Adams, p. 35; cf. Skinner, p. 43.
27 Machiavelli, *The Prince*, ch. XII; Adams, p. 36; cf. Skinner, p. 44.
28 Machiavelli, *The Prince*, ch. XIII; Adams, p. 40; cf. Skinner, p. 49.
29 Machiavelli, *The Prince*, chs XII-XIII; Adams, pp. 36, 42; cf. Skinner, pp. 44, 51.
30 Machiavelli, *The Prince*, ch. XII; Adams, p. 38; cf. Skinner, pp. 46–7.
31 Machiavelli, *The Prince*, ch. XII; Adams, p. 34; cf. .Skinner, p. 41.
32 Machiavelli, *The Prince*, ch. XIII; Adams, p. 39; cf. Skinner, pp. 48–9.
33 Machiavelli, *The Prince*, ch. IV; Adams, p. 13; cf. Skinner, p. 16.
34 Machiavelli, *The Prince*, ch. XXVI; Adams, pp. 72–3; cf. Skinner, pp. 87–8.
35 Machiavelli, *The Prince*, ch. IX; Adams, p. 29; cf. Skinner, p. 35.
36 Machiavelli, *The Prince*, ch. XII; Adams, p. 35; cf. Skinner, pp. 42–3.
37 Machiavelli, *The Prince*, ch. VI; Adams, p. 18; cf. Skinner, p. 21.
38 Machiavelli, *The Prince*, ch. VI; Adams, p. 18; cf. Skinner, p. 21.
39 Machiavelli, *The Prince*, ch. IX; Adams, p. 31; cf. Skinner, p. 37.
40 Machiavelli, *The Prince*, ch. XVIII; Adams, pp. 49–50; cf. Skinner, pp. 61–2.
41 Machiavelli, *The Prince*, ch. XVIII; Adams, p. 50; cf. Skinner, p. 62.
42 Machiavelli, *The Prince*, ch. XVII; Adams, pp. 47–8; cf. Skinner, p. 59.
43 Machiavelli, *The Prince*, ch. VI; Adams, p. 16; cf. Skinner, p. 19.
44 Machiavelli, *The Prince*, ch. XIX; Adams, p. 54; cf. Skinner, p. 67.
45 Machiavelli, *The Prince*, ch. XVIII; Adams, pp. 50–1; cf. Skinner, p. 62.
46 Machiavelli, *The Prince*, ch. XI; Adams, p. 33; cf. Skinner, p. 40.
47 Machiavelli, *The Prince*, ch. XVIII; Adams, pp. 49–50; cf. Skinner, p. 61.
48 Machiavelli, *The Prince*, ch. XVIII; Adams, p. 50; cf. Skinner, pp. 61–2.
49 Machiavelli, *The Prince*, ch. XIX; Adams, p. 56; cf. Skinner, p. 69.

50 For analytical discussion of some of these issues, see Snyder, *Citizen-Soldiers*; Carol Cohn, 'Gays in the military: texts and subtexts', in Marysia Zalewski and Jane Parpart, eds, *The 'Man Question' in International Relations* (Boulder, CO: Westview, 1998), pp. 129–49.

51 For further reflections on these themes, see Terrell Carver, 'Men and IR/Men in IR', in Louiza Odysseos and Hakan Seckinelgin, eds, *Gendering the International* (Basingstoke: Palgrave, 2002), pp. 86–105; Dubravka Zarkov, 'The body of the other man: sexual violence and the construction of masculinity, sexuality and ethnicity in Croatian media', in Caroline O.N. Moser and Fiona C. Clark, eds, *Victims, Perpetrators or Actors? gender, armed conflict and political violence* (London: Zed, 2001), pp. 69–82.

CHAPTER SIX

Hobbes: materialism, mechanism, masculinity

Sovereignty and gender

The most famous visual representation of unitary state sovereignty is undoubtedly the frontispiece of Hobbes's *Leviathan* of 1651. Hobbes's representation is indubitably corporeal and male, or at least visually coded as such. Like any number of monarchical images he is crowned, holds a sword and sceptre, and overawes his domain, pictured as town and country. Unlike other representations of the king's sovereign body, though, his body seems to be composed of the bodies of his subjects collectively amassed. They give the general impression of being all male (though it is rather hard to tell), or at least all adult. Or perhaps the surface of his body reflects his subjects, limning a constitutive relationship. And again, unlike other representations, Hobbes's sovereign overawes both secular and ecclesiastical powers, portrayed as castle and church, because he is himself neither, but rather a '*Mortall God*', brought into existence by '*Acquisition*' involving 'Naturall force', or by '*Institution*' involving 'mutuall Covenants' amongst a multitude. In the both cases they agree, 'every man with every man', to authorise all his actions and judgements.[1]

Hobbes's frontispiece thus displays certain radical differences from earlier *representations* of kingly sovereignty, just as is argued in his book with respect to *conceptions* of kingly sovereignty. But there are also strong lines of similarity – otherwise both the representation and the conceptions would be unintelligible as interventions in a debate on the nature of the best state. Hobbes's text, and his frontispiece, also draw on conceptions of masculinity almost too obvious to notice. Or rather, given the normality of the link between masculinity and sovereignty, it was genuinely little noticed until feminist studies drew out the implications of what it is not – a representation of a woman, of women, of things which – for one reason or other – are characteristically done by women, or more complicatedly, 'coded feminine'. Note that this kind of analysis in terms of 'coding' accommodates women participating in things 'coded masculine', e.g. Elizabeth I calling herself 'your Prince', and Margaret Thatcher's Hobbesian handbag doing service for the sovereign's sword.

Whether there is anything much else to know about the traditional connections between over-awing masculinity and state sovereignty – other than that it is not about, by, with, or for women – is really the question this chapter is posing. This is a question that has been posed before, very largely in a feminist context outside political theory at first, and then later in a feminist context within it. What I am proposing to do here is to draw on a rather different literature than previous studies have generally done, in order to move the discussion on a bit further. This is going to mean that the discussion will be more complex, and I hope more interesting and useful, while not negating or marginalising previous achievements.

Sovereignty itself is a concept that is politically deployed, in just the way that Hobbes intended, to create states of a certain sort, rather than merely to represent them. The Hobbesian representation of state sovereignty could almost do as a recruiting poster for the military, calling and commanding men to come forward bodily and to fit a bodily image. The image, of course, is that of armed pursuit of, and defence of, the bodily self, and hence of a calculating rationality to match – reading the text into the image, as presumably one is intended to do. Just as real armies are created with reference to, and once created are cross-cut by, highly varied binaries of race/ethnicity, language, class and religion, sex and sexual orientation, age and culture, so the Hobbesian representation of state sovereignty is deployed to mask this diversity amongst states, as well as amongst the constituent males (and masculinised females) in armies.[2] Even in Hobbes himself, however, the mask slips and masculinity emerges as complex and various. Men are not all in the same mould, hence masculine in the same way (despite presumed bodily similarity), in Hobbes's text. In considering conscription, and consequent risk of life, a variant suddenly emerges. In other circumstances, there would no doubt be further variations from the warrior theme:

> Upon this ground, a man that is commanded as a Souldier to fight against the enemy, though his Soveraign have Right enough to punish his refusall with death, may nevertherlesse in many cases refuse, without Injustice; as when he substituteth a sufficient Souldier in his place: for in this case he deserteth not the service of the Common-wealth. And there is allowance to be made for naturall timorousnesse, not onely to women, (of whom no such dangerous duty is expected,) but also to men of feminine courage.[3]

Making rare appearances in *Leviathan*, women (and children, often collectively grouped together, as against ideal-typical males)[4] are portrayed by Hobbes as dependent, needing help. This passage occurs in his lengthy typology of human psychology and picks out an exception to a general, masculine norm of emotional control:

> ... *Sudden Dejection*, is the passion that causeth WEEPING; and is caused by such accidents, as suddenly take away some vehement hope, or some prop of their power: And they are most subject to it, that rely principally on helps externall, such as are Women, and Children.[5]

Rather than pursue the familiar imagery of the masculine/feminine binary, which Hobbes is as willing to deploy for his purposes as anyone, I aim to take the discussion along a different track, in order to illuminate both political action (by states, groups, individuals) and modern hegemonic masculinity (by drawing explicitly on metaphor, rather than on Weberian typologies). To do this, however, I need to consider the over-arching metaphors of Hobbes's very philosophy.

Science and nonsense

Famously Hobbes wrote a 'science of politics', making explicit use of the latest and most radical science of the time.[6] One of the delights of *Leviathan* is the scorn and ridicule he pours on the 'Schoolmen', who espoused an Aristotelian array of concepts relating to the physical world, which Hobbes considers not just unscientific but nonsensical. By contrast with the ambiguous Aristotelian 'essences', his view of science is relentlessly and non-dualistically materialist, founded on 'bodies in motion' exclusively and employing the Gallilean principle of inertia throughout:

> That when a thing lies still, unlesse somewhat els stirre it, it will lye still for ever, is a truth that no man doubts of. But that when a thing is in motion, it will eternally be in motion, unless somewhat els stay it, though the reason be the same, (namely, that nothing can change it selfe,) is not so easily assented to.[7]

Typically the Schoolmen come in for another swipe here:

> For men measure, not onely other men, but all other things, by themselves: and because they find themselves subject after motion to pain, and lassitude, think every thing els growes weary of motion, and seeks repose of its own accord ... From hence it is, that the Schooles say, Heavy bodies fall downwards, out of an appetite to rest, and to conserve their nature in that place which is most proper for them; ascribing appetite, and Knowledge of what is good for their conservation, (which is more than man has) to things inanimate absurdly.[8]

Again, the motions of animate 'things' (such as 'man') are then likened to inanimate motions, presented as analogous to mechanical systems ('wind' and 'waves') and no different in kind:

> When a Body is once in motion, it moveth (unless something els hinder it) eternally; and whatsoever hindreth it, cannot in an instant, but in time, and by degrees quite extinguish it: And as wee see in the water, though the wind cease, the waves give not over rowling for a long time after; so also it happeneth in that motion, which is made in the internall parts of a man, then, when he Sees, Dreams, etc. ... IMAGINATION therefore is nothing but *decaying sense*; and is found in men, and many other living Creatures, as well sleeping, as waking.[9]

The sensations one experiences in dreaming that are apparently sensory (e.g. seeing images) but in fact take place with the sense organs 'benummed' (e.g. closed eyes), are explained by Hobbes in terms not just of motion but of a mechanism or 'connexion'. This is not described directly through sensible experience:

> The imaginations of them that sleep, are those we call *Dreams*. And these also (as all other Imaginations) have been before, either totally, or by parcells in the Sense ... and therefore [there can be] no Dreame, but what proceeds from the agitation of the inward parts of mans body; which inward parts, for the connexion they have with the Brayn, and other Organs, when they be distempered, do keep the same in motion ...[10]

Orderliness, such as there is, in all these motions, waking or dreaming, is explained through a mechanical analogy, clearly described though not in fact understood (the theory of surface tension being somewhat down the road of scientific 'discovery' from Hobbes's careful but non-theoretical observation):

> And those motions that immediately succeeded one another in the sense, continue also together after Sense: In so much as the former coming again to take place, and be praedominant, the later followeth, by coherence of the matter moved, in such manner, as water upon a plain Table is drawn which way any one part of it is guided by the finger.[11]

Methodologically Hobbes's prime definition for science begins with strict definitions that are never varied, and which function in logical reasoning very like the numbers in arithmetic calculations and the logical deductions of Euclidean geometry. This is previewed in relation to 'Beasts':

> The Imagination that is raysed in man (or any other creature indued with the faculty of imagining) by words, or other voluntary signes, is that we generally call *Understanding*; and is common to Man and Beast. For a dogge by custome will understand the call, or rating of his Master; and so will many other Beasts. That Understanding which is peculiar to man, is the Understanding not onely his will; but his conceptions and thoughts, by the sequell and contexture of the names of things into Affirmations, Negations, and other formes of Speech …[12]

More formally and explicitly, Hobbes defines truth:

> Seeing then that *truth* consisteth in the right ordering of names in our affirmations, a man that seeketh precise *truth*, had need to remember what every name he uses stands for; and to place it accordingly; or else he will find himselfe entangled in words, as a bird in lime-twiggs; the more he struggles, the more belimed.[13]

Much the same occurs when Hobbes recommends accurate and consistent definitions, contrasting this method again with the practices of the Schools:

> By this it appears how necessary it is for any man that aspires to true Knowledge, to examine the Definitions of former Authors; and either to correct them, where they are negligently set down; or to make them

> himselfe. For the errours of Definitions multiply themselves, according as the reckoning proceeds; and lead men into absurdities ... From whence it happens, that they which trust to books, do as they that cast up many little summs into a greater, without considering whether those little summes were rightly cast up or not; and at last finding the errour visible, and not mistrusting their first grounds, know not which way to cleere themselves; but spend time in fluttering over their bookes; as birds that entring by the chimney, and finding themselves inclosed in a chamber, flutter at the false light of a glasse window, for want of wit to consider which way they came in.[14]

The human is more cleverly organised, it seems, but only potentially; obviously Hobbes thinks that many misuse this capacity to keep to clear definitions, to order them consistently, and thus to keep their mental and bodily motions running in an efficient and self-protective way. Birds are more subject to chance, not having such a built-in system of accident-avoidance.

For Hobbes, ideas are correct when they are accurate reflections of, or better, material analogues for, the objects of which the world outside the brain consists. Second-order concepts, such as numerical and logical relationships, enable these primary thoughts to be rightly ordered:

> Of Names, some are *Proper*, and singular to one onely thing ... and some are *Common* to many things ... in respect of all which together, it is called an *Universall*; there being nothing in the world Universall but Names; for the things named, are every one of them Individuall and Singular.[15]

Right ordering is then a primarily mathematical process, even when what are added and subtracted are words, rather than numbers:

> When a man *Reasoneth*, hee does nothing else but conceive a summe totall, from Addition of parcels; or conceive a Remainder, from Substraction of one summe from another: which (if it be done by Words,) is conceiving of the consequence of the names of all the parts, to the name of the whole; or from the names of the whole and one part, to the name of the other part ... For as Arithmeticians teach to adde and substract in *numbers*; so the Geometricians teach the same in *lines, figures* (solid and superficiall,) *angles, proportions, times,* degrees of *swiftnesse, force, power,* and the like; The Logicians teach the same in *Consequences of words*; adding together *two Names*, to make an *Affirmation*;

and two *Affirmations*, to make a *Syllogisme*; and *many Syllogismes* to make a *Demonstration*; and from the *summe*, or *Conclusion* of a *Syllogisme*, they substract one *Proposition*, to find the other ... In summe, in what matter soever there is place for *addition* and *substraction*, there also is place for *Reason*; and where these have no place, there *Reason* has nothing at all to do.[16]

To test out reason, Hobbes invents a confrontation between a 'natural Fool' and a clock, an invocation of the orderly archetype of predictable and predictive reasoning:

A naturall foole that could never learn by heart the order of numerall words, as *one*, *two*, and *three*, maybe observe every stroak of the Clock, and nod to it, or say one, one, one; but can never know what houre it strikes ... So that without words, there is no possibility of reckoning of Numbers; much lesse of Magnitudes, of Swiftnesse, of Force, and other things, the reckonings whereof are necessary to the being, or well-being of man-kind.[17]

This neatly closes the gap between arithmetical calculations with numerals and correct reckoning with other words, which are non-numerical, but similarly closely and consistently defined.

When the sense impressions at the basis of the thoughts are one's own, according to Hobbes, then there is certain knowledge; when reasoning is from the reports of others, as in the science one learns, then there is knowledge conditional, though repetition and care in demonstrating this knowledge lowers the level of conditionality, and raises the level of certainty to a scientific sufficiency, so Hobbes says:

There are of KNOWLEDGE two kinds; whereof one is *Knowledge of Fact*: the other *Knowledge of the Consequence of one Affirmation to another*. The former is nothing else, but Sense and Memory, and is *Absolute Knowledge*; as when we see a Fact doing, or remember it done: And this is the Knowledge required in a *Witnesse*. The later is called *Science*; and is *Conditionall*; as when we know, that, *If the figure showne be a circle, then any straight line through the Center shall divide it into two equall parts*. And this is the Knowledge required in a Philosopher; that is to say, of him that pretends to Reasoning.[18]

The geometric truth that '*Every triangle hath its three angles equall to two right angles*' is for Hobbes a product of meticulous logical demonstration, rather than sense experience (triangles not being sensory objects).[19] The conditionality, rather than certainty, of this knowledge as science (rather than memory or sense as such) shows Hobbes's dedication to an empiricism of sense-impressions as the only foundation for certain knowledge, whilst allowing considerable credence to logical and quasi-mathematical reasoning, hence to (near certain) truths of science, clearly distinguished in his mind from nonsense and 'insignificant speech'.

> But the Philosophy-schooles, through all the Universities of Christendome, grounded upon certain Texts of *Aristotle*, … say, For the cause of *Vision*, that the thing seen sendeth forth on every side a *visible species* (in English) a *visible shew, apparition*, or *aspect* or *a being seen*; the receiving, whereof into the Eye, is *Seeing* … Nay for the cause of *Understanding* also, they say the thing Understood sendeth forth *intelligible species*, that is, an *intelligible being seen*; which coming into the Understanding, makes us Understand. I say not this, as disapproving the use of Universities: but because … I must let you see on all occasions by the way, what things would be amended in them; amongst which the frequency of insignificant Speech is one.[20]

Animate objects, such as people and animals, are defined by Hobbes's science in terms of his matter-in-motion materialism, explicitly including all the phenomena of human thought and action. God becomes a 'first cause' about which little can be known, and therefore almost nothing said. The language of religious belief is sanctioned by Hobbes as words to inspire men to obedience (to their rulers), and to fill them with awe – anything but to make descriptive claims about the divine or anything beyond sensory experience.

> Hee that will attribute to God, nothing but what is warranted by naturall Reason, must either use such Negative Attributes, as *Infinite, Eternall, Incomprehensible*; or Superlatives, as *Most High, most Great*, and the like; or Indefinite, as *Good, Just, Holy, Creator*; and in such sense, as if he meant not to declare what he is, (for that were to circumscribe him within the limits of our Fancy,) but how much wee admire him, and how ready we would be to obey him …[21]

A further delight in *Leviathan* is Hobbes's scathing scepticism concerning priests, witches, and anyone attempting to befuddle others with tales of ghostly things (obviously for their own material benefit). Religious observance, for Hobbes, resides in a realm of commandment by one's earthly sovereign, and constitutes neither knowledge nor science. The Almighty, Hobbes cautions, is well capable of making miracles, but not nearly so much as greedy schemers are wont to claim:

> For as for Witches, I think not that their witchcraft is any reall power; but yet that they are justly punished, for the false beliefe they have, that they can do such mischiefe, joyned with their purpose to do it if they can; their trade being neerer to a new Religion, than to a Craft or Science. And for Fayries, and walking ghosts, the opinion of them has I think been on purpose, either taught, or not confuted, to keep in credit the use of Exorcisme, of Crosses, of holy Water, and other such inventions of Ghostly men. Neverthelesse, there is no doubt but God can make unnaturall Apparitions: but that he does it so often, as men need to feare such things, more than they feare the stay, or change of the course of Nature, which he also can stay, and change, is no point of Christian faith.[22]

> Miracles are Marvellous workes: but that which is marvellous to one, may not be so to another. Sanctity may be feigned; and the visible felicities of this world, are most often the work of God by Naturall, and ordinary causes. And therefore no man can infallibly know by naturall reason, that another has had a supernaturall revelation of Gods will; but only a beliefe; every one (as the signs thereof shall appear greater, or lesser) a firmer, or a weaker belief.[23]

Hobbes leaves himself an 'out', as ever, with respect to Christian belief in miracles and all the supernatural events of the creed, but the message of scepticism is there, and in his own time he rather properly had the reputation of a closet atheist. Once God is identified with a first cause, and the doctrinal confession of Christianity (by implication) with the faeries, sprites and 'Gentile' gods mentioned in *Leviathan*, then it is hard to resist the conclusion that God is just as material as anything and everything else, humans included.

Hobbes's chapter 12 on religion is an extraordinary cultural anthropology of religious phenomena, within which Christianity is nothing particularly out of the ordinary:

> Seeing there are no signes, nor fruit of *Religion*, but in Man onely; there is no cause to doubt, but that the seed of *Religion*, is also onely in Man; and consisteth in some peculiar quality ... And first, it is peculiar to the nature of Man, to be inquisitive into the Causes of the Events they see

... Secondly, upon the sight of any thing that hath a Beginning, to think also it had a cause, which determined the same to begin, then when it did, rather than sooner or later ... The first two make Anxiety ... This perpetuall feare, always accompanying mankind in the ignorance of cause, as it were in the Dark, must needs have for object something. And therefore when there is nothing to be seen, there is nothing to accuse, either of their good, or evill fortune, but some *Power*, or Agent *Invisible* ...[24]

Metaphor and mechanics

Judging from Hobbes's straightforward materialism and empiricism – and it could hardly be more straightforward and forthright – it would seem that he would be a prime candidate for sticking to the literal language that Michael Shapiro rightly identifies with this philosophical position, and indeed with the language of modern science generally. That is, discourses of science that follow from a view of knowledge that is empiricist and a view of the world that is materialist. These discourses adopt a distinction between literal, descriptive language, and the language of metaphor or 'fancy'. On this view, the latter kind of language needs to be kept clearly separate from science and pursued for other purposes altogether, presumably poetry or other fictions. This non-literal language, and the discourses and genres which favour it, are then implicitly devalued as untruthful, indeterminate and seductively misleading. Better to stay on the straight and narrow of factual description and compelling logic, a realm more certain, more real and more useful, than to flirt with any extravagances and effusions at a remove from material certainties and scientific proofs.[25]

Rather surprisingly then, Hobbes employs language that strikes one today as highly metaphorical, and tropes or imagery that seem bizarrely extravagant. His vivid language, even in passages detailing the workings of material phenomena, is again one of the delights of his masterwork. While Shapiro rightly notes that the distinction between literal and metaphorical language is itself a trope, indeed the foundational trope for constituting materialism and empiricism in the first place, it is worth exploring exactly how this distinction is made and sustained in *Leviathan*. Hobbes's literal language is not exactly the 'plain' language of (supposed) non-metaphorical description (as

Locke later recommended in his *Essay on the Origin of Human Understanding*, on which Shapiro focuses). Rather Hobbes prioritises a necessarily abstract language of mathematical concepts and logical relationships, though as mentioned above, these are second-order ideas used to organise thoughts that result directly from the materiality of sense impressions themselves.

The language that expresses the basics of Hobbes's materialism, and provides the descriptive concepts and analogies for his empiricism, is then a metaphorical (rather than literal) language of mechanics:

> The cause of Sense, is the Externall Body, or Object, which presseth the organ proper to each Sense ... All which qualities called Sensible, are in the object that causeth them, but so many several motions of the matter, by which it presseth our organs diversly. Neither in us that are pressed, are they anything else, but divers motions; (for motion, produceth nothing but motion.) ... So that Sense in all cases, is nothing els but originall fancy, caused (as I have said) by the pressure, that is, by the motion, of externall things upon our eyes, Eares, and other organs thereunto ordained.[26]

> The impression made on the organs of Sight, by lucide Bodies, either in one direct line, or in many lines, reflected from Opaque, or refracted in the passage through Diaphanous Bodies, produceth in living Creatures ... an Imagination of the Object, from whence the Impression proceedeth; which Imagination is called *Sight*; and seemeth not to bee a mere Imagination, but the Body it selfe without us; in the same manner, as when a man violently presseth his eye, there appears to him a light without, and before him, which no man perceiveth but himselfe; because there is indeed no such thing without him, but onely a motion in the interiour organs, pressing by resistance outward, that makes him think so.[27]

Hobbes does not so much describe mechanisms as employ them as an analogy and a metaphorical resource in order to convince his readers that there are literal 'bodies in motion' to which mathematical concepts can be assigned, and logical deductions drawn, with the high truth-values he associates with science. Mechanism is the major trope of *Leviathan*, appearing in 'The Introduction' in a very particular guise – Automata, or 'Engines that move themselves by springs and wheeles as doth a watch'. This passage has its puzzles. Hobbes says that 'man' can imitate 'Nature' (itself the 'Art whereby God hath made and governes the World') by making an 'Artificial Animal'. What exactly can this be? Hobbes's mention of automata, and then watches, suggests a (highly) imaginative contraption along the lines of Phillip K. Dick's artificial pets in *Do Androids Dream of Electric Sheep?*[28] The linking idea for Hobbes between life and mechanism is that 'life is but a motion of limbs', so limbs in motion are life, as in the (hypothetical) artificial animal. Hobbes then enquires, 'why may we not say, that all Automata ... have an artificiall life?' And indeed, why can 'man' not make 'an Artificiall Man'? This is famously not an individual robot or Frankenstein 'monster' but 'a COMMON-WEALTH, or STATE'.[29] Sovereignty is then:

> ... an *Artificiall Soul*, as giving life and motion to the whole body; The *Magistrates*, and other *Officers* of Judicature and Execution, artificiall *Joynts*; *Reward and Punishment* ... are the *Nerves*, that do the same in the Body Naturall; The *Wealth and Riches* of all the particular members, are the *Strength*; ... *Counsellors* ... are the *Memory*; *Equity* and *Lawes*, an artificiall *Reason* and *Will*; *Concord*, *Health*; *Sedition*, *Sicknesses*; and *Civill war*, *Death*, Lastly, the *Pacts* and *Covenants*, by which the parts of this Body Politique were at first made ... resemble that *Fiat*, or *Let us make man*, pronounced by God in the Creation.[30]

It would be hard to be more extravagantly metaphorical than this. Metaphors, of course, work two ways, as they draw a likeness between two things. The main direction of the Hobbesian metaphor is from the natural to the artificial, from natural bodies to artificial ones, from natural life to artificial life. But what exactly is artificial life? In what way are the artificial man (Leviathan), the (hypothetical) artificial animal and the (existing) self-moving watch (with its wheels and springs) only alive artificially, and not alive naturally? How are God (who moves mysteriously), natural 'men' (who move predictably when 'well ordered' in political society) and natural animals (who are always well ordered, even when social, like bees and ants)[31] alive in any way that is different? The metaphor also runs from the artificial to the natural, too, and gives us the answer. The human (or animal) heart is a (kind of) 'spring'; the human (or animal) nervous system is a set of 'strings'; the human (or animal) joints are so many 'wheels'. Modern medical science could hardly have put it better, and current debates in medicine and elsewhere over 'the medical [i.e. mechanistic] model' and 'the social [i.e. person/emotion/mind] model' attest to the continuing power and scientific practicality of Hobbes's image of 'man' as a mechanical system.

'Life', as Hobbes is saying, is 'but a motion of limbs' – whatever the limbs are made of.[32] The supposed distinction between the organic and living, on the one hand, and the inorganic or non-living, on the other, is abolished here, both in the way that God functions only through Nature to create everything that moves as a mechanism, and in the way that inorganic automata are in terms of a rhetorical question, said to be alive. The inorganic automata may be really existing (like watches), fictionally teasing (like the 'artificial animal') or immaterially collective (like the commonwealth or state). Not everything in the world that moves is alive, on this view (presumably rivers are not). However, anything alive is mechanical (as fluids are),[33] but crucially different only in being self-moving, as an automaton is. 'Soveraignty', as Hobbes says, gives 'life and motion to the whole body', and it is the binding character of pact or covenant that creates the self-acting mechanism.[34] Reading Hobbes this way throws the apparently important distinction between the artificial and natural into some doubt; not that Hobbes makes the distinction substantively, but rather that he makes it in passing in order to collapse it into a consistent materialism that accounts for God, 'man' and the 'state', and in so doing licences a highly mechanical, and normatively mechanistic, view of 'man', the state and politics.

As a materialist Hobbes has evaded the whiff of extravagance that I am arguing surrounds his metaphor, precisely because the central trope is so material in its mechanics, and because the abiding image is so mechanical in its materiality, namely the watch. It seems a literal kind of language, because it is the kind of language that a non-dualistic materialist and a scientific empiricist would like, precisely because we tend to think of the material as the literal. Hobbes's mechanistic metaphors enhance his ontological materialism and his epistemological empiricism. The materiality, predictability and mechanics of his automata mirror perfectly the matter-in-motion materialism and mechanical theory of 'thoughts' and 'passions' that he goes on to expound:

> There be in Animals, two sorts of *Motions* peculiar to them: One called *Vitall*; begun in generation, and continued without interruption through their whole life; such as are the *course* of the *Bloud*, the *Pulse*,

the *Breathing* ... to which Motions there needs no help of Imagination: The other is *Animall motion*, otherwise called *Voluntary motion*; as to *go*, to *speak*, to *move* any of our limbes, in such manner as is first fancied in our minds ... And that Fancy is but the Reliques of the same Motion, remaining after Sense ... And because *going*, *speaking*, and the like Voluntary motions, depend alwayes upon a precedent thought of *whither*, *which way*, and *what*; it is evident, that the Imagination is the first internall beginning of all Voluntary Motion ... These small beginnings of Motion, within the body of Man, before they appear in walking, speaking, striking, and other visible actions, are commonly called ENDEAVOUR.[35]

Hobbes then parses all human behaviour into motion towards some objects, and aversion from some others: 'This Endeavour, when it is toward something which causes it, is called APPETITE, or DESIRE ... and when the Endeavour is fromward something, it is generally called AVERSION.'[36] Defending his mechanistic view against the Schools, Hobbes has to argue carefully for the real existence of unobservable motions (because they are so small) against the view that the absence of visible motion can be explained away as *by nature* metaphorical:

And although unstudied men, doe not conceive any motion at all to be there, where the thing moved is invisible; or the space it is moved in, is (for the shortnesses of it) insensible; yet that doth not hinder, but that such Motions are ... For the Schooles find in meere Appetite to go, or move, no actuall Motion at all; but because some Motion they must acknowledge, they call it Metaphoricall Motion; which is but an absurd speech: for though Words may be called metaphorical; Bodies, and Motions cannot.[37]

Thus Hobbes seems as literal as Locke recommends in the *Essay on Human Understanding*, whilst – perhaps unsurprisingly – venturing into the realm of science fiction (and possibly schizophrenia) for his controlling trope: that living conscious bodies, whether animal or human (animal) are automata, only different in scale, materials and capacities, from watches – not different in some essence or nature, and in particular, not different in some relationship to God. Whether life comes with God's fiat, or 'man's' winding up a watch, or 'men's' making pacts or covenants to create sovereignty and thereby the state, is not the interesting intellectual issue for Hobbes. The issue is making all these processes the same in intellectual reflection, and thus helping to ensure (as was Hobbes's hope) their mechanical regularity in practice.

Masculinity and mechanism

The links between Hobbes's metaphors and masculinity on the one hand, and mechanisms on the other, has been noted in some detail by Christine di Stefano in her pioneering feminist work *Configurations of Masculinity*.[38] Offering a 'reading of Hobbes', she writes:

> ... Hobbes's thought reflects and advances a distinctively modern masculinist orientation to the realm of social life. This reading of Hobbes by no means supersedes or replaces all others. Rather, it is offered as another interpretive angle on the work of a theorist who defies canonical packaging along limited and mutually exclusive axes of interpretation.[39]

In much the same spirit I wish to take this kind of reading further and draw out exactly what this 'masculinist orientation' implies, using the mechanical and mechanistic metaphors that Hobbes employs in his materialistic approach to 'man', society and politics. As a result Hobbes's view of the state will look even more mechanistic, and his view of 'man' even more mechanical, quite literally so. This will leave us the task of enquiring into the extent that Hobbes is right about modern states and modern masculinity. Does a mechanistic model of hegemonic masculinity produce a political world-machine?

Di Stefano gets the discussion going:

> Those who would refute Hobbes by pointing out various features of human behavior or sensibility that are conducive to peaceful social relations are taking the wrong tack, for these are never enough to override the fundamental anarchy of social interaction. Hobbes's point is not that human beings are especially evil or deliberately antisocial. It is rather that we inevitably get in one another's way. As appetitive machines that engage incessantly in the pursuit of pleasure and avoidance of pain, we cannot help 'bumping' into and thereby impeding the 'motion' of others. Totally impeded motion is what we commonly refer to as death.[40]

Her conclusion is not that Hobbes's 'chronicle of the passions' is 'an ugly portrait of human nature', but rather 'that it presents a view of desire, motivation, and identity that is strictly *self*-originating and self-driven'.[41] What I am arguing can be added to this is an explicit and informative link back to Hobbes's foundational mechanistic materialism and his extravagantly metaphorical concepts of automata, particularly watches and clocks.[42] Di Stefano rightly says that modern masculinity studies suggest that this is a masculinised and male-identified concept of selfhood: 'strict differentiation of self from others, identity conceived in exclusionary terms, and perceived threats to an ego thus conceived which is vulnerable to displacement or dissolution by an invader'. To which she opposes a 'female material presence', one not only less strictly differentiated from others but also open to the embodied multiple selves of pregnancy.[43] Hobbes's mushroom metaphor (in *De Cive*) suits di Stefano's analysis well, in terms of drawing the contrast between the masculinised concept of 'man' and the female/maternal contrast in 'woman':

> [Hobbes's] grand artifice consists of a clever recombination of the given elements of the state of nature. These elements are 'natural' males atomistically conceived along egoistic masculine lines. This masculine tenor may be found initially in Hobbes's conception a self-possessed and discrete ego, one that is unassailable except in combative terms, and is socially approachable only on the terms of contracted and nominalist exchanges. It is an ego constituted in strict either-or terms of total integrity unto itself or total disintegration at the hands of a similarly constructed opposing ego. We can discern modern masculinity at work in the fantasy pattern that underlies this account: men magically sprung like mushrooms, unmothered and unfathered. While such a fantasy deals a blow to parenthood and to the organic notion of generational continuity, it strikes especially hard at the maternal contribution, whose denial is uniquely remarkable and difficult to implement since it is so biologically and socially apparent (even to Hobbes). Hobbes's omniscient and self-sprung ego owes no dues to others except those that are freely and individually contracted.[44]

Intriguingly many of the same concepts, and indeed similar metaphors, help to explicate both the mushroom and the watch, e.g. 'self-sprung' and 'self-generated movement'. It is easier, though, to see the components of a watch in a relationship with each other that is (metaphorically) 'calculating and instrumental', and certainly controlled by an overall regulatory system that stops the 'wheels and springs' from 'bumping' into each other.[45] The mushroom cluster does not quite live up to this, however well it illustrates the (apparently) motherless quality of self-generation and (apparently) history-less appearance of individuals as interchangeable and uniform entities. Ultimately, as di Stefano says, we confront today the Hobbesian solution to the inevitable civil war of all against all that his masculinised egos generate: 'narrowly calculating leaders' ruling social and political worlds.[46] An honest look at (so-called) democratic governments will make us realise that the Locke/Hobbes contest concerning restrained or unlimited power, divided or singular sovereignty, and accountable or absolute government has not gone as overwhelmingly in the Lockean direction as most people are led to believe, not least by the governments themselves. She rightly concludes that in so far as we live in a world of 'self-sprung men', it is not surprising to find authorities who follow the Hobbesian model of sovereignty in imposing order on what would (so it seems) be an 'unredeemable anarchy'.

Hobbes's conception of 'LIBERTY, or FREEDOME' is notoriously counter-intuitive, as he argues that liberty and fear, liberty and necessity are entirely consistent, viz. that 'when a man throweth his goods into the Sea for feare the ship should sink' he does it nevertheless 'very willingly', and similarly paying debts for 'feare of Imprisonment' is also a free action. This of course follows from his mechanical definition of freedom as the 'absence of Opposition ... [or] externall Impediments of motion'. Once again, Hobbes melds the natural and the artificial, the animate and the inanimate, into one, saying that this applies 'no less to Irrationall, and Inanimate creatures, than to Rationall':

> For whatsoever is so tyed, or environed, as it cannot move, but within a certain space, which space is determined by the opposition of some externall body, we say it hath not Liberty to go further. And so of all living creatures, whilest they are imprisoned, or restrained, with walls, or chayns; and of the water whilest it is kept in by banks, or vessels, that otherwise would spread it selfe into a larger space, we use to say, they are not at Liberty, to move in such manner as without those externall impediments they would.[48]

Absence of impediment, of course, allows bodies (of whatever kind) to career about, bumping into one another, which in the case of humans, is civil war, the greatest disaster, Hobbes reckons, that can befall a (former) community.⁴⁹ The proper liberty of subjects comes with the establishment of singular sovereignty and hence the commonwealth or state, wherein impediments to injurious actions are attained through the imposition of 'Artificial Chains, called *Civill Lawes* ... fastened at one end, to the lips of that Man, or Assembly, to whom they have given the Soveraigne Power; and at the other end to their own Ears.'⁵⁰ Unsurprisingly the paradigmatic liberties are those of commercial calculation and markets-in-motion:

> For if wee take Liberty in the proper sense, for corporall Liberty; that is to say, freedome from chains, and prison ... the Liberty of a Subject, lyeth therefore only in those things, which in regulating their actions, the Soveraign hath praetermitted: such as is the Liberty to buy, and sell, and otherwise contract with one another ...⁵¹

My supplementary question to this is: what does the Hobbesian exposition of this masculinised self have to tell us about modern hegemonic masculinity? My hypothesis is that mechanics, mechanisms, automata and disciplinary uniformities all flow from Hobbes's central trope and his mechanistic metaphorical extravagances. R.M. Connell, in his foundational work *Masculinities*, takes up the overall metaphor of 'the body as machine'.⁵² He does this when he discusses sociobiological accounts of gender that set up supposed facts of male and female difference, and in particular, accounts of masculinity that link it with (supposed) hormonal difference and (allegedly) innate aggression:

> [T]he power of this perspective lies in its metaphor of the body as machine. The body 'functions' and 'operates'. Researchers discover biological 'mechanisms' in behaviour. Brains are 'hardwired' to produce masculinity; men are generically 'programmed' for dominance; aggression is in our 'biogram'.⁵³

Rather closer to the Hobbesian model of material interaction in mechanical systems, though, is Connell's historical account of a transition in masculinised labour from a working-class association between males and heavy machinery and a more recent re-masculinisation (and de-feminisation) of sedentary jobs, which have become iconically middle class and masculinised:

The class process alters the familiar connection between masculinity and machinery. The new information technology requires much sedentary keyboard work, which was initially classified as women's work (key-punch operators). The marketing of personal computers, however, has redefined some of this work as not working-class. These revised meanings are promoted in the text and graphics of computer magazines, in manufacturers' advertising that emphasizes 'power' ... and in the booming industry of violent computer games. Middle-class male bodies, separated by an old class division from physical force, now find their powers spectacularly amplified in the man/machine systems (the gendered language is entirely appropriate) of modern cybernetics.[54]

The analysis that really puts this together in the starkest, most Hobbesian terms, is James der Derian's work on the most obvious and most violent nexus between men and machines, the modern military. The interchangeability between 'natural' (i.e. masculinised humans) and 'artificial' components of a metaphorically mechanical, and therefore literally mechanistic, system or 'machine' constitutes one of the main features of his analysis. That is, humans not only tell machines what to do, but machines acting as super-sense perceptors tell humans what to do ... and they do it. Der Derian discusses a variety of circumstances and incidents in which the 'machine' view or analysis directs human thinking. He also notes that disaster occurs (e.g. an Iranian airbus was shot down from the USS *Vincennes*), when truth (factual and moral) is defined as that which corresponds with the machines' sensory apparatus and conceptual programming (i.e. what is or is not a threat or target).[55]

In so far as the military system is acting within itself to preserve the lives of those who have opted for obedience to its singular internal sovereignty (as it is in the military's portrayal of itself), then an orderly system of command acts on the 'society' of obedient 'men' in the way that Hobbes advised, namely it commands them and they obey. The last thing that a military organisation will tolerate is 'civil war' within, and indeed the first thing that generates credible threats of martial justice is disobedience to a sovereign command. Unsurprisingly metaphors of cogs and wheels, well-oiled machines and conservation-of-motion efficiencies represent and reinforce the disciplinary norms amongst the overt categorisations of functional and interchangeable parts that constitute 'the ranks'.[56] In volunteer armies the Hobbesian subjects of the sovereign have even got into that position through, as he says, 'pact or covenant', obliging them to (almost) unconditional obedience.[57]

It is another question how similar to, or different from, so-called civilian life this military-cybernetic model actually is. Armed forces have an investment in both hegemonic masculinity[58] (witness the struggles over women and gays in the military) and in a distinction between themselves and 'civvies'. The former – ensuring that the military continues to exemplify an alpha-rated hegemonic masculinity – helps to secure the latter – ensuring that the military is paid and rewarded, resourced and unregulated in a manner commensurate with corporate cultures. Corporate cultures may look less alpha-masculine ... but only just. Charlotte Hooper's persuasive analysis of the ways that representations of international warriordom help construct current images of corporate masculinity illustrates precisely the point at issue:

> A contribution to the project of exploring the politics of masculinities is the mapping of Anglo-American hegemonic masculinity. The ideal types of citizen-warrior and bourgeois-rational man, and to a lesser extent Judeo-Christian patriarch and honor/patronage aristocrat ... have proved useful guides to the various constructions of Anglo-American masculinities ... Indeed, they have matched so well the various representations of masculinity that have been discussed here that it seems clear that Anglo-American hegemonic masculinity is indeed largely made up of shifting combinations of elements from these particular ideal types. While the bourgeois-rational model may be in the ascendant, it is important not to underplay the influence of the others, which continue to provide an elitist element of contemporary constructions, even as the twenty-first century opens.[59]

It should now, at the end of this discussion, come as no surprise that Hobbes's God is not only confirmed masculine in his mechanistic regularity (even his supernatural interventions seem mechanical), he is also likened to a five-star general with an additional and particular command:

> It is true that God is King of all the Earth: Yet may he be King of a peculiar, and chosen Nation [the Jews]. For there is no more incongruity therein, than that he that hath the generall command of the whole Army, should have withall a peculiar Regiment, or Company of his own.[60]

The Hobbesian world of automata, singular and material, neither 'natural' nor 'artificial' in any important sense, requiring regulations, barriers, apparatuses of rigid control, simply *is* the dominant metaphor of modern, 'rational', calculating hegemonic masculinity. For confirmation, *circumspice*. For a satire, try *Dr. Strangelove*. As Carol Cohn concludes, 'The dominant voice of militarized masculinity and decontextualized rationality speaks ... loudly in our culture'.[61]

Notes

1. Thomas Hobbes, *Leviathan*, ed. C.B. Macpherson (Harmondsworth: Penguin, 1968, repr. 1985; hereafter 'Macpherson'), ch. 17, pp. 227–8; ed. Richard Tuck (Cambridge: Cambridge University Press, 1991; hereafter 'Tuck'), pp. 120–1.
2. See Tarak Barkawi, 'Peoples, homelands and wars? Ethnicity, the military and battle among British imperial forces in the war against Japan', *Comparative Studies in Society and History*, 46 (2004), pp. 134–63.
3. Hobbes, *Leviathan*, ch. 21, Macpherson, pp. 269–70; Tuck, p. 151.
4. For a discussion of this practice, see Terrell Carver, 'Men and IR/men in IR', pp. 99-100; see also Adam Jones, ed., *Genocide and Gendercide* (Nashville, TN: Vanderbilt University Press, 2004), where there are discussions of the collective 'women and children' set against males and a masculinised norm.
5. Hobbes, *Leviathan*, ch. 6, Macpherson, pp. 125–6; Tuck, p. 43.
6. See M.M. Goldsmith, Hobbes' *Science of Politics* (New York: Columbia University Press, 1966).
7. Hobbes, *Leviathan*, ch. 2, Macpherson, p. 87; Tuck, p. 15.
8. Hobbes, *Leviathan*, ch. 2, Macpherson, p. 87; Tuck, p. 15.
9. Hobbes, *Leviathan*, ch. 2, Macpherson, p. 88; Tuck, p. 15.
10. Hobbes, *Leviathan*, ch. 2, Macpherson, p. 90; Tuck, p. 17.
11. Hobbes, *Leviathan*, ch. 3, Macpherson, p. 94; Tuck, p. 20.
12. Hobbes, *Leviathan*, ch. 2, Macpherson, pp. 93–4; Tuck, p 19.
13. Hobbes, *Leviathan*, ch. 4, Macpherson, p. 105; Tuck, p. 28.
14. Hobbes, *Leviathan*, ch. 4, Macpherson, p. 105–6; Tuck, p. 28.
15. Hobbes, *Leviathan*, ch. 4, Macpherson, p. 102; Tuck, p. 26.
16. Hobbes, *Leviathan*, ch. 5, Macpherson, p. 110–11; Tuck, pp. 31–2.
17. Hobbes, *Leviathan*, ch. 4, Macpherson, p. 104; Tuck, p. 27.
18. Hobbes, *Leviathan*, ch. 9, Macpherson, p. 147–8; Tuck, p. 60.
19. Hobbes, *Leviathan*, ch. 4, Macpherson, p. 104; Tuck, p. 27.
20. Hobbes, *Leviathan*, ch. 1, Macpherson, p. 86–7; Tuck, p. 14.
21. Hobbes, *Leviathan*, ch. 31, Macpherson, p. 403; Tuck, p. 251.

22 Hobbes, *Leviathan*, ch. 2, Macpherson, pp. 92–3; Tuck, pp. 18–19.
23 Hobbes, *Leviathan*, ch. 26, Macpherson, p. 332; Tuck, p. 198.
24 Hobbes, *Leviathan*, ch. 12, Macpherson, pp. 168–70; Tuck, pp. 75–6.
25 Michael J. Shapiro, 'Metaphor in the philosophy of the social sciences', *Culture and Critique* 2 (1985–86), pp. 192–3.
26 Hobbes, *Leviathan*, ch. 1, Macpherson, pp. 85–6; Tuck, pp. 13–14.
27 Hobbes, *Leviathan*, ch. 45, Macpherson, pp. 657–8; Tuck, p. 440.
28 Phillip K. Dick, *Do Androids Dream of Electric Sheep?* (London: Gollancz, 1999).
29 Hobbes, *Leviathan*, Introduction, Macpherson, p. 81; Tuck, p. 9.
30 Hobbes, *Leviathan*, Introduction, Macpherson, pp. 81–2; Tuck, pp. 9–10.
31 Hobbes, *Leviathan*, ch. 17, Macpherson, pp. 225–7; Tuck, pp. 119–21; Hobbes taxes Aristotle for making these creatures, who 'live sociably', also 'Politicall creatures', citing six points of crucial distinction between them and humans, which make the latter the only political creatures, i.e. requiring an artificial order to ensure peace and therefore society (as opposed to the natural dissociation that renders 'men apt to invade, and destroy one another'; ch. 13, Macpherson, p. 186; Tuck, p. 89).
32 Hobbes, *Leviathan*, Introduction, Macpherson, p. 81; Tuck, p. 9.
33 As indeed everything must be, even thoughts, on Hobbes's matter-in-motion monist materialism; see the discussion below.
34 Hobbes, *Leviathan*, Introduction, Macpherson, pp. 81–2; Tuck, p. 9.
35 Hobbes, *Leviathan*, ch. 6, Macpherson, pp. 118–19; pp. 37–8.
36 Hobbes, *Leviathan*, ch. 6, Macpherson, p. 119; Tuck, p. 38.
37 Hobbes, *Leviathan*, ch. 6, Macpherson, p. 119; Tuck, p. 38.
38 Christine di Stefano, *Configurations of Masculinity: a feminist perspective on modern political theory* (Ithaca, NY and London: Cornell University Press, 1991).
39 di Stefano, *Configurations*, p. 70.
40 di Stefano, *Configurations*, p. 80.
41 di Stefano, *Configurations*, pp. 80–1.
42 This image of the bird struggling 'belimed' in the twigs must surely be the pathetic 'other' to the orderly tickings of the watch, its self-driving energies channeled by mechanical wheels and springs into purposeful, meaningful and efficient motions (till the energy in its spring is eventually exhausted). The bird not only expires quickly but also self-destructively and with appalling confusion in its exterior and interior motions. Hobbes, *Leviathan*, ch. 4, Macpherson, p. 105; Tuck, p. 28. The fluttering bird in the chimney also comes to mind; ch. 4, Macpherson, p. 105–6; Tuck, p. 28.
43 di Stefano, *Configurations*, pp. 82–3.
44 di Stefano, *Configurations*, pp. 88–9.
45 di Stefano, *Configurations*, p. 92.

46 di Stefano, *Configurations*, p. 103.
47 di Stefano, *Configurations*, pp. 103–4.
48 Hobbes, *Leviathan*, ch. 21, Macpherson, pp. 261–3; Tuck, pp. 145–6.
49 Hobbes, *Leviathan*, ch. 3, Macpherson, p. 98; Tuck, p. 23; also ch. 13, Macpherson, pp. 185–6; Tuck, pp. 89–90.
50 Hobbes, *Leviathan*, ch. 21, Macpherson, pp. 263–4; Tuck, p. 147. The chains are a kind of mechanical metaphor here, representing not just restraint and constraint, but an active process of information-transmission (i.e. the word and will of the sovereign) through mechanical linkages. In Hobbes's time chains were certainly part of mechanisms that transmitted motion, but not yet information as such. There is an element of science fiction in Hobbes's science of politics; electronic tagging is perhaps a contemporary evocation of Hobbes's vision.
51 Hobbes, Leviathan, ch. 21, Macpherson, p. 264; Tuck, pp. 147–8.
52 Connell, *Masculinities*.
53 Connell, *Masculinities*, p. 48.
54 Connell, *Masculinities*, pp. 55–6.
55 James der Derian, *Virtuous War: mapping the military—industrial—media—entertainment network* (Boulder, CO: Westview, 2001), p. 14.
56 Carol Cohn draws attention to the connection between militarised masculinity and 'imagery that reverses sentient and nonsentient matter' in 'Sex and death in the rational world of defense intellectuals', *Signs* 12, pp. 687–718.
57 The exception is a sovereign command to kill oneself or another.
58 The role of the military in constructing and reinforcing 'sexual citizenship' is detailed in Snyder, *Citizen-Soldiers*.
59 Hooper, *Manly States*, p. 221.
60 Hobbes, *Leviathan*, ch. 12, Macpherson, pp. 178–9; Tuck, p. 83.
61 Cohn, 'Sex and death', p. 717.

CHAPTER SEVEN

Locke: overtly and covertly gendered narratives of political society

Gender theory, gender politics and masculinities

In this chapter I use the gender lens to explore narratives in Locke's *Two Treatises of Government* that have become foundational for the documents and practices of liberal democracy.[1] I review what has previously been conceptualised in commentary as the family and household, parental and filial obligations, the 'sexual contract', patriarchy, the public/private 'split' and gender-neutral concepts of 'man'.[2] The literature on men and masculinities starts from the feminist insight that men have presented an idealised image of themselves as generically human, and that this has had the effect of marginalising women in practice and devaluing the activities with which they have been stereotypically associated.[3] Recent research in sociology and history has further demonstrated that this image of 'man' is itself untrue to many men's experiences, and politically selective in its portrayal of an apparently singular masculinity.[4]

It is clear from feminist critique that the traditional conceptualisation of 'man' as generically human was certainly not a woman nor subject to specifically female experiences. It was masculinised, rather than androgynous. However, it does not follow that this conception 'man' represents the actual and potential experiences of men, nor the range of masculinities, including practices of sex and sexuality, with any degree of subtlety beyond the merely stereotypical. More nuanced understandings are needed to drive critical and constructive theorisations of political issues concerning men, and therefore men in relation to women. These issues were salient in Locke's time, and are still so in ours. Texts such as Locke's exclude and devalue women, but they are also hierarchically validating with respect to some kinds of men, in terms of some kinds of masculinities. In short, they are normative constructs requiring deconstruction, and the new, feminist-inspired literature on men and masculinities represents an important resource for doing this.[5]

Feminist critique has identified generic 'man' with a male body, that is, a body unable to give birth, and with a competitive and self-interested persona, rather than one attuned to nurturing and emotion. Feminists have also identified an apparent paradox in that generic 'man' is also made to seem sexless, or de-gendered, a figure abstracted from sexual activity, reproductive attributes, and even the body itself. This, of course, fits well with a public/private 'split' that feminists have identified, namely that sex and reproduction are conceptualised as (somehow) 'private', and so women (stereotypically associated with these activities) are then consigned to that realm in practice. Conversely men, operating in a 'public' realm to which sex and reproduction (supposedly) do not belong, are conceptualised as apparently sexless and almost disembodied beings, monopolising 'public' powers for themselves. There is thus an *apparently de-gendered* narrative of 'public man' through which political theory makes its most crucial claims about humanity, but in a falsely generic way.[6]

However, in Locke's text, and in any theoretical account of the human community, there are also *overtly gendered* narratives. These include the association of women with reproduction and motherhood, and the relegation of those activities to a 'private' (or domestic, non-public) realm that is presumed to be pre-political. That, of course, is the foil that makes 'public man' seem apparently de-gendered, because gender issues are stereotypically defined as 'private' and so out of the 'public' realm. Yet the textual narratives of political theory do not maintain a consistent boundary line in this respect, since the 'private' sphere is not exclusively reserved for females, nor are all gender issues overtly female-related. There are moments in those texts when men have a life as gendered beings in private and in public. Indeed the public/private 'split' tends to collapse at that point because it is an inherently patriarchal and anti-feminist device deployed to marginalise women and the feminine side (as it were) of certain social activities.

The overtly gendered narrative relating to men in political theory gives them a generative role in reproduction, a husbandly role in marriage, a fatherly role in relation to children (especially sons), and a head of household role in relation to servants. In feminist thought this overtly gendered narrative about men has a sharply political edge, since feminism is by definition anti-patriarchal. The men and masculinities perspective is a useful one, though, because it draws on the breadth and variety of men's experiences of *differences within masculinities*. In that way it establishes the dynamics of patriarchy more clearly, in relations between men as well as in relations between men and women, and also points up critical areas where diversity among men could be mobilised politically. This could be done in ways that feminists might find constructive.[7]

Locke is an exceptionally interesting theorist in this regard, because he was an adamant opponent of seventeenth-century 'patriarchalism'. He portrayed it as a dangerous doctrine, in which absolute monarchical authority was said to be the only correct theory of rulership. This was supposedly the case because God had granted that power (which was said to be the *same* as husbandly, fatherly and householder powers) to Adam and his heirs, who were assumed to be males in male lines of descent. It was thus an overtly gendered theory of rulership. Patriarchal theories of that kind obviously relied on contemporary assumptions, doctrines and laws that comprehensively privileged men over women.[8] In seeking to undermine contemporary claims to divine right and absolute authority as the foundation of rulership, Locke attacked patriarchalism in terms that border on the burlesque. His contrary view concerning political power made bold claims for equality,[9] and he took delight in referring to women as contracting wives, parents, householders and rulers. This was in specific rebuttal to the 'truths' about men and women that patriarchalists had argued were natural, God-given features of human society and fundamental relationships.

However, Locke was concerned at certain points to limit his claims regarding equality in order to fit in with unequal power relationships already existing in society,[10] provided that these did not touch (as he thought) on the fundamental dimension of political power with which he was principally concerned, and which he distinguished from the powers appropriate to other relationships (marriage, parenthood, householdership). Thus he tempered his bold egalitarianism with a certain conventional hindsight respecting equality generally and male/female relations specifically,[11] and so became perforce a patriarchal theorist in feminist eyes, or at least partly so. Locke would not, of course, have recognised his own residual patriarchalism as a serious fault, nor would he have seen the analogy with the partriarchalists he so despised. However, it is apparent that he used egalitarian arguments enthusiastically as a way of ridiculing patriarchalists, and hence their absolutist claims to divine right of kings. Later in his discussions he reined in his egalitarianism, perhaps to avoid any charge of fomenting undue radicalism elsewhere in the social order, most particularly in marriage, parenthood and householdership.[12]

In common with other 'mainstream/malestream' political theorists, Locke's narratives were about the 'straight' men and patriarchal households presumed to be foundational for the polity. This set up hierarchies of disadvantage, marginalisation and exclusion that were both explicit and implicit. My aim is not to reveal that Locke's texts were written by 'the straight mind' of a 'straight man' but rather to engage critically with the argumentative strategies deployed there and continuously reappropriated in overt and covert gender politics since 1689. This requires a view of gender that deploys it to represent binaries and hierarchies beyond the M/F distinction, including sexuality differences, as they are framed within familiar 'cleavages' – property, class, race/ethnicity, religion, language and so on. It is through these concepts and practices that marriage, parenthood, householdership and other gradations of esteem in citizenship are defined and take effect.[13] In that way the gender lens reveals not just that sex and sexuality relations are cross-cut with other kinds of social difference, but that those forms of difference may themselves be genuinely hybridised with sex and sexuality, and thus 'gendered' always and already.

The overtly gendered narrative about men that occurs in Locke's *Two Treatises* 'genders' power-relations in society. I aim to draw out what he has to say about rulership, householdership, parenthood and conjugal relations by showing that there are effectively three kinds of dominant masculinities at issue in his *Two Treatises*. One is related to the rational/bureaucratic masculinity of modern commerce, which he endorsed, and another is related to concepts of masculine tenderness and solicitude, of which he also approved. The third is related to the warrior mode of absolutism, conquest and tyranny, to which he was deeply opposed. The advantage of reading Locke's text this way is that it shows how he reconciled a residual patriarchy with his egalitarian principles of equality, legitimacy and consent. He did this by drawing a strong contrast between an absolutist and irrational masculinity, on the one hand, and a dual masculinity not just of competitive individuality but of fatherly care, on the other. He deployed these historically in relation to archaic societies, and politically in relation to contemporary society. Feminists are rightly critical of Locke's residual patriarchy as regressive in practice with respect to his principles. Liberals are today puzzling over how to reconcile egalitarian principles with the practical exigencies of gender. This chapter argues that the literature on men and masculinities can be deployed to aid both those political processes.

Overtly gendered narratives of women and men

Locke's *Two Treatises of Government* were published anonymously in a single volume in 1689. The 'Second Treatise' is probably the most successful political tract of all time. It is often used to interpret the founding documents and later legislation of liberal democracies, and oftentimes serves as the raw material for judicial interpretations in the English-speaking world. As a founding narrative it was translated (in part and in anonymity) into French in 1691, and republished, for example, in Boston in 1773, just before the American Revolution.[14] In any case, it is a reasonably concise conflation of power/knowledge, served up in a discourse that now sounds like 'plain truths' about liberal democracy. Those 'plain truths' persist through cultural processes that do not reference the work explicitly, and Locke's ideas have thus entered democratic discourse generally.

The 'First Treatise' has been explored by feminists because of its close connection with patriarchalism, since Locke engaged directly and at length with Sir Robert Filmer's text, recently published by 'divine right' monarchists as *Patriarcha, or the Natural Power of Kings* (written c. 1628–21, published 1679–1680).[15] In mainstream/malestream political theory the 'First Treatise' is generally less read and cited than the 'Second Treatise'. This is because mainstream/malestream theory is not particularly interested in the divine right of kings as such, nor in the gender issues about women and women's roles, and about men and men's roles, that patriarchalism raised explicitly. In short, it lacks the gender lens.

The 'Second Treatise' became canonical for 'mainstream/malestream' theory, because it contained formulations of equality and legitimacy that are foundational for liberal democracy. These employ a conception of 'public man' that effectively feminises and so marginalises gender issues, a situation that mainstream/malestream theorists have found very normal, not least because their world is already organised that way. I make use of both Locke's texts. Schochet rightly criticises the literature on Locke for taking his version of patriarchalism, and in particular of Sir Robert Filmer's doctrines, on trust.[17] However, for my purposes, Locke's version of Filmer is important because it represents the kind of patriarchalism from which he wished to distinguish himself very sharply, and which functioned as a foil to his own residual patriarchalism when this surfaced in his thinking.

Locke's text was not only covertly gendered in relation to 'public man', as feminists have demonstrated, but also overtly gendered in relation to women and men. This is because an account of human society and political community requires a narrative of reproduction, birth, infant care, transition to adulthood, and many other things connected with an inter-generational and continuing polity.[18] To do that, sex and sexuality must be confronted out in the open (which is not to say that there is much subtlety about it in Locke's text – rather the opposite). So Locke discussed mammalian reproduction, conjugal society, marriage, husbands and wives, fathers and mothers, legitimate and illegitimate offspring, the care of children, the obligations of adult offspring to parents, and other gender and 'gendered' relationships in the household and community, including class relations (as master/servant) and rulership (as magistracy).

Chapter 1 of the 'Second Treatise' begins with an overtly gendered narrative, in the sense that not only is the sexual binary introduced, but the two sexes are also set hierarchically in relation to each other in very explicit ways. Locke was keen to distinguish the power of 'magistrate over subject' from that of 'a father over his children' and a 'husband over his wife'.[19] Of course Locke was not constructing his text as some theory or doctrine in isolation from contemporary politics, but rather still pursuing – in the 'Second Treatise', as well as in the 'First Treatise' – a polemical riposte to Filmer's overtly gendered narrative of patriarchal authority. In Locke's reading, Filmer was arguing that political power arose from, and was in essence the same as, the patriarchal power attributed to fathers/husbands with respect to children/women.[20] While Locke could have claimed merely that patriarchal and political powers were different in kind, without challenging fatherly/husbandly authority over children/women, he actually cited biblical teaching and contemporary practice to make an egalitarian-sounding case with respect to men and women – though he did not pursue this consistently. Thus in Chapter 6 'Paternal power' he appealed to biblical injunctions to obey both father and mother, or 'parents', mentioning that mothers had 'a share' in this 'parental authority' and then referring to 'two persons jointly' as holders of it.[21] This had already been argued out more fully and prominently in the 'First Treatise', beginning in Chapter 2:

> I hope 'tis no injury to call a half quotation a half reason, for God says, 'honour thy father and mother'; but our author [Filmer] contents himself with half, leaves out 'thy mother' quite, as little serviceable to his purpose.[22]

This passage continued with a scornful Lockean riposte to Filmer's identification of fatherly with regal power, again, making an egalitarian-sounding claim with respect to mothers and female rulers:

> [Filmer says] 'to confirm this natural right of regal power, we find in the Decalogue, that the law which enjoins obedience to kings, is delivered in the terms, "honour they father", as if all power were originally in the father.' And why may I not add as well, that in the Decalogue, the law that enjoins obedience to queens, is delivered in the terms of 'honour thy mother', as if all power were originally in the mother. The argument, as Sir Robert puts it, will hold as well for one as t'other.[23]

The argument returned later in Chapter 6 of the 'First Treatise', with what Locke intended as an ultimate *épater* to Christian patriarchalists:

> For had our author set down this command without garbling, as God gave it, and joined mother to father, every reader would have seen that it had made directly against him, and that it was so far from establishing the 'monarchical power of the father', that it set up the mother equal with him ...

Thus noting Scriptural equality between the sexes, Locke acidly mentioned that Scripture did not actually support exclusively patriarchal authority over children anyway:

> The Scripture joins mother too in that homage, which is due from children, and had there been any text, where the honour or obedience

of children had been directed to the father alone, 'tis not likely that our author [Filmer], who pretends to build all upon Scripture, would have omitted it.

And even better for Locke, in scripture mothers sometimes come first!

> Nay, the Scripture makes the authority of father and mother, in respect of those they have begot, so equal, that in some places it neglects, even the priority of order, which is thought due to the father, and the mother is put first, as *Leviticus* 19:3.[24]

Thus in the 'Second Treatise' II§53 established an apparently egalitarian concept of parental authority in 'two persons jointly', yet the immediately following II§54 then explicitly qualified the apparently unlimited egalitarianism of the preceding Chapters 2–5 that has thrilled so many liberal readers, and indeed defined the liberal project. Locke mentioned 'age or virtue', 'excellency of parts and merit', 'birth' and 'alliance or benefits' as significantly qualifying his opening salvo concerning the equality of all 'men'. To establish his initial egalitarianism at the opening of the 'Second Treatise', Locke had firstly asserted the negative, namely that no man is bound to another by any natural tie of unfreedom. At the beginning of Chapter 2 he stated:

> ... we must consider what state all men are naturally in ... a state of perfect freedom to order their actions, and dispose of their possessions, and persons as they think fit ... without asking leave, or depending upon the will of any other man.

He then continued to argue that those relations among free men were also equal in a crucially important respect:

> A state also of equality, wherein all the power and jurisdiction is reciprocal, no one having more than another: there being nothing more evident, than that creatures of the same species ... should also be equal one amongst another without subordination or subjection ...[25]

However, in II§54, where Locke qualified his initial egalitarianism, he did not include inequality between husbands and wives, or fathers and mothers, or indeed men and women. Perhaps surprisingly the starkly gendered juxtaposition men/women did not seem to occupy him very much in his thinking in the text (though see the overtly procreative 'male' and 'female' in II§§79–80). Instead he carefully traced out the implications for children when their father dies, commenting that 'everywhere' parental power is then exercised by the mother, and that children should fulfil their duties to her in exactly the same way as if the surviving single parent were the father.

That line of argument had the useful consequence that Locke could taunt his patriarchalist enemies by appealing not only to moments of apparent biblical egalitarianism but also to contemporary practice, in that widows did indeed exercise parental power and other powers as head of household, until remarriage. So keen was Locke on this argumentative tack that he also attempted (astonishingly) to undermine patriarchalist claims concerning the naturalism of the two-parent family by appealing in apparently factual terms to polyandry in unspecified places, and even to normalised practices of maternal single-parenting in America, presumably amongst 'Indians'![26]

Unsurprisingly Locke's own version of residual domestic patriarchy, i.e. gender inequality between husbands/wives and fathers/mothers, came back with a vengeance in the succeeding Chapter 7 'Political power' in the 'Second Treatise'. There he reintroduced in II§82, as it were, a subordination of wife/mother to husband/father, the 'sexual contract' with which Carole Pateman has been so productively occupied. Moreover all Locke's examples of inheritance in the 'Second Treatise' were of father to son (e.g. II§58), though in his own time daughters (of the right social class) certainly inherited, and many would-be husbands looked not merely for wives but for heiresses. Prior to the Married Woman's Property Act of 1882, of course, a husband became sole proprietor of what his bride had previously owned, and moreover a father had a clear right to custody over any children. This was legally superior to a mother's claim, a situation first modified only in the Custody of Children Act of 1839.[27]

In the 'Second Treatise' Locke did not consider female rulers explicitly, either by inheritance or by usurpation/conquest, as anyway the overall argument of the tract was to refute all theories of political power that derive rulership, not from consent, but from anything else, e.g. divine right to rule descending patriarchally from father to son (or exceptionally, descending patriarchally through the female line). However, female rulers were considered explicitly in the 'First Treatise', and in properly respectful terms. Locke referred to 'our queens Mary [I] or Elizabeth [I]', arguing the absurdity of believing that their (presumably legitimate) monarchical authority would have been forfeited should they marry any of their subjects, *contra* Filmer's view that God's grant of authority to Adam over his wife Eve was part of Adam's grant of authority as absolute monarch over all peoples. Queenly marriage, of course, was a famous sixteenth-century political issue in both cases, viz. Mary's marriage to Philip II of Spain, and Elizabeth's presumed need to marry, both in relation to their personal will and in relation to their monarchical role.[28] Philip II was conspicuously absent during Queen Mary's marriage, and was never King of England anyway, and Queen Elizabeth was notoriously and in the end deliberately unmarried in order to function as 'prince'.

Surprisingly, though, Locke went on to argue that the curse of the Fall in Genesis not only gave Adam no monarchical authority over anyone or everyone, never mind any 'succession', but also no authority over Eve, 'or to men over their wives'.[29] Locke portrayed Eve as a 'helper in the temptation, as well as a partner in the transgression', who 'was laid below' Adam, giving him 'accidentally a superiority over her, for her greater punishment'. But then strangely Locke went on to argue that Adam, having 'had his share in the fall, as well as the sin' was 'laid lower' as 'a day labourer for life'. That wonderfully refuted Filmer by absurdly suggesting that God 'in the same breath' should make Adam 'universal monarch over all mankind' while condemning him 'to till the ground'.[30] But it also raised apparently irresolvable issues concerning gender (in)equality in Locke – who is lower than whom? Rather similarly the authority of 'husbands over wives' was said by Locke to be both accidental (due to the Fall) (I§44) and 'ordinary' in normal practice (I§47), and in any case strictly limited by the purpose of the association and also as specified in a marriage contract.[31] Moreover he argued that Genesis merely foretold 'what should be the woman's lot', and did not actually establish a form of natural subjection:

> But there is here no more law to oblige a woman to such a subjection [in marriage], if the circumstances either of her condition or contract with her husband should exempt her from it, that she should bring forth her children in sorrow and pain, if there could be found a remedy for it, which is also part of the same curse upon her.[32]

This is an unusually de-naturalising argument in relation to women, interestingly viewing marital subjection as potentially remediable, like pain in parturition (and perhaps with a similar moral obligation to bring this amelioration about?). But before anyone today gets too excited about this passage, it has to be noted that Locke followed it with comments that 'generally the laws of mankind and customs of nations have ordered it [i.e. wives subject to husbands] so; and there is, I grant, a foundation in nature for it'.[33] This then reappeared at II§82, where he identified men as 'abler and stronger' than women, and so apparently entitled to execute the last 'determination' in any conflict of wills between husband and wife.[34] Returning to his previous argument – that any subjection of wives to husbands is nothing to do with any 'original grant of government and the foundation of monarchical power' – Locke explained that 'conjugal power' is different: 'the power that every husband hath to order the things of private concernment in his family ... and to have his will take place before that of his wife in all things ...'.[35] However, it is clear that for Locke 'wife' and 'woman', at least, were not necessarily the same, and in certain cases, neither were 'queen' and 'wife', whereas, according to him, they were all the same to Filmer.

The only other female ruler mentioned by Locke was Athaliah, 'a woman, who reigned six years [over the Hebrews] an utter stranger to royal blood', *contra* Filmer's argument (as presented by Locke) that the succession of monarchical authority amongst the Hebrews could be reckoned consistently with an inheritance from father to son.[36] (Rather predictably Locke's text at I§93 and I§98 wanders indiscriminately between 'child' and 'son' in discussing inheritance more generally.)[37] Elsewhere Locke had considerable fun with Filmer's naivete concerning the rules of monarchical succession, which marks a rare point at which 'daughter', as well as 'sister' and 'widow', entered Locke's text explicitly. The discussion broadened out again from monarchy to reproductive relations, and marital (and non-marital) relations, particularly those of consanguinity and inheritance, with interesting glances at the effects of reproductive technologies on naturalistic presumptions about birth-order ('dissection of the mother', i.e. Caesarian section, is mentioned below) and at nature's indifference to the whole customary (and Christian) apparatus of marriage and legitimacy:

> I go on then to ask whether in the inheriting of this paternal power, this supreme fatherhood, the grandson by a daughter, hath a right before a nephew by a brother? ... Whether the daughter before the uncle? Or

> any other man, descended by a male line? Whether a grandson by a younger daughter, before a granddaughter by an elder daughter? Whether the elder son by a concubine, before a younger son by a wife? From whence also will arise many questions of legitimation, and what in nature is the difference betwixt a wife and a concubine? For as to the municipal or positive laws of men, they can signify nothing here …

Locke was evidently taking a hard-headed doctor's view of human reproduction, evincing a remarkably unmoralised view of humanity that queried conventional presumptions concerning a supposed natural order of precedence by birth-order and by matrimonial legitimacy. He then went on to ridicule a strict patriarchalism, i.e. rulership by males in male lines of inheritance, as unworkable, again drawing on medical circumstances and legal conundrums:

> Who has the paternal power, whilst the widow queen is with child by the deceased king, and nobody knows whether it will be a son or a daughter? Which shall be heir of two male twins, who by the dissection of the mother, were laid open to the world? Whether a sister by the half blood, before a brother's daughter by the whole blood?[38]

Locke's overtly gendered engagement with women and men unsurprisingly covered issues of parental care, marriage, childbirth, legitimacy, widowhood, inheritance, householdership and rulership. Arguing inconsistently from both moralised and non-moralised presumptions, he pursued his case against what he presented to his readers as Filmer's patriarchalism. Filmer's besetting sin, according to Locke, was an absurd insistence on absolute precedence for males and the male line, for which neither nature nor science nor scripture nor conventional practice could provide a justification. Filmer had rolled up fatherhood, husbandhood, householdership and rulership into one patriarchalist package, and had perforce produced a complementary view of motherhood, wifehood and female subjection right across the board. In arguing against such ridiculous consistency, Locke produced any inconsistency with it that looked good at the moment, and in so doing promoted (unwittingly, of course) both the emancipation of women along gender-egalitarian lines and their continued subjection *within a residual patriarchalism* that he found comfortable (again, arguing from various inconsistent premises). Relentless in his pursuit of Filmer, Locke ventured into areas and issues that other political theorists merely touch on, or simply omit. In doing that he (inadvertently, no doubt) helped to push gender egalitarianism and political emancipation much further than he had in mind. However, he also provided us with a useful way in to many issues that are of political importance today, precisely because he articulated so many 'traditional' presumptions so thoroughly and so variously. At least in his texts they are out in the open, if one cares to look.

Overtly gendered narratives of men and women

The terms of Locke's discussion of masculinised citizenship are only slightly archaic. The operation of the gender binary that he outlines is recognisable today with minimal translation. The apparently degendered (yet covertly gendered) narrative that makes women second-class citizens is visible now in Locke, and in practical politics, thanks to feminist analysis. The overtly gendered narrative in Locke does not only cover women as gendered beings. In those terms it certainly gives the lie, as we have noted above, to his generically human egalitarianism (and his occasional egalitarian comments concerning women as parents, as contracting wives, and as rulers). The overtly gendered narrative in Locke also covers men as gendered beings. In those terms it makes explicit the political obverse to the subordination and exclusion of women. It positions some men over others in crucial ways with respect to power, property and full citizenship, as well as over women generally.

Locke's text gives a portrait not just of patriarchy, but of dominant masculinities that privilege some men over others (as well as men over women).[39] Those dominant masculinities are heavily inflected (overtly or covertly) with race/ethnicity, class, religion, language and numerous categories that appear to be other than gender. However, it is worth considering the extent to which those categories are already defined in gender terms, provided that gender is itself allowed to represent hierarchical differences *within* the sexual and sexuality binaries. Locke's privileged males, the ones who were not servants or foreigners or children and could thus become a 'perfect member' of the community,[40] were propertied householders and fathers, precisely because they were marriageable. Marriage was an important way that property came to men, through marriage settlements (as husbands) and subsequent inheritance (as sons). It was just as important for Locke that some men dominate other men in certain social relationships, such as propertied/unpropertied in commercial society, master/servant in the household, 'industrious and rational'/'wild Indian' territorially,[41] as it was that men in general dominate women. Marriageable men were the 'men' of the 'Second Treatise', not because they were heterosexual rather than homosexual (in modern terms), but because marriage was the public face of sexuality, as well as the public face of property, and therefore a defining factor in the dominant masculinities of the time. Servants, foreigners, boys and e.g. 'several nations of the Americans'[42] all belonged to different and subordinate masculinities, and as such were treated as inferiors, making them objects of domination, *within* the male gender order, in various different ways.

In particular, overt gendering of men in Locke reinforces a modern, rather commercial type of dominant masculinity, by contradicting an old-fashioned, rather Old Testament archetype of patriarchy. Locke's text thus marks a point where a rational/bureaucratic concept of masculinity overthrows (theoretically, at least) a 'warrior' masculinity associated with physical force and lethal violence.[43] The latter masculinity appeared in Locke's portrayal of the Filmerian patriarchal tyrant, absolute and arbitrary, as father, as husband, as householder and as ruler. The Filmerian ruler as absolute monarch was portrayed by Locke as violent, aggressive, sub-human and animal-like in unpredictability and ferocity. Filmerian patriarchal powers were all of a piece, whether those of father, husband, householder or ruler: 'In absolute monarchies indeed … if it be asked, what security, what fence is there in such a state, against the violence and oppression of this absolute ruler? The very question can scarce be borne. They are ready to tell you, that it deserves death only to ask after safety …'. Locke cannot imagine 'men' bargaining their way out of the state of nature only to set up so dangerous a tyranny: 'This is to think that men are so foolish that they take care to avoid what mischiefs may be done them by polecats, or foxes, but are content, nay think it safety, to be devoured by lions'.[44]

The superior claim of *some* (presumptively) male agents over others in terms of a competitive, individualistic and commercial cast of mind, was famously and sweepingly announced by Locke in this passage:

> God gave the world to men in common; but since he gave it them for their benefit, and the greatest conveniences of life they were capable to draw from it, it cannot be supposed he meant it should always remain common and uncultivated [i.e. unenclosed for commercial agriculture]. He gave it to the use of the industrious and rational, (and labour was to be his title to it); not to the fancy or covetousness of the quarrelsome and contentious.[45]

The executive power of the law of nature, held (presumptively by *some* males, and later transferred to magistrates as rulers, again presumptively male) fits into this pattern of orderly and bounded restraint:

> And thus in the state of nature, one man comes by a power over another; but yet no absolute or arbitrary power, to use a criminal when he has got him in his hands, according to the passionate heats, or boundless extravagancy of his own will, but only to retribute to him, so far as calm reason and conscience dictates, what is proportionate to this transgression, which is so much as may serve for reparation and restraint.[46]

Lockean 'masters' (of households, and over servants and labourers generally) were thus defined in terms of this masculinised vision of rationality and industry. Note the positioning of (presumptively but not necessarily male) servants in this passage alongside their fellow (animal) laborers: 'Thus the grass my horse has bit; the turfs my servant has cut; and the ore I have digged in any place where I have a right to them in common with others, become my property …'[47] In terms of 'conjugal society' between husband and wife, once again the orderly and purposive, contractual and limited qualities of a relationship were contrasted with Filmerian absolutism. For Locke even the marriage relationship was not perpetual, and there was 'no necessity in the nature of the thing, nor to the ends of it'. A wife may be 'in the full and free possession of what by contract is her peculiar right', and thus a husband has 'no more power over her life, than she has over his', and indeed the 'power of the husband' is 'so far from that of an absolute monarch, that the wife has, in many cases, a liberty to separate from him'.[48] In terms of parental relations, Locke argued similarly that fathers had paternal powers to guide and protect their charges, but no absolute power over their lives as such, and therefore no legitimate powers to destroy or disadvantage them.[49]

The concepts of fatherhood, husbandhood, householdership and magistracy that Locke endorsed stand in contrast to the absolute, arbitrary powers of murder and enslavement that he rejected as 'force without right'.[50] He condemned those illegitimate powers in his portraits (explicit and implied) of tyrannical rulers, householders, husbands and fathers. In his view they all pretended to a right that no one could ever have, namely the right to harm others who were themselves innocent of any evil-doing. The Lockean household thus comprised conjugal, parental and master/servant relationships, none of which represented or assigned 'absolute power of the whole family', as Filmerian patriarchy was supposed to entail, and all of which reflected an 'industrious and rational' form of dominant masculinity. Filmerian tyranny, Locke argued, would fall apart even in the domestic context, paralleling his later argument, that such tyranny in the political context is a standing invitation to rebellion and disorder:[51]

> ... if it [the family] must be thought a monarchy, and the paterfamilias the absolute monarch in it, absolute monarchy will have but a very shattered and short power, when 'tis plain, by what has been said before, that the master of the family has a very distinct and differently limited power, both as to time and extent, over those several persons that are in it ...[52]

Locke argued that rulers acted legitimately when and only when they ruled for the public good, and therefore had no such absolute powers as life and death over the community or individuals, independent of that justification.[53] It follows that in his theory no one can consent to absolute and arbitrary power in a ruler, precisely because it would expose the citizenry to public evil, rather than good.[54] That situation, Locke noted, was one of slavery, and totally inconsistent with the freedom which only legitimate government could provide, as opposed to Filmerian absolutism. Locke's sole justification for slavery (defined as an *ad hoc* suspension of the death sentence due to prisoners from an unjust war) was, of course, a situation in which an evil was rightly owed as punishment.[55] This was carefully distinguished even from Old Testament slavery, which Locke said gave the master no right to kill those whom they (mistakenly) called slaves.[56]

While arguing that legitimate government arises only from consent of the people, as would be true with the Old Testament

Judges of the 'First Treatise' or the contemporary 'magistrates' of the 'Second Treatise', Locke also felt that he needed to reconcile his theory of popular sovereignty with the historical existence of legitimate rulers who were *apparently* patriarchal monarchs, *contra* Filmer's general thesis that this was no mere appearance but a God-given reality for all time. However, arguing that patriarchal monarchy was not what it seemed then turned out to be a rather difficult task for Locke, in terms of evidence, and it also posed a problem vis-à-vis his theory of 'express consent'. His theory of 'express consent' was a defining feature of the 'perfect member', i.e. marriageable householder, of his political society.[57] In so far as Locke could solve his problems, he did so by again contrasting a different type of dominant masculinity of which he approved – the kindly father – with Filmer's 'warrior' absolutism – which he was at pains to reject.

For Locke there was a masculinity of fatherhood that is gendered just as much masculine as feminine, and distinctly different from Filmer's 'warrior' absolutism. Jointly as parents both men and women were said by Locke to have a similar authority to match their duty of care. It was, however, a power tempered with 'suitable inclinations of tenderness and concern' for 'the children's good'.[58] Moreover the power of fathers and mothers over children was temporary: 'The bonds of this subjection are like the swaddling clothes they [i.e. babies] are wrapped up in, and supported by, in the weakness of their infancy'.[59] Thus the 'subjection of a minor places in the father a temporary government, which terminates with the minority of the child … The nourishment and education of their children is a charge so incumbent on parents for their children's good, that nothing can absolve them from taking care of it'.[60] Locke's portrait of the kindly father thus presents a contrast with its opposite, the Filmerian patriarch, imbued with 'absolute, unlimited power':[61]

> And therefore God Almighty when he would express his gentle dealing with the Israelites, he tells them, that though he chastened them, 'he chastened them as a man chastens his son' (*Deuteronomy* 8:5), i.e. with tenderness and affection, and kept them under no severer discipline than what was absolutely best for them, and had been less kindness to have slackened.[62]

Locke relied on a classical image of dominant masculinity that was not overtly in the warrior mode, namely the 'nursing' father as lawgiver – Moses, Lycurgus, Solon and Numa Pompilius were the usual models.[63] In the scholarship and literature of the time they were seen as carers for 'their' peoples. Locke had no difficulties idealising classical and Old Testament rulership when he could make it wise and kindly, because he saw it as functioning within the God-given moral frame, through which God's property in human life was preserved and promoted. However, he objected to the (presumed) Filmerian idealisation of rulership as fatherly and *absolute*, seeing absolute power as nothing to God's purpose and quite against reason. Filmer's patriarchalism thus promoted the wrong kind of masculinity, falsely identifying the fatherly role with the untrammelled powers of a 'wild beast, or noxious brute'.[64] Men who behaved in that way, even in war, were not welcome in Locke's moral universe.[65]

When Locke dealt with the historical problem of (apparently) patriarchal monarchy, he shifted his ground on consent very considerably. 'Express consent' is the 'actual agreement' and 'express declaration' that binds all who make it 'perpetually and indispensably' to the government[66] and makes each of them a 'perfect member'[67] of the community. But in archaic times the very consent that instituted legitimate rulership was (paradoxically) so utterly tacit as to be virtually imperceptible to the parties giving and receiving it:

> Thus, whether a family by degrees grew up into a commonwealth, and the fatherly authority being continued on to the elder son, everyone in his turn growing up under it, tacitly submitted to it, and the easiness and quality of it not offending anyone, everyone acquiesced, till time seemed to have confirmed it, and settled a right of succession by prescription ...[68]

That argument merely justified patriarchal rule by consent, but did not catch what was for Locke the point behind consent and legitimacy in the first place, namely 'All for the public good'.[69] To bring that in, but in the archaic context, he needed to add something further about the kind of fathers he had in mind: 'without such nursing fathers tender and careful of the public weal, all governments would have sunk under the weakness and infirmities of their infancy; and the prince and the people had soon perished together'.[70] That way of forming legitimate government was ascribed to a distant but happy past when in simple societies 'the people' moved effortlessly from filial obedience to political obligation, due to the excellent ministrations of their 'nursing fathers'. Those legitimated rulers presumably noted the difference between one role and another, i.e. their role as father with respect to children, and their role as magistrate with respect to consenting adults. Locke's 'nursing fathers' were thus model males, not just fatherly, but fatherly in the right way. From the children's point of view such a father sustained them with his care and brought them up with a 'tenderness for them all'.[71] In the past those men had been so thoroughly accepted as excellent fathers, husbands and heads of household that they were then ultra-tacitly legitimised as ruler-magistrates, a sequence that Locke said he could not then recommend to a more corrupt age, as material temptations for both sides were so much more prevalent.[72]

Unfortunately, though, ultra-tacit consent of that sort makes Locke's concept of express consent – the only consent that makes one a 'perfect member' (i.e. full citizen) of a modern community[73] – even more mysterious than it already is, as notoriously Locke never really envisions a practical process through which such contracts among *some* men are drawn up and executed. Indeed Locke himself was somewhat mystified about what counted as express and what counted as tacit in his imagined historical situation: '… since without some government it would be hard for them [i.e. a family] to live together, it was likeliest it [i.e. some government] should, by the *express or tacit* consent of the children, be in the father …' [emphasis added].[74]

How can the consent that makes one a 'perfect member' be an express declaration as a matter of principle (self-imposed obligation), and also an unstated understanding? An unstated agreement, of course, would not necessarily be the same for everyone, anyway. The explicit and usual concept of tacit consent in Locke was really quite different in function and form. Tacit consent, as Locke explained in detail,[75] was very much parasitic on an existing 'political society', and it could only arise when a binding obligation has been expressly incurred on the part of *some* men to be 'concluded by the majority'.[76] Those persons merely enjoying even minimal advantages of the life, liberty and property that legitimate government secured, without consenting expressly, were then obliged to obey it, and were said to have consented tacitly. That, of course, did not give them the same status as 'perfect member', although the obligations may apparently be similar in practice.

How then could another form of tacit consent also flow from 'the people' (i.e. adult sons in the primitive familial society) to their erstwhile father, such that he was legitimised as magistrate in the imperceptible way that Locke wanted, and such that they became 'perfect members' of a 'political society'? Obviously there are two kinds of tacit consent at work here: tacit-express (an ultra-tacit consent in relation to 'nursing fathers'), and tacit-tacit (a mere use of facilities in relation to political societies that have already been formed). Intriguingly, express consent, and tacit-tacit consent, occur in the apparently de-gendered narrative that is popular with contemporary liberals. Tacit-express consent occurs in an overtly gendered narrative concerned with 'nursing fathers' who are legitimised silently as magistrate-monarchs, a scenario that liberals would not much favour and would prefer to forget, as it were. The 'nursing father' version of dominant masculinity cancelled out the need for marriageable males to make an explicit declaration of obligation to be 'concluded' by the majority, which could then devolve government by majority decision to a smaller body or to an individual person. The 'sons' of the archaic era were evidently not up to making that kind of 'rational' declaration in favour of a bureaucratic ruler who would act as magistrate, in Locke's view. Rather the kindly 'nursing father' salvaged the nexus between consent and legitimacy for all times, past and present, by contrast with the Filmerian patriarchy of absolute rule by a 'warrior', which in Locke's view never created legitimacy, and was certainly not an archaic origin of government.

Locke's text was not, even in part, about genderless values (relating anyone and everyone equally to the 'public good'). Rather those values were expressed in his text through the construction of different dominant masculinities (along with their subordinate 'others'). In the archaic world Lockean masculinity for rulers was that of the 'nursing father', tender and solicitous. In his modern world, Locke's preferred masculinity for rulers was rational/bureaucratic and contractual/commercial. In both worlds Locke's residual patriarchalism was effected through a unified portrait of fathers, husbands and householders that mingled both those masculinities together. Fatherhood was more tender than contractual; husbandhood more contractual than commercial; and householdership more contractual/commercial than tender. In none of those roles, however, was a Filmerian, tyrannical 'warrior' male in evidence, holding absolute and arbitrary power over the very lives of children, wives, servants and fellow citizens.

Thus Locke's principles of equality, articulated explicitly between men and women, and between *some* men and other men, were made to fit into a politics of pre-existing masculinities, ancient and modern. Locke was concerned to theorise society and politics that way round. Many of his readers, feminists especially, have been concerned to drive the argument in reverse, and to use the principles of equality to re-envision and reform the social relationships that Locke conceptualised as conjugal, parental, household and political. Given that feminists have an interest in just that kind of politics, it follows that overtly gendered narratives of masculinities, such as those that Locke reinforced as foundational, are very much an issue. All of the issues that Locke raised are issues today for men, as well as women, not because they are 'male' issues, or 'gender' issues, in some sense, but because the narrative construction of dominant masculinities, such as those he articulated, represents the most important site of all in society where power is accumulated and deployed politically.

Notes

1 On this point, see Jeremy Waldron, *God, Locke, and Equality: Christian foundations in Locke's political thought* (Cambridge: Cambridge University Press, 2002), pp. 6–12.
2 The feminist literature on these issues is very large. With respect to Locke the foundational account is Pateman, *The Sexual Contract*. For some recent studies that I have found useful, see Mary Lyndon Shanley, 'Marriage contract and social contract in seventeenth century English political thought', in Jean Bethke Elshtain, ed., *The Family in Political Thought* (Amherst MA: University of Massachusetts Press, 1982); Sharon Cooney, 'A Revolution in the Household: Locke's Reconstitution of the Family', unpublished paper presented at the American Political Science Association 1995 Annual Meeting; Peter C. Myers, 'Locke on the Constitution of the Liberal Family', unpublished paper presented at the American Political Science Association 1997 Annual Meeting.
3 Harry Brod, 'Introduction', and 'The case for men's studies', in *The Making of Masculinities*, pp. 1–18, 39–62; Jeff Hearn, *The Gender of Oppression: men, masculinity and the critique of Marxism* (Brighton: Wheatsheaf, 1987).
4 Peter Filene, 'The secrets of men's history', in Brod, ed., *The Making of Masculinities*, pp. 103–20; R.W. Connell, *Gender and Power: society, the person and sexual politics* (Cambridge: Polity Press, 1987); Jeff Hearn and David Collinson, 'Unities and differences between men and between

masculinities', in Harry Brod and Michael Kaufmann, eds, *Theorizing Masculinities* (Newbury Park CA: Sage, 1994), pp. 97–118; Tim Edwards, *Erotics and Politics: gay male sexuality, masculinity and feminism* (London: Routledge, 1994); Lynne Segal, *Slow Motion: changing masculinities, changing men* (London: Virago, 1990).

5   For a detailed discussion of these points, see Carver, '"Public man"', pp. 673–8.
6   Carver, '"Public Man"', pp. 676–9.
7   Terrell Carver, *Gender is not a Synonym for Women* (Boulder, CO: Lynne Rienner, 1996), pp. 32–6.
8   Gordon J. Schochet discusses varieties of seventeenth-century patriarchalism, and hence gives a critical view of Locke's account of their theories, in his *Patriarchalism in Political Thought: the authoritarian family and political speculation and attitudes especially in seventeenth-century England* (Oxford: Blackwell, 1975).
9   John Locke, *Two Treatises of Government*, ed. Mark Goldie (London: Dent, 1993), II§§4–5, p. 116; cf. *Two Treatises of Government*, ed. Peter Laslett (Cambridge: Cambridge University Press, 1988); page references below are to the Goldie edn; readers can use the § references below to find passages in the Laslett edn.
10 Locke, *Two Treatises*, II§54, p. 141.
11 Locke, *Two Treatises*, II§82, p. 155.
12 Waldron views this as a philosophical inconsistency; see *God, Locke, and Equality*, pp. 21–43.
13 See Evans, *Sexual Citizenship*, pp. 5–6.
14 Peter Laslett, 'Introduction', *Two Treatises*, ed. Laslett, pp. 13–14.
15 Mark Goldie, 'Glossary', in Locke, *Two Treatises*, p. 243.
16 See, for example, Richard Ashcraft, *Revolutionary Politics and Locke's Two Treatises of Government* (Princeton, NJ: Princeton University Press, 1986).
17 Schochet, *Patriarchalism*, pp. 1–4.
18 Carver, '"Public Man"', pp. 679–82; see Stevens, *Reproducing the State*.
19 Locke, *Two Treatises*, II§2, pp. 115–16.
20 Locke, *Two Treatises*, II§1, p. 115.
21 Locke, *Two Treatises*, II§§52–53, pp. 140–1.
22 Locke, *Two Treatises*, I§6, p. 8.
23 Locke, *Two Treatises*, I§11, p. 12.
24 Locke, *Two Treatises*, I§61, pp. 43–5.
25 Locke, *Two Treatises*, II§4, p. 116.
26 Locke, *Two Treatises*, II§65, p. 146.
27 These issues are discussed in Mary Astell, *Some Reflections on Marriage* [1700], in Marie Mulvey Roberts and Tamae Mizuta, eds, *Perspectives on*

    the History of British Feminism, The Wives: the rights of married women (London: Routledge/Thoemmes Press, 1994), pp. 1–98.
28 John Guy, *Tudor England* (Oxford: Oxford University Press, 1988, repr. 1991), pp. 226–49, 250–2, 268–71, 282–3.
29 Locke, *Two Treatises*, I§47, pp. 34–5.
30 Locke, *Two Treatises*, I§44, pp. 32–3.
31 Locke, *Two Treatises*, II§82, p. 155.
32 Locke, *Two Treatises*, I§47, pp. 34–5.
33 Locke, *Two Treatises*, I§47, p. 35.
34 Locke, *Two Treatises*, II§82, p. 155.
35 Locke, *Two Treatises*, I§48, p. 35.
36 Locke, *Two Treatises*, I§161, p. 108.
37 Locke, *Two Treatises*, I§§93, 98, pp. 66, 68–9.
38 Locke, *Two Treatises*, I§123, p. 84.
39 Connell, *Masculinities*, pp. 67–86.
40 Locke, *Two Treatises*, II§119, p. 176.
41 Locke, *Two Treatises*, II§§26, 34, pp. 127–8, 131.
42 Locke, *Two Treatises*, II§41, p. 135.
43 Jean Bethke Elshtain, *Public Man/Private Woman: women in social and political thought*, 2nd edn (Princeton, NJ: Princeton University Press, 1993), pp. 100–31; Connell, *Masculinities*, pp. 185–203; Hooper, *Manly States*, pp. 64–76.
44 Locke, *Two Treatises*, II§93, p. 161.
45 Locke, *Two Treatises*, II§34, p. 131.
46 Locke, *Two Treatises*, II§8, p. 118.
47 Locke, *Two Treatises*, II§28, p. 129.
48 Locke, *Two Treatises*, II§81, p. 155.
49 Locke, *Two Treatises*, II§69, p. 149.
50 Locke, *Two Treatises*, II§19, p. 124.
51 Locke, *Two Treatises*, II§§222–226, pp. 226–30.
52 Locke, *Two Treatises*, II§86, p. 157.
53 Locke, *Two Treatises*, II§131, pp. 180–1.
54 John Dunn, *The Political Thought of John Locke: an historical account of the argument of the 'Two Treatises of Government'* (Cambridge: Cambridge University Press, 1982), pp. 131–47.
55 Locke, *Two Treatises*, II§23, p. 126; see James Farr, '"So Vile and Miserable an Estate": the problem of slavery in Locke's political thought', *Political Theory* 14 (1986), 263–9.
56 Locke, *Two Treatises*, II§24, pp. 126–7.
57 Locke, *Two Treatises*, II§119, p. 176.
58 Locke, *Two Treatises*, II§63, p. 145.
59 Locke, *Two Treatises*, II§55, p. 141.
60 Locke, *Two Treatises*, II§67, pp. 147–8.

61 Locke, *Two Treatises*, II§61, p. 144–5.
62 Locke, *Two Treatises*, II§67, p. 148.
63 Locke, *Two Treatises*, II§110, p. 171–2; the 'nursing father' image comes from *Isaiah* 49:23.
64 Indeed the Filmerian father is likened by Locke to Peruvian cannibals [sic], who are so far sunk below the level of beasts (including male ones), that they are reported (by Garcilasso de la Vega) to 'farm' children for the table, and to eat any mothers that are past child-bearing! (*Two Treatises*, I§§56-59). I owe this reference to Jennet Kirkpatrick, 'Thinking the Unthinkable: Lockean Reason and the Figure of Woman', unpublished paper, presented at the Midwest Political Science Association, 61st National Conference, Chicago, IL, 3–6 April 2003, and email correspondence.
65 Locke, *Two Treatises*, II§§177–180, pp. 206–8.
66 Locke, *Two Treatises*, II§121, p. 177.
67 Locke, *Two Treatises*, II§119, p. 176.
68 Locke, *Two Treatises*, II§110, p. 171.
69 Locke, *Two Treatises*, II§131, pp. 180–1.
70 Locke, *Two Treatises*, II§110, pp. 171–2.
71 Locke, *Two Treatises*, II§75, p. 152.
72 Locke, *Two Treatises*, II§111, p. 172.
73 Locke, *Two Treatises*, II§119, p. 176.
74 Locke, *Two Treatises*, II§74, pp. 151–2.
75 Locke, *Two Treatises*, II§§119, 122, pp. 176, 177–8.
76 Locke, *Two Treatises*, II§96, p. 163.

CHAPTER EIGHT

Rousseau: fantasising men

Humans, animals, technologies

Rousseau is probably the most gender-conscious of political theorists, and the most conscious of sexual difference and sexuality. Throughout his massive and complicated *oeuvre*, Rousseau's thought on gender is a dizzying experience, as he travels from the utter depths of individual self-examination and revelation to the highest reaches of moralised pontification and idealised civic virtue.[1] To make matters that much more difficult, it has to be noted that for all his interest in gender (that is, sex, sexuality and power), Rousseau is not these days the gender-theorist of choice. His views on sexual difference go against the intellectual and social grain in contemporary circles by oftentimes emphasising difference in physical bodies and reproductive biology (and attendant emotions, so he opines) in pronouncing on roles and capacities, rather than consistently following a more 'progressive' programme. That would mean suiting activities to individual capacities first (e.g. for citizenship and other 'public' activities), and considering sexual difference as in principle no bar to anyone's inclusion and equality, unless specific exceptions can be warranted. This line in gender politics tends to reduce the effect of ascribed sexual difference, to denaturalise and destabilise sex as a fixed principle of discrimination, and to flatten the gender-hierarchy of male domination in spheres commonly denominated as public and private by including women on an equal basis with men. It may not yet attack the overall masculinisation of society; it may not yet be really woman-friendly; and it may be compatible with any number of economic and other oppressions that bear harder on (most) women than on (some) men. But there is no doubt that factoring out sexual difference (to a certain extent, and to a certain extent counter-productively) has altered many women's lives and the character of gender-relations in some societies, notably those on the upside of global capitalism.

Yet Rousseau is no more popular with theorists who work in the other direction in terms of gender politics, emphasising sexual difference and the need for this to stand in principle as a crucial and inescapable feature of private and public relationships. The extent to which that politics is rooted in 'woman' as the vessel of sexual difference (rather than in 'man as male') is striking, whether we are looking at religious politics (e.g. traditional Catholic, Christian 'fundamentalist', Islamic theocratic, or numerous other faiths) or at feminisms that are of the radical or 'standpoint' variety (where the political goals may, of course, be quite different). 'Woman' on this model tends to be 'womb', and a metonymy for 'child', 'family' and 'reproduction', conceptualised either as God-given or as species-competitive (or sometimes both). Rousseau is rather an exception here in including disquisitions on female sexual desire (which he construes as delightful yet dangerous *for men*).

Only occasionally is 'man as male' located firmly in the repro-ductive sphere by theorists, and then almost always with less constraint, less responsibility, less emotion. Putting the situation that way almost tells you what 'man as male' is, according to commonplace representations, namely emotionally limited, sexually promiscuous and morally irresponsible, that is, 'free' and rightly so, as trite charac-terisations will have it. Those characteristics are themselves often projected onto male biology and behaviour, usually illustrated with views of selected male animals which are thought to act this out in nature, and thus to validate the picture. Interestingly 'woman' is some-what less often located in the biological world of animal behaviour, or at least when she is, the trope is politically less exciting than rutting stags and strutting peacocks. Possibly there are sufficient command-ments and exemplars in religious thought (and in 'western' morals and public policies until extremely recently) to keep women apprised of the 'biology' of sexual difference and its 'obvious' role in defining what is and is not possible or suitable for them in private and public relations, so imaginative trips to the zoo are perhaps not so necessary.

This is not to say that animals are not conveniently used on occasion to teach lessons to women about mothering and family life, but rather that these exercises tend to reinforce what is already 'known' about women: they have a destiny or function in motherhood, and this entails responsibilities and emotions that are at root 'other' to men, who would have to work at those tasks and experiences even to approach the 'natural' female experience with any sense of understanding or competence. The film *Junior*, in which Arnold Schwarzenegger becomes (ectopically) pregnant, raises these issues, though needless to say, the intent is humorous rather than critical. Men can't do it, they aren't like that, it's unnatural and it won't happen ... or so we might think. The point, of course, is not whether a man will ever have an ectopic pregnancy (at all, or to term) but whether men with their bodies (cf. Arnie for choice!) will actually have and indeed desire and enjoy (most of) the (typical and highly various) female experiences of childbirth and motherhood (as the Arnie character, Dr Hesse, does in the film). The film thus does a good job of constructing man-as-woman in reproductive terms by taking Dr Hesse through morning sickness and food fetishes, mood swings including sexual desire, bodily changes including nipple sensitivity, and eventually the oddities of infant-kicking. Attendant emotions, ups and downs, anxieties and highs are all written into his script, including bonding with his biological co-parent and with other pregnant women.[2]

While the film is evidently a Hollywood transposition gag-vehicle, the script and editing seem to work quite hard to deconstruct woman-as-biology. The Emma Thompson character, Dr Reddin, another masculinised doctor/scientist, discourses dismissively on hormones, periods, menopause and similar markers of femaleness (and markers of male-non-experience), apart from the pregnancy that Dr Hesse has (and she hasn't had). *Junior* thus destabilises (fictively) the male/female biological boundary of (supposedly) irremovable sexual difference, and in so far as it is dramatically convincing (the actors work hard at this), it presents a denaturalisation of biology and sex. In the dramaturgical background, though, the screenplay is also working hard to show us that this denaturalisation is the product of both individual human behaviour in doing things however one pleases and the outcome of modern medicalisation that technologises the body and the mind in formulaic and disciplinary ways. Dr Hesse's business partner in this novel enterprise of male pregnancy is Danny DeVito's character Dr Arbogast. His ex-wife Angela 'gets herself pregnant' by a roadie at an Aerosmith concert, simply because she wants a child (as did Dr Arbogast, when they were married). This vignette and sub-plot thus deconstructs all of the romance, happy-couple, emotional-involvement and nest-building paraphernalia that Dr Hesse (and Dr Reddin) are working so hard to put together, though only semi-consciously most of the time (as often in real life). Angela has all the same physical experiences of pregnancy as Dr Hesse; they just got there in apparently opposite ways (existential choice in the one case and scientific career-building in the other), albeit in apparently (and supposedly) opposite biologies. They are also in apparently similar non-relationships to conventional moralities, exemplars, teachings and institutions that tell us what responsible parenthood is like for women and men in 'the family'.[3] Family life doesn't figure in the film, of course, until the end, when the two 'odd' families have the children and bond together in loving parenthood.

In the background there are the tell-tale animals, in this case jovial chimps that are (presumably) capable of biological reproduction but are in fact having embryo implants (just like people!). While the apparent purpose of the setting (a university laboratory) is medical research to find a drug to stave off tissue-rejection (and therefore to secure lucrative contracts with drug companies – which is what makes the plot go), the overall picture is one of humans, animals and machines all involved in the vagaries of the creation of new life (a thunderstorm during the in-vitro conception and implantation procedures explosively recalls the Frankenstein myth of 'man playing God'). The technological side of the screenplay ruthlessly deconstructs every physical and emotional aspect of 'normal' reproduction in 'the family', from sperm donations ('all the latest pornography'), to frozen eggs ('the dairy section'), to intrusive extraction and implantation technologies (graphic depictions), to medical services and 'patient-care' (chilling and haphazard). Even bodily differences between men and women as such are dismissed as mere 'fat', and the very specially female character of maternity garments gets decisively deconstructed when an overweight salesman in a men's store instantly empathises with Dr Hesse's need for roomy, expandable clothes. Dr Hesse's male body, and his masculine outfits, only adapt to his situation. He doesn't become in either respect a woman in gender terms until near the end, when he is forced into drag in order to pass as female in a private maternity clinic. He explains his appearance, again in impeccably deconstructive terms, by saying (as a woman) that East

German athletic coaches had forced her to take steroids, thus giving her a masculine appearance (general sadness all round).

The sacredness and mystique of science and medicine are also an easy target throughout; all the ethics and scruples go by the board in a hail of laughter. Scientists are not machines and they are not animals; they are wacky, corrupt and (supposedly) lovable humans, each in their own way. However, they are notably different in principle and in practice from the stereotypes ('woman', 'man', 'morals') that they are supposed to mirror and to which indeed they are supposed to subordinate themselves. Those are all in the minds of the audience, and are not represented in any of the characters. The one major character with no angle on sex or sexuality is the head of the research unit, an obviously evil figure, who sniffs a breach of the legal and ethical regulations. However, his only intent is to use this to get ahead selfishly, through fair means or foul, the latter being to him the more familiar method of career management.

This discussion raises a well-known paradox that Rousseau tackles throughout his highly gendered political theory. If humans have to *discover* what is 'natural' and have to *learn* what is 'biological', in order to teach themselves how to behave and what to think, and moreover to prevent themselves from doing the opposite (i.e. being *un*natural), in what sense then can 'biology' and 'nature' ever be said to be determinants or constraints on individual and collective choice? There should certainly be constraints, and behaviour may indeed have its determinants, but how seriously should we take 'biology' and 'nature' (perhaps as handed down through varying cultural traditions) as determinants of identities and boundaries in society? If 'biology' and 'nature' already answer the questions we have about identity and boundaries, why then are we having the discussion at all?

Moreover there is a related question for us. If, on the supposition that 'biology' and 'nature' had *not* constructed us with these determinants and constraints 'wired in', would they then indeed be repositories of knowledge for us about ourselves? The 'truths' of 'biology' and 'nature' (as conceptualised according to various objects of study) are assumed to be applicable universally across individuals (of whatever kind), across all species as such, and indeed ultimately throughout the material universe. If we could find this knowledge about ourselves, it would thus be usefully general and certain. In a post-Nietzschean world, where God and morality have failed to tell us what is what, and what to do (and not to do), will we be any better off with 'biology' and 'nature' for guidance? If we rebel against that, where then will we be? How much do we want to rebel against the intellectual traditions (and the tradition of intellectualising) that have got us into the unhappy and unequal state (in gender terms, and every other) that we bemoan? If we do rebel, and thus cease looking for universalities and certainties, will all our identities and boundaries collapse for want of justification? Could we find justification in some other quarter? Would it be universal and certain? If not, in what sense would it be justification? Do we need justification in any sense? Rousseau is paradigmatic here as rebel, and I shall be considering him in this chapter as questioner, rather than as giver-of-an-answer. This will not be a reassuring experience.

'Man' and society

Rousseau has left us major meditations on the human animal and comparator animals, on sexual difference in nature and in biology, on pre-history and the history of technology, on sexual and reproductive technologies and emotions, on gender-difference and power-relations, and on 'public man' and 'private woman'. He has also notably left us meditations on 'private man', and his (now intensely provocative) condemnation of 'public woman'. Most of our current obsessions are rehearsed in his writings, but as with many other thinkers, his reputation has suffered through appalling over simplification (e.g. 'noble savage') and a relentless reading of his texts for 'truth'. Both speak to poor reading strategies: the first represents intellectual laziness, and the second intellectual dependency. Rousseau has also suffered more than most political theorists from our contemporary aversion to what appear to be his conclusions. Standpoint feminists dislike his views on woman's relationship to man (that way round); religious and 'family values' campaigners can't bear his scorn for biblical revelation and the Christian church; liberals are mystified by his bucolic obsessions and anti-commercialism. Almost everyone thinks he 'wants to turn the clock back', which in our days of (minimal) post-Marxism is utterly *verboten*. While Hobbes has few political followers arguing for undivided sovereignty and no-nonsense authoritarianism, he is appreciated as methodologist and 'father' to rational choice theory. Even *The Republic* gets some credit for raising the issue of justice in the community, although commentators never have much time for the three-class solution. Rousseau has fans only amongst greens and ecologists, who rally to his ideals of the small-scale community, limitations on technology and commerce, and some aspects of his participatory and deliberative ideals for inclusive decision-making. But even those writers keep their distance, given his in-your-face reputation for self-authorised coercion and his very out-of-line views on gender-difference generally and femininity in particular.

Perhaps what has tarred Rousseau with the blackest of brushes is his notorious 'forced to be free' comment in the *Social Contract* (1762), which has sounded ominous since the days of Fascism and Totalitarianism (and the surrounding politics of political theory, keen to find intellectual genealogies for these twentieth-century disasters).[4] To make matters worse, where gender, women and sexual difference have been noticed at length and argumentatively in political theory (and this interest pretty much marks such work as 'feminist'), Rousseau's declared sexism – or bluntly, the subordination of women to men – has made him anathema, or only to be read 'against the grain'. Such readings strive to salvage his masculinised concept of man as 'man' (the 'individual' citizen) and then – rather as in the film *Junior* – to stretch this rather abstract creature around female experiences and feminine stereotypes as much as 'he' will stand. Rousseau is thus the theorist to whom so many readers turn … with instantly professed reservations.[5]

I propose to examine some of Rousseau's political theory for what it has to say about 'man', that is 'public man', making it clear that I am attending to this conceptualisation as the apparently degendered, yet covertly gendered, masculinised and male 'citizen'.[6] While we know that this person is not a woman, I shall work to unfold in what ways this citizen is actually man-as-male, and what kind of masculinity Rousseau is contriving. As a kind of masculinity, what, if anything, does it have to recommend it? How does it construct relationships in (homosocial) society as 'man to man'? And (bearing with me here) what relationships does it construct with 'women and children'? What do we learn about masculinity past and present, masculinised societies real and ideal, and sex-difference (rooted in biology, or not) from a civic perspective? Rousseau's 'civil religion' is not popular, either, in these days of (supposed) secularism, yet it can be investigated and evaluated as a value-system. Rousseau's 'man', and his men, will bear at least as much interest.

Rousseau's 'Discourse on the Origins of Inequality among Men' (or 'Second Discourse', 1755) is a landmark work, notably for its thoroughness in addressing the physical side of human power-relations in complex conjunction with the political side, namely the realm of law and other forms of social regulation. He addresses the question of human identity in a unique historical way within the canon of political theory. Rather than tracing some cultural boundary (such as Greeks/barbarians) or religious boundary (such as Jews/Christians/unbelievers), Rousseau conceptualises history quite differently, reflecting the development of knowledge (chiefly by colonial discovery) that had come into circulation since the sixteenth century. Contact with the 'exotic' and technologically varied cultures and populations of the African coast, the East Indies and the Americas had raised questions of an anthropological, historical and biological character for Rousseau's contemporaries, particularly when taken in conjunction with an understandable interest in exotic animals, especially the larger primates.[7] Where was the human/animal boundary line? Were there boundary lines of a similar significance between humans? Was there a developmental progression among species, and within our species? If so, what behaviour did this license from 'superiors' to 'inferiors', that is, more developed to less developed? If there were no line of progressive development, what other rules would then apply, and on what basis? Rousseau's analytical gifts enabled him to pose issues of this kind with extraordinary clarity, and thus to draw into political theory the (still open) debates that we have concerning the history of our sub-species (from, say, 20,000 years ago) and of our place in primate 'development' (from, say, 2.5 million years ago). Intriguingly, and rather against most trends, Rousseau argues that the achievements of 'western' civilisation mark a *decline* for our species, and his account of any remedy is rather pessimistic and unconvincing (in the 'Discourse on the Origins of Inequality' and in the *Social Contract*).[8] This has not been a popular message.

Central to Rousseau's questioning of the commonplace simple and optimistic 'truths' about humans as a species are numerous physical issues, some rooted in phenomena that do not (in his view) reflect sexual difference (so at least in some ways males and females belong to the same species), and some rooted in phenomena that do reflect the physical features that he conceptualises as sexual difference itself (and so drive his analysis towards a radical divide between men and women). His discussion as to when and how the animal-primate/human-person boundary line is crossed is extraordinarily well argued and subtle, but also contradictory, ambiguous and subject to different interpretations. His account of male/female differences, what they have been and what they should be, is similarly difficult to present with coherence and consistency. It takes a great deal of theoretical work to argue Rousseau's sexism into something else, and of course comparatively little to demonstrate it. What I am doing in this chapter is looking at Rousseau's sexism in relation to men, not where he locates it in his writings (in his novelised discussion of education *Émile* of 1762), but back in the 'Discourse on the Origins of Inequality', where I think it all began. In my view that work is *inter alia* a 'Discourse on the Origins of Masculinity' and *hence* a 'Discourse on the Origins of Inequality'. This is so even in Book I, where among the animals, so one would think (and indeed Rousseau himself says), males and females were equal.

Rousseau opens the work with a distinction between two sorts of inequality 'in the human species':

> ... one which I call natural or Physical, because it is established by Nature, and which consists in the differences in age, health, strengths of Body, and qualities of Mind, or of Soul; The other, which may be called moral, or political inequality, because it depends on a sort of convention ... It consists in the different Privileges which some enjoy to the prejudice of the others, such as to be more wealthy, more honored, more Powerful than they, or even to get themselves obeyed by them.[9]

Rousseau's account is straightaway iconoclastic (and downright rude), since he first announces that 'natural' inequality is basically a tautology (i.e. physical differences occur and simply are differences), and second he dismisses any 'essential connection between the two' kinds of inequality (such as Aristotle and Aristotelians had attempted to prove):

> ... whether strength of Body or of Mind, wisdom or virtue, are always found in the same individuals, in proportion to their Power, or their Wealth: A question which it may perhaps be good for Slaves to debate within hearing of their Masters, but not befitting rational and free Men who seek the truth.[10]

The whole discourse speaks to Rousseau's tendentiously political outlook, stated already on the opening page: '... to explain by what chain of wonders the strong could resolve to serve the weak, and the

People to purchase an idea of repose at the price of real felicity'.[11] Or in other words, physical differences, and in particular supposed characteristics of bodily strength and weakness, have no bearing for Rousseau on the orders of privilege and authority that were so evident in his society. The masculinity here probably lies more in the author's bumptious challenge (to his presumed male audience) than in his characterisation so far of the human species. Where the male/female 'divide' comes to bear on the issue of physical difference (and on how that difference is conceptualised – thus creating the 'divide') are further issues. What is interesting is not that Rousseau raises these to the detriment of women but that he raises the 'woman' question at all, and in such direct ways. It would also seem that his later conclusion contradicts his premise, namely that with respect to 'woman', physical characteristics *do* have a 'some essential connection' with patterns of inequality (in terms of wealth and power) in modern societies, whereas for men (for we will later see the maleness in his original conception), these physical characteristics when exhibited by men (e.g. 'weakness', parenthood) do not create or license the differentials that Rousseau recognises as inequality *par excellence*.

Thus the contradiction (patterns of inequality in human society are – and are not – essentially connected with physical differences) was merely apparent; the 'human species' is cast as male at the outset. This happens in two ways: firstly, the argument about physical characteristics and power-relations works differently for women, so they are evidently not part of the human social relations that Rousseau really has his eye on; and secondly, physical differences are cast as degrees of 'strength' relative to age, health, mind and soul (presumably 'soul' means 'character' here). These differences are thus conceptualised in terms of power, either as physical strength, or on analogy with physical strength. Against this simple (and indeed simplistic) scale, the physical phenomena associated with femaleness (fertility cycles, reproductive phenomena, muscular development) do not appear to merit discussion as yet, and indeed the definition of 'strength' itself is basically assumed from an unproblematic masculine view.

These are important areas of contemporary debate, most usually as workplace and employment issues, and as issues in competitive athletics and feminine lifestyle. What counts as strength or weakness on a spaceship? in a submarine? in physical activity? Rousseau makes masculinised assumptions and treats feminine 'weakness' as natural (and he makes matters worse by finding it sexually attractive).[12] My point here, however, is that his homogenisation of men as relatively strong or weak works for him only to undercut naturalistic theories that the strong should rule, or more likely in conventional arguments, that those who rule *are* strong in the relevant way already and therefore should not be challenged. Relative strength and weakness among men-as-men then tells Rousseau nothing about them in society that he finds politically significant; they are all homogenised and suddenly equalised as men, bodily and intellectual differences notwithstanding. One 'man', in his guise as 'equal' to any other (male) 'citizen', is the same as any other. Some bodily differences in the human species are crucially different, though, with respect to politics, and those are the ones that Rousseau finds determining in femaleness as incontrovertible markers.[13] As we shall see, these are 'weakness' and child-bearing. However, what marks a man? Why is this not interesting? Rousseau's masculinised perspective is supported by this characteristic lack of enquiry.

Not short on iconoclasm and chutzpah, Rousseau dismisses both state of nature theories and scriptural readings by confounding them with each other. States of nature merely transpose 'Civil man' anachronistically into 'Savage' times (NB Rousseau eventually charges 'civilised man' with being far more cruel and savage than so-called savages are or ever were); the Bible relates that the 'first Man' was never in that state, anyway. Rousseau then proceeds into a realm of 'hypothetical and conditional reasonings' not far removed from current methodologies of pre-history,[14] and startlingly he likens his work to that of 'Physicists … regarding the formation of the world'. Again this is an analogy that bears up against the current practice of cosmologists on slender assumptions and less evidence. With that he then addresses the whole of the human species throughout history and in times to come, suggesting that he will praise the 'earliest forebears' and advise his contemporaries (and those who will come after) that they might 'perhaps wish to be able to go backward'. This perspective, more than ever, is difficult now to get hold of, but it is essential to do so in order to follow the course of Rousseau's argument, his distinctions and his judgements.

Rousseau's opening shot at paleoanthropology and evolutionary primatology is not a bad satire on scientific efforts today 'to piece together' the biological development of *homo sapiens* from an imperfect record of highly imperfect fossils:

> I shall not examine whether, as Aristotle thinks, his ['man's'] elongated nails were at first hooked claws; whether he was as hairy as a bear and whether, walking on all fours, his gaze directed to the Earth, and confined to a horizon of a few paces, determined both the character and the limits of his ideas ... so that ... without taking into account the changes that must have occurred in man's internal and the external conformation, as he gradually put his limbs to new uses, and took up new foods, I shall assume him always conformed as I see him today, walking on two feet, using his hands as we do ours ... I see an animal less strong than some, less agile than others ...[15]

Rousseau then builds up a picture of 'man' as 'sturdy, agile, courageous', skilled at evading any 'ferocious Beasts', and not much troubled by predators anyway. Sexual difference first enters the text in a perhaps rather unexpected way: children (unsexed) have 'Fathers':

> Accustomed from childhood to the inclemencies of the weather ... hardened to fatigue ... Men develop a robust and almost unalterable temperament; The Children, since they come into the world with their Fathers' excellent constitution and strengthen it by the same activities that produced it, thus acquire all the vigor of which the human species is capable.[16]

Rousseau then continues this passage as a polemical comparison of the Spartan practice of exposing weak infants, which he praises, against the contemporary practice of abortion in his own society, undertaken to further sexual and economic pursuits of which he thunderously disapproved.[17]

Rousseau's view is almost a fantasy of male generation, a tribe of male Amazons, as it were, providing themselves with male children in their own image, and excluding females, whether mothers or infants, altogether.[18] This picture is completed in Rousseau's invocation of the near-contemporary (and still existing) exotic realm of Savages. While this picture might indeed be of a mixed group, the context here (warriors/hunting, see below) suggests it is exclusively male:

> These are undoubtedly the reasons why Negroes and Savages worry so little about the ferocious beasts they might meet up with in the woods. In this respect the Caribs of Venezuela, among others, live in the most profound security ... Although they are almost naked ... they do not hesitate to take their chances ... armed only with bow and arrow; yet nobody has ever heard of a single one of them being devoured by beasts.[19]

Unsurprisingly 'woman' then (and first) enters the picture as 'Mother',[20] though this happens when Rousseau's mind turns to 'natural infirmities ... old age, and illnesses of every kind'. Human males (as 'man'), in comparison, were differentiated from the other animals by Rousseau in terms of learning:

> But Savage man, living dispersed amongst the animals, and early finding himself in the position of having to measure himself against them, soon makes the comparison, and feeling that he surpasses them in skill more than they do him in strength, learns to fear them no more.[21]

Rousseau's introduction of 'woman' and motherhood (as feeding of the young) follows a sexual divide in not mentioning males at all at that point, in conceptualising her relationship to female animals as one of natural advantage (rather than mental agility), and in brutally reducing her weakness to a likelihood (unspecified) of death (whereas his hearty males, once past infancy, appear to live in an alternative world, surviving to old age, thanks to their 'excellent constitution'):

> As regards Childhood, I even note that, since the Mother carries her child with her everywhere, she can feed it much more readily than can the female of a number of animals, forced as they are to wear themselves out going back and forth, one way to find their food, the other to suckle or feed their young. It is true that if the woman happens to perish, the child runs a considerable risk of perishing with her, but this danger is common to a hundred other species ... And since Savage life keeps gout and rheumatisms from them,[22] and old age is the one of all ills which human assistance can least alleviate, they eventually expire ...[23]

The payoff for Rousseau comes in a contrast between his Savages, 'at least of those we have not ruined with our strong liquors', and the 'soft and effeminate' ways of civilisation, where bad food, excess sensuality and useless doctors (who torment us with incisions and poison us with drugs) contribute to short and unhappy lives. To reinforce his point, Rousseau develops a further contrast between wild and domesticated animals, the latter losing their natural constitutions 'in our homes', hence declining in 'vigor, force, and courage', a mirror to the degeneration Rousseau sees in civilised humans, compared with Savagery.[24] While Rousseau's association of woman with domesticity, sensuality and effeminisation of males is well known, his envisioning of savagery as male-exclusive is less remarked, since the contrast with 'woman' is less overtly drawn at that point, than in his discussions of civilised degeneracy. Women in savagery are (apparently) only 'mothers', who carry infants naturally (inside, presumably, as well as outside the body). In civilisation women are dangerous to Rousseau's men, because they threaten their masculinity, which he respects only in so far as it limns his boyish fantasy of Savage life (albeit transposed to a restrained concept of virtue). It is tempting to say that Rousseau's crisis of civilisation is, for him, a crisis of an ideal masculinity, threatened by feminisation.[25] He is outraged that civilised women do not want to be mothers at all, and it seems to follow that, turning the clock back, as he recommends, we would arrive at the sturdy masculinity that male Savages achieve with their bodies (albeit tempered with the *education sensible* of Émile), and the motherly femininity that females weakly embody, apparently by nature (tempered with the alluring sexuality of Sophie).[26]

While the implications of this vision of 'woman' have been debated for some two centuries, and while Rousseau's picture of savagery has been investigated anthropologically, the latter has been conducted in a way rather complicit with Rousseau's arguments: men are hunters, women are mothers. Whether or not such societies did or do produce sturdy male warriors and women whose lot in life is bearing and carrying infants is not the question here. What requires our attention is the continuing role that male-hunter fantasies play in the construction and sustenance of modern masculinities, together with a consideration of the institutions and representations that perpetuate this 'no girls allowed'/'women are mothers' view of human society at its origins. In itself this fantasy does not entail Rousseau's strong thesis that civilisation is degenerate. What it does entail, though, is some account of how masculinity has moved from this (allegedly) admirable savagery to something more modern that is significantly different. Rousseau himself is interested in the intervening stages, and in charting them he moves from the level of physical difference rooted in nature (as he sees it, but mostly in female bodies) to a realm of intellectual and moral difference rooted in language and issuing in technologies.

Boys and toys

Writing, as he says, in the hypothetical and conditional, Rousseau gives himself no easy options in getting 'man' on the road to 'civilisation', which encompasses material technologies and ever more refined and complex modes of thought. He wrestles with the paradox that there can be no obvious stimulus to change (usually conceptualised as 'improvement') if generations of animal-like creatures are living as they do, and nothing tells or provokes them to do otherwise. As he says, 'he who first made himself clothes or a Dwelling thereby provided himself with things that are not very necessary'.[27] While Savage man is already different from other animals in having some element of 'free' agency,[28] Rousseau is determined not to make his demonstration circular by reading into this creature all the desires that other theorists have inscribed there in order to naturalise 'civilisation' and therefore to give it an unimpeachable 'natural' justification.[29] Rousseau's use of assumptions is more sparing and more critical; other than agency, he employs language, but with language come social relations, and with social relations we are back with Mother and Child. (Note that in the previous theorisation of life-before-language fatherhood is merely passing on physical constitution genetically, though apparently only to sons.) Rousseau warns against projecting the family group ('Fathers, Mothers and Children') back into the pre-linguistic state, and gives an alternative view: '… without Houses or Huts or property of any kind, everyone bedded down at random and often for one night only; males and females united fortuitously, according to chance encounters, opportunity, and desire …'[30] These creatures had virtually no need for each other (children for mothers being sole exception):

> Indeed, it is impossible to imagine why, in that primitive state, a man would need another man any more than a monkey or a Wolf would need his kind, or, assuming this need, to imagine what motives could induce the other to attend to it, or even, if he did, how they might agree on terms.[31]

Mischievously Rousseau locates the creation of language in the child, rather than in the mother, but even this will not be enough to create sociability of the sort that Rousseau expects to find in Savagery, that is, a sociability quite opposite to that of competitive self-interest in commercial civilisation.[32] This Savage sociability depends on a sentiment of pity, which Rousseau locates in animals generally and in human 'Mothers':

> I speak of Pity, a disposition suited to beings as weak and as subject to so many ills as we are [cf. Rousseau's prior depiction of Woman in exactly these terms – TC] ... and so Natural that even the Beasts sometimes show evident signs of it. To say nothing of the tenderness Mothers feel for their young and of the dangers they brave in order to protect them, one daily sees the repugnance of Horses to trample a living Body underfoot ...[33]

Mysteriously this spark of moral sentiment is passed along to Savage man (in his mother's milk, perhaps? or from working with horses?), who reappears in conjunction with the (good) market women of civilisation – good because close to Savage man in outlook, and probably because they are (in Rousseau's eyes) child-bearing mothers (unlike the 'fine women' he detests):

> Savage man ... is always seen to yield impetuously to the first sentiment of Humanity. In Riots, in street-brawls, the Populace gathers, the prudent man [of 'civilisation' – TC] withdraws; it is the rabble, it is the Marketwomen who separate the combatants, and keeps honest folk from murdering one another.[34]

The finale to Rousseau's depiction of Savage man (and sometimes woman-and-child) and to his hypothetical derivation of human sociability (at first in its essence, and then in its contrasting degradation in contemporary upper-class life), is a disquisition on male sexuality, both in its natural Savage form and its present-day perversion, the latter perversely blamed on women!

> Limited to the Physical aspect of love alone, and fortunate enough not to know preferences that exacerbate its sentiment and increase its difficulties, men must feel the ardors of temperament less frequently and less vividly ... everyone peacefully awaits the impulsion of Nature, yields to it without choice with more pleasure than frenzy, and, the need once satisfied, all desire is extinguished.[35]

The above description might, of course, apply to both sexes ('the passions that ... [make] one sex necessary to the other ...'),[36] if the discussion were not framed by reference to 'men ... daily feuding over their loves at the cost of their blood'. It is rather the 'Moral' aspect of love, developed under 'civilisation', which causes the trouble, and that appears to be with men:

... the vengeance of Husbands daily cause Duels, Murders, and worse, where the duty of eternal fidelity only makes for adulteries, and where even the Laws of continence and of honor inevitably increase debauchery, and multiply abortions.[37]

In any case Rousseau's Savage: '... heeds only the temperament he received from Nature, and ... any woman suits him'.[38] Oddly what causes the problem by creating a 'Moral' aspect to love is (modern) women:

Now it is easy to see that the moral aspect of love is a factitious sentiment; born of social practice, and extolled with much skill and care by women in order to establish their rule and to make dominant the sex that should obey.[39]

Rousseau's conclusion that the state of nature has little or no inequality in it, beyond minor physical differences of no great importance, is really a conclusion about men-as-males. While they are said not even to understand notions of domination and subjection, the text itself announces that one sex (female) is inferior there in various respects (through physical difference) to the other, and that considerable chaos is caused when, as 'civilisation' develops, the female sex artfully perverts the nature of the sexual act such that men become murderous. The ever-useful Caribs, of course, are different from moderns, *as men*:

... the Caribs, which of all existing Peoples has so far deviated least from the state of Nature, are in fact also the most peaceful in their loves and the least given to jealousy, even though they live in a scorching Climate which always seems to rouse these passions to greater activity.[40]

Once Savage man, the free agent, has language, life changes, and he changes life. Intriguingly Rousseau draws an analogy with animal communication, but does not explore how and why human communication became so different, other than to detail what language, together with the ever more complex social relationships it allows, had brought about (again, referencing the ever-useful contemporary 'exotics'):

It is easy to understand that such dealings [hunting in a homosocial 'herd' or 'association' – TC] did not require a language much more refined than that of Crows or of Monkeys, which troop together in approximately the same way. Some inarticulate cries, many gestures, and a few imitative noises must, for a long time, have made up the universal Language, [and] the addition to it, in every Region, of a few articulated and conventional sounds – the institution of which is, as I have already said, none too easy to explain – made for particular languages, crude, imperfect and more or less such as various Savage Nations have now.[41]

Partly this transition is a story of technology introduced to solve 'difficulties'. Evidently the notions of 'free agent' and linguistic potential gave rise to such a conception in Savage man, whereas for Rousseau animals merely obey what 'Nature' commands.[42] The technologies again are those of the hunter (and now warrior) male fantasy:

> On seashores and Riverbanks they invented line and hook; and became fishermen and Fish-eaters. In forests they made bows and arrows, and became Hunters and Warriors; In cold Countries they covered themselves with the skins of the beasts they had killed; Lightning, a Volcano, or some happy accident acquainted them with fire, a new resource against the rigors of winter: They learned to conserve this element, then to reproduce it, and finally to prepare the meats they had previously devoured raw.[43]

The paradigm for social relationships (of co-operation and competition) is the hunt:

> Taught by experience that love of well-being is the sole spring of human actions, he [Savage man] was in a position to distinguish between the rare occasions when common interest should make him count on the help of his kind, and the even rarer occasions when competition should make him suspicious of them. In the first case he united with them in a herd, or at most in some kind of free association that had formed it. In the second case everyone sought to seize his own advantage, either by open force if he believed that he could do so; or by skill and cunning, if he felt he was the weaker.[44]

Reaching the subject of a sexual differentiation of labour, Rousseau comments that family life in Huts ('husbands and Wives, Fathers and Children together in a common dwelling') marked the point when 'the first difference was established in the ways of living of the two Sexes, which until then had had but one'.[45] This is somewhat belied by his previous picture where 'woman' functioned as mother and sole parent, and his evident belief in males as the 'dominant' sex.[46] We are in the realm of symbolic fantasy here, where 'woman' functions as mother and sex-object (again, working from Rousseau's explicit comments about 'man' and his 'need for a female'), rather than in the realm of realistic or at least thoroughgoing imaginative speculation about life (for both sexes) in distant pre-historic times at the dawn of language and technology. Partly this is the result of Rousseau's evident male-centric perspective: 'the habit of living together [in Huts] gave rise to the sweetest sentiments known to man, conjugal love, and Paternal love'.[47] Mentioning maternal love here, by contrast, would represent a shift out of a male-centric view into a more objective perspective, in which women (and children) mattered in and of themselves, rather than merely in relation to what men are doing, feeling, wanting. The difficulty in reading Rousseau is really in dispensing with the apparent generality of 'man', which other authors commonly invoke to make their semi-covert subordination of women less visible. Rousseau is almost the other way around, apparently invoking a generic 'man' almost by accident, as his perspective on the inferiority and subordination of women (or in his view, their dichotomously different nature as 'mothers') is so deep-seated.

Partly this results, I suspect, from Rousseau's view that men-as-hunters will make fishhooks, whereas women actually inventing and making technologies would be against their nature and the natural order that he sees disrupted when women behave inappropriately, and thus in ways not successfully contained by men. Certainly he has little difficulty in bringing women in explicitly when the hut needs cleaning: 'Women became more sedentary and grew accustomed to looking after the Hut and Children, while the man went in quest of the common subsistence.'[48] The effects on women of this moralising (or rather demoralising) perspective have been well researched and critiqued. The issue here is the meaning that these fantasies have *for men*, and in particular, the way that hunter-and-warrior masculinities impact symbolically on more modern forms of masculinities (in hierarchies of domination, within the male gender order, as well as in relation to women). Most importantly, looking at Rousseau in this light reveals how thin the line is between 'knowledge' generated in archaeology, paleo-history and anthropology (much of which still startlingly resembles his work), and the fantasies of popular culture and media representation that reinvoke the symbolic homosociality of the hunter/warrior world, updated to today's hegemonic masculinities (both 'warrior' and commercial).[49] Very few popular cultural fantasies deconstruct masculinities, and even maleness, in the manner of *Junior*.[50]

Rousseau's own updating of this masculinity has two parts. The first is an idyll, where language and technology have arrived at a point that balances co-operation and competition, happiness and sadness, individual achievement and collective safety, comfort and rigour, bonding love and desiring jealousy:

> So long as men were content with their rustic huts, so long as they confined themselves to sewing their clothes of skins with thorns or fish bones,[51] to adorning themselves with feathers and shells, to painting their bodies different colors, to perfecting or embellishing their bows and arrows, to carving a few fishing Canoes or a few crude Musical instruments with sharp stones; In a word, so long as they applied themselves only to tasks a single individual could perform, and to arts that did not require the collaboration of several hands, they lived free, healthy, good, and happy as far as they could by their Nature be …[52]

As Rousseau tells the tale, it is metallurgy and agriculture (interestingly, in that order) that make the difference, in that 'one man' will need the help of another, and it will be 'useful for one to have provisions for two'. Both the property system, and the concomitant need for government, are institutions that define and guarantee an inequality, for Rousseau, that brings an end to the golden age (vividly described in terms of contemporary 'exotics') that he endorses with self-conscious anachronism:

> … equality disappeared, property appeared, work became necessary, and the vast forests changed into smiling Fields that had to be watered with the sweat of men, … slavery and misery were soon seen to sprout and grow together with the harvests.[53]

Rousseau directly attributes government to the need for 'the rich' to protect their hold over the poor through the property system by an ingenious and speciously defended scheme to use 'attackers' forces' in their favour, by creating rules of 'justice' and institutions of 'peace' that would benefit themselves. Famously Rousseau says that the rich found other people foolish enough to believe them, and so 'crude, easily seduced men … ran toward their chains in the belief that they were securing their freedom'.[54] What follows in political theory terms is a three-stage typology charting a decline to contemporary despotism (and desperation):

> If we follow the progress of inequality through these different revolutions, we will find that the establishment of the Law and Right of property was its first term; the institution of Magistracy, the second; the conversion of legitimate into arbitrary power the third and last; so that the state of rich and poor was authorized by the first Epoch, that of powerful and weak by the second, and by the third that of Master and Slave, which is the last degree of inequality, and the state to which all the others finally lead, until new revolutions either dissolve the Government entirely, or bring it close to legitimate institution.[55]

The *Social Contract*, prefigured in the 'Discourse on the Origins of Inequality' under examination here, famously defines legitimacy in terms of an agreement in which 'each, by giving himself to all, gives himself to no one, and since there is no associate over whom one does not acquire the same right as one grants him over oneself, one gains the equivalent of all one loses, and more force to preserve what one has'.[56] The moderation that Rousseau recommends for the economy will give rise, so he argues, to only moderate degrees of power-differentiation within an inclusive framework of legitimacy for those contracting to create the general will and then obeying the authorities that it institutes:

> … with regard to equality, this word must not be understood to mean that degrees of power and wealth should be absolutely the same, but that, as for power, it stop short of all violence and never be exercised except by virtue of rank and the laws, and that as for wealth, no citizen be so very rich that he can buy another, and none so poor that he is compelled to sell himself. Which assumes, on the part of the great, moderation in goods and influence and, on the part of the lowly, moderation in avarice and covetousness.[57]

Devices, desires and fantasies

With all due self-conscious reference Rousseau has ended up in somewhat the same position as Locke:[58] invoking a modern masculinity of moderation as a guarantor of political stability amongst the well-off (presumptively male) citizenry. In Rousseau's case, while not in Locke's, this invocation represents a nostalgia for the intermediate stage between the true state of (animal or near-animal) nature and the current state of depravity and despotism. Locke's focus on patriarchalism entailed a barrage of (apparently) egalitarian remarks about women, which are not sustained, so I have argued, because of his commitment to residual patriarchy.[59] Lacking patriarchalist opponents, Rousseau had little need to remark at any level on women's equality to men, and so produced a (mostly) feminist-unfriendly text. Rousseau took his state of nature far more seriously as a (pre-)historical question than Locke did (the differing approaches may or may not be to the credit of either), and in doing so he gave free rein to hunter/warrior fantasies about men-as-men to fill out his picture and drive his speculations. Rousseau paused on patriarchalism only just long enough to dismiss it out of hand, taking care to rescue a conception of kindly domestic fatherhood that – much as Locke had argued[60] – had nothing to do with despotism in the home nor in the state, but everything to do with a modernised patriarchy of republican virtue:

> As for paternal authority, from which some have derived absolute Government and the whole of Society, without invoking Locke's or Sidney's proofs to the contrary, it suffices to note that nothing in the world is farther from the ferocious spirit of Despotism than the gentleness of this authority which looks more to the advantage of the one who obeys than to the utility of the one who commands ...[61]

Locke's use of the apparently generic 'abstract individual' genuinely flickers between the androgynous and the male-gendered, though as I have argued, the *overall* narrative strategy is not one of female emancipation in the home, much less in the public world of politics, but rather one of residual patriarchy.[62] Rousseau, so I am arguing here, should be read as never really invoking the apparently generic 'man', except by accident or falsely, because his argument is founded on an inferiority and subordination of women to which he simply alludes when the discussion, as he propels it along, requires some notice of 'the second sex'. This takes the form of woman-as-mother and female-as-sex-object; femaleness is also clearly a marker for physical weakness (and early death), and apparently for inaptitude for mental agility and technological inventiveness. Additionally the human capacity for sympathy for others ('pity') appears to come from the female side (an obvious 'other' to male hunting and warriordom, where opposite feelings would be the norm), though it is woman's job to teach it to men, who must none the less retain their 'natural' dominance.

The shock and horror of Rousseau's views on women commonly registered in contemporary feminist scholarship should, in my view, be matched by a thorough-going scorn for his hunter/warrior fantasies about men. This should also raise some accompanying criticism of the ways that ersatz versions of this 'primitive' life are invoked and represented in contemporary society as masculine ideals and visions of a 'human nature' that is primarily and developmentally male. As in Rousseau's text, these representations instantiate a dichotomy between male and female that works, in contemporary economic and social terms, to the disadvantage of the latter. Moreover these representations also work to the disadvantage of many men who do not, cannot or otherwise will not conform to those archetypes.

Male fantasies about men are potent. They marginalise women and subordinate some men to others through symbolic oppressions, institutional disciplines and systematic violence. They are not pictures of what is 'natural', nor even if they were, should they have the political force that they currently evoke.

Notes

1 For an overview of Rousseau's life and writings, see Robert Wokler, *Rousseau* (Oxford: Oxford University Press, 1995), esp. pp. 100–3 on men, women and sexuality. For an historian's perspective on feminism and Rousseau, see Joan Landes, *Women and the Public Sphere in the Age of the French Revolution* (Ithaca, NY: Cornell University Press, 1988), pp. 66–89.

2 Interestingly Rousseau was a correspondent of the Chevalier/ière d'Eon (1728–1810), who (we now know) was male but lived approximately half his life as a man and half as a woman (though at the time he made his transposition from man to woman in the 1770s, it was thought that he had been a female raised as a male, in which role he had had a successful and decorated military career). While this does not raise the pregnancy issues of *Junior*, it does raise intriguing issues about gender,

especially given d'Eon's *resistance* – after 'confessing' to being a woman – to wearing female clothing, which is rather similar to Dr Hesse's resistance in the film. D'Eon is also said to have been influenced by Rousseau's highly dichotomous views on gender difference; see Gary Kates, *Monsieur d'Eon is a Woman: a tale of political intrigue and sexual masquerade*, new edn (Baltimore, MD: Johns Hopkins University Press, 2001), pp. 141–4, 145–9, 166–71.

3 Their childbirth experiences are also not different from those of many women. Dr Hesse has a Caesarian; Angela has a normal delivery (though she shouts 'give me drugs'). This functions as a metaphor for the pastiche of individual differences generally, e.g. some women do not breastfeed, some mothers are adoptive, etc., etc.

4 Jean-Jacques Rousseau, *The Social Contract and other Later Political Writings*, ed. and trans. Victor Gourevitch (Cambridge: Cambridge University Press, 1997), p. 53; Elizabeth Rose Wingrove tackles this in a positive way as 'consensual nonconsensuality' or willing 'the circumstances of one's own domination', particularly in (mutual) heterosexual relations; *Rousseau's Republican Romance* (Princeton, NJ: Princeton University Press, 2000), pp. 4–6.

5 See Wingrove, *Rousseau's Republican Romance*, pp. 6–8, for a useful categorising overview of the literature on Rousseau and gender. While Wingrove aims to unify Rousseau on gender by viewing all his works through the lens of a performative heterosexuality, my focus is rather on debunking the 'insipid biologism' that she identifies in the texts most popularly read as political theory (especially the 'Discourse on the Origins of Inequality'). This is because with or without Rousseau this 'biologism' is still an influential picture, and Rousseau's fantasies about men are so far little studied (as opposed to his fantasies about women, which Wingrove interestingly attempts to salvage as metaphors for citizen/lover relationships legitimated by consent). I part company from her and others (such as Penny A. Weiss) in discounting Rousseau's professions of androgyny in the 'state of nature' in favour of his self-contradictory relapses into biological sexism detailed below. While there is little that is biological in any detailed way about Rousseau's view of Savage woman as mother and Savage man as (non-)father, it is difficult to see what else drives his account other than a conventional biologism; see Penny A. Weiss, *Gendered Community: Rousseau, sex and politics* (New York: New York University Press, 1993), pp. 3–5, 10–53. For thoughtful discussions of Rousseau, biology and sex that contrast with Weiss, see Joel Schwartz, *The Sexual Politics of Jean-Jacques Rousseau* (Chicago, IL: University of Chicago Press, 1984), pp. 1–40, 151–4; Tracey B. Strong, *Jean-Jacques Rousseau: the politics of the ordinary* (Thousand Oaks, CA: Sage, 1994), pp. 131–8; Ursula Vogel, '"But in a Republic, men are

needed": guarding the boundaries of liberty', in Robert Wokler, ed., *Rousseau and Liberty* (Manchester: Manchester University Press, 1995), pp. 213–31; Linda M. G. Zerilli, *Signifying Woman: culture and chaos in Rousseau, Burke, and Mill* (Ithaca, NY: Cornell University Press, 1994), pp. 16–59.
6 On this analytical point, see Pateman, *The Sexual Contract*; and Carver, '"Public Man"', pp. 673–8.
7 See Christopher Frayling and Robert Wokler, 'From the orang-utan to the vampire', in R.A. Leigh, ed., *Rousseau after Two Hundred Years* (Cambridge: Cambridge University Press, 1982), pp. 109–24.
8 Jean-Jacques Rousseau, 'Discourse on the Origins of Inequality among Men', in *The Discourses and other early Political Writings*, ed. and trans. Victor Gourevitch (Cambridge: Cambridge University Press, 1997), pp. 186–7; Rousseau, *Social Contract*, pp. 117–52.
9 Rousseau, 'Discourse on the Origins of Inequality among Men', p. 131.
10 Rousseau, 'Discourse on the Origins of Inequality among Men', p. 131.
11 Rousseau, 'Discourse on the Origins of Inequality among Men', p. 131.
12 See the discussion in Wokler, *Rousseau*, pp. 100–3; see also Weiss, *Gendered Community*, pp. 41–2.
13 Vogel makes a similar point; '"But in a Republic, men are needed"', p. 214.
14 See Michael Shanks and Christopher Tilley, *Social Theory and Archaeology* (Cambridge: Polity Press, 1987).
15 Rousseau, 'Discourse on the Origins of Inequality among Men', p. 134.
16 Rousseau, 'Discourse on the Origins of Inequality among Men', p. 135.
17 Rousseau, 'Discourse on the Origins of Inequality among Men', p. 135.
18 See Hobbes, *Leviathan*, Macpherson, pp. 253–4, cf. Tuck, p. 140, for a famous theoretical discussion of female equality with males via the Amazons; for views on 'the Amazon' contemporary with Rousseau, see Kates, *M. d'Eon is a Woman*, pp. 157–8, 160–2, 203–9, 290–1 (D'Eon 'herself' appeared for money as an Amazonian fencer at exhibitions; p. 256); for a scholarly discussion of Amazonian myths and combat realities, see Joshua S. Goldstein, *War and Gender: how gender shapes the war system and vice versa* (Cambridge: Cambridge University Press, 2001), pp. 11–19 and passim.
19 Rousseau, 'Discourse on the Origins of Inequality among Men', p. 136; 'nobody has ever heard' seems a rather enthusiastic extrapolation from limited evidence, to say the least.
20 The film *Junior* opens with the quintessential male nightmare – being alone with a baby and looking vainly for 'the mother' to take it back – because maleness is conceptualised as dichotomously 'other' to babies and childcare.
21 Rousseau, 'Discourse on the Origins of Inequality among Men', p. 136.

22 I think that Rousseau, having finished (temporarily) with 'woman', reverts back to his vision of Savage life for the hardy and agile males at this point.
23 Rousseau, 'Discourse on the Origins of Inequality among Men', p. 137.
24 Rousseau, 'Discourse on the Origins of Inequality among Men', pp. 138–9.
25 See the discussion in Kates, *M. d'Eon is a Woman*, pp. 169–71.
26 See the discussion in Wingrove, *Rousseau's Republican Romance*, pp. 58–168, where her concern is the construction of political identities through heterosexual ones, rather than through a construction of 'woman' and man-as-male with political consequences (then and now). See also the discussion in Lori Jo Marso, *(Un)Manly Citizens: Jean-Jacques Rousseau's and Germaine de Staël's subversive women* (Baltimore, MD and London: Johns Hopkins University Press, 1999), pp. 72–5, where her concern is to read what Rousseau's women (Sophie and Julie) actually say and to figure it as a (marginalised) discourse of 'democratic and participatory citizenship' that highlights and potentially overcomes the 'dangers of manly citizenship'.
27 Rousseau, 'Discourse on the Origins of Inequality among Men', p. 139. Rousseau also famously comments: 'The only goods he [Savage man] knows in the Universe are food, a female and rest …'; p. 142.
28 Intriguingly humans are distinguished from animals via machines: 'I see in any animal nothing but an ingenious machine to which nature has given senses in order to wind itself up … I perceive precisely the same thing in the human machine, with this difference, that Nature alone does everything in the operations of the Beast, whereas man contributes to his operations in his capacity as a free agent'; Rousseau, 'Discourse on the Origins of Inequality among Men', p. 140. See the discussion regarding Hobbes on this point, pp. 142–3 above.
29 Civilisation will involve foresight, not just agency; the exotics re-enter here, as representatives of pre-historic Savagery: 'Such is still nowadays the extent of the Carib's foresight: he sells his Cotton bed in the morning and comes weeping to buy it back in the evening, for not having foreseen that he would need it for the coming night'; Rousseau, 'Discourse on the Origins of Inequality among Men', p. 143.
30 Rousseau, 'Discourse on the Origins of Inequality among Men', p. 145.
31 Rousseau, 'Discourse on the Origins of Inequality among Men', p. 149.
32 This view of sociability is developed against Hobbes explicitly as an 'other'; Rousseau criticises him for projecting the evils of civilised selfishness back onto Savage man; 'Discourse on the Origins of Inequality among Men', pp. 151–2.
33 Rousseau, 'Discourse on the Origins of Inequality among Men', p. 152.
34 Rousseau, 'Discourse on the Origins of Inequality among Men', p. 154.

35 Rousseau, 'Discourse on the Origins of Inequality among Men', p. 156.
36 Rousseau, 'Discourse on the Origins of Inequality among Men', p. 154.
37 Rousseau, 'Discourse on the Origins of Inequality among Men', p. 157.
38 Rousseau, 'Discourse on the Origins of Inequality among Men', p. 155.
39 Rousseau, 'Discourse on the Origins of Inequality among Men', p. 155.
40 Rousseau, 'Discourse on the Origins of Inequality among Men', p. 156; I take this passage to refer to men only, rather than to men and women, because of its textual relationship with Rousseau's comments on duels and murders prompted among males by 'civilised' sexuality. Carib women seem to be represented by the notorious 'hutwives' of the post-linguistic but pre-technological social relations that Rousseau sketches; see below, p. 195.
41 Rousseau, 'Discourse on the Origins of Inequality among Men', p. 163.
42 Rousseau, 'Discourse on the Origins of Inequality among Men', p. 141.
43 Rousseau, 'Discourse on the Origins of Inequality among Men', p. 162.
44 Rousseau, 'Discourse on the Origins of Inequality among Men', p. 163.
45 Rousseau, 'Discourse on the Origins of Inequality among Men', p. 164.
46 Animals do not have gender, as power-relations derived from – or projected onto – sex and sexuality. Male animals are not 'dominant' and female animals are not 'weak', either in particular species or in general. They do not (so far as we know) pursue and experience 'relations' in the required sense. It is certainly not the case that female animals are 'weak' in some sense because they bear offspring. Having (rightly) criticised Hobbes for reading 'civilised' traits back into 'natural man' (e.g. competitiveness, acquisitiveness), Rousseau is clearly – despite his otherwise ruthless analysis – reading the gender relations of civilisation (as hierarchical sexual difference and socialised disadvantage for 'mothers') back into his state of nature, his own protestations notwithstanding.
47 Rousseau, 'Discourse on the Origins of Inequality among Men', p. 164.
48 Rousseau, 'Discourse on the Origins of Inequality among Men', p. 164.
49 See the discussion of modern masculinities in Hooper, *Manly States*.
50 For a contrary view about popular culture and commercial media, see Paul Nathanson and Katherine K. Young, *Spreading Misandry: the teaching of contempt for men in popular culture* (Montreal and Kingston: McGill-Queen's University Press, 2001).
51 I think we are looking at male tailors here.
52 Rousseau, 'Discourse on the Origins of Inequality among Men', p. 167.
53 Rousseau, 'Discourse on the Origins of Inequality among Men', pp. 167–8.
54 Rousseau, 'Discourse on the Origins of Inequality among Men', pp. 172–3.
55 Rousseau, 'Discourse on the Origins of Inequality among Men', p. 182.
56 Rousseau, *Social Contract*, p. 50.

57 Rousseau, *Social Contract*, p. 78.
58 Rousseau was, of course, self-consciously and sympathetically rewriting what he called 'Locke's Civil Government'; 'Discourse on the Origins of Inequality among Men', for example, pp. 212–16.
59 See above, pp. 155–7, 161, 172.
60 See above, pp. 169–72.
61 Rousseau, 'Discourse on the Origins of Inequality among Men', p. 177.
62 Waldron reads Locke the other way round, emphasising the (at least potential) radical egalitarianism of (selected parts of) the text, and reiterating Richard Ashcraft's point that few conservatives ever use Locke to reinforce their inegalitarian views (whether between the sexes or in terms of other social relationships); *God, Locke, and Equality*, pp. 114–19.

CHAPTER NINE

Marx: (non)critique of the gender categories

Marx and gender politics

At present Marx's record on these issues – sex and gender – looks much the same as that of any other (dead, white, male) social theorist. Neither sex nor gender is an especially important analytical category in his scheme of things, in theoretical works or in political activities. Nor is there any really extended discussion – however marginal or ancillary – of the topics that are most usually pointers to interests cognate with the ones that are today grouped together under headings such as these: family life, childhood, dependency, reproduction, sensual pleasure, 'the body', sexualities, identity, etc. This is not to say that Marx never mentioned these things, nor that he failed to remark on various 'fundamentals' which generally include these ideas and practices. Indeed, as will become evident below, he did have things to say. Rather that with the best will in the world, and whether reading 'with the grain' or against it, there are considerable difficulties in either adjudicating on Marx as an authority worth reading in, say, feminist theory, gender studies, or men's studies, or in simply finding material to cite that would constitute any very impressive contribution, one way or another, to contemporary debates.

This 'lack' is in itself grounds for considerable criticism. These criticisms range from fairly generous excuses for his evident 'gender-blindness' on grounds that few, if any of his (male) contemporaries did any better, to harsh rejections of virtually all of his work on grounds that it is predicated on a 'masculinist point of view' that is always (or at least currently) unacceptable to women, and perhaps now (or eventually) also unacceptable to men (or at least to some of them). From the broader perspective of sexuality studies, it is further evident that a gay, or at least non-binary and non-heterosexist recovery of Marx would be even more difficult and problematic. None the less there are moments in the feminist and gay literatures when Marx surfaces, and not necessarily as someone who 'got it wrong' or did not 'get it' at all with respect to sex, sexuality and gender. In so far as writers in those literatures concern themselves with commodification as a general phenomenon, and with the commodification of human beings as 'wage-labour' in particular, then Marx has a role to play in their discussions of the 'sex and gender' issues listed above. Moreover, in so far as feminist and gay writers envisage large-scale social change, proceeding from movements with a basis in mass democracy, then Marx figures large by analogy. If there are class struggles, then there are sex struggles; if class war, then sex war; if there are chains of economic exploitation, then there are chains of gender oppression.[1]

(Re)production in *The German Ideology*

There is certainly no space here to pretend to a comprehensive survey of Marx's record on gender issues, conceptualised in the way I have elaborated above. Nor is there probably much need to do this. Rather I shall take a number of illustrative examples from Marx, and read them in what I hope is an interpretively imaginative and useful way.

Probably the best place to start is in *The German Ideology*, jointly written with Engels. While there may be authorial issues of significance here, I am going to leave them to one side, taking the published passages to be ones that Marx wrote, or at least could plausibly have agreed with, given evidence elsewhere.[2] They certainly seem to me to chime well with, rather than to grate against, both his earlier and later writings in so far as he alludes to such 'basics' as sexual reproduction in human species-life. Given the scattered character of Marx's and Engels's thoughts as they appear physically on the manuscript sheets of *The German Ideology* – giving rise, I realise, to insoluble interpretive difficulties – I have constructed the following excerpt with free use of ellipses:

> Since we are dealing with the Germans ... we must begin by stating the first premise of all human existence and therefore, of all history ... namely, that men must be in a position to live in order to be able to

'make history'. But life involves before everything else eating and drinking, a habitation, clothing and many other things ... The second point is that the satisfaction of the first need ... leads to new needs; and this production of new needs is the first historical act ... The third circumstance which, from the very outset, enters into historical development, is that men, who daily remake their own life, begin to make other men, to propagate their kind: the relation between man and woman, parents and children, the *family*. The family, which to begin with is the only social relationship, becomes later, when increased needs create new social relations and the increased population new needs, a subordinate one ... and must then be treated and analysed according to the existing empirical data ... These three aspects of social activity are not of course to be taken as three different stages, but just as three aspects or ... three 'moments', which have existed simultaneously since the dawn of history and the first men, and which still assert themselves in history today.[3]

The first interpretive (and contextually constructive) point to make here is that *The German Ideology* was intended to be a satire on the 'German ideologists' Ludwig Feuerbach, Bruno Bauer and Max Stirner, a triumvirate of Marx's own making. In that way much of Marx's discussion is structured by views on what those three had got wrong. Hence the whole business of developing 'premises' for history is manifestly suspect to Marx in terms of the discussion that survives, though whether this kind of over-arching narrative – 'premises for history' – is wholly or merely partly suspect is unclear. I pursue this point below.

Although responding to others, but undaunted by their mistakes, Marx elaborates conceptual premises, not so much for the explication of historical stages as for an understanding – in aid of contemporary political campaigns, assuredly – of human society, any society perhaps, but most pertinently European industrialising society, and its recent history. The narrative outcome of *The German Ideology*, such as we have it, is a theory and demonstration of the class struggle in modern history and modern society. While it may seem odd that reproduction of the species only emerges as number three in the list that Marx constructs – albeit a list of historically and empirically simultaneous 'moments' or 'aspects' in an analytical structure – none the less there is some overall sense in this. Given that Marx was arguing against philosophical idealists whose account of history and society depended crucially on 'ideas' or 'concepts' (which had a supposed logic and attributed 'development'), it follows that he would think first of production for subsistence, secondly of further needs, and only then of social relationships, of which he considered the family – a presumed sexual and reproductive unit – the evident origin.

There are certainly similar ways of making a narrative out of what we know, or presume to know, about human history, pre-history and supposed 'basic requirements'. One famous example occurs in Rousseau's 'Discourse on the Origins of Inequality' (1755). There are certainly other very different ways of doing this, such as Sigmund Freud's or Max Weber's, depending on what contrary positions are being addressed in debate. My point is that taking *The German Ideology* to express presumptions about human life that were effectively immovable for Marx is a dubious strategy for readers and commentators to follow. A good deal of Marx's narrative (which I have mostly omitted in the ellipses but have recounted above) pursues a serious debate on the nature of society, albeit in tandem with intense ridicule of a threesome who can do no right philosophically or politically. We still ask these questions, and we still do not have the answers.

Elsewhere in *The German Ideology* Marx's discussion of these matters takes on a form more akin to that of claim and evidence in the most general sense, in that relations between 'different nations' (presumably in recent history, or possibly including classical history) are stated to 'depend upon the extent to which each has developed its productive forces, the division of labour and internal intercourse (i.e. socio-economic relationships and activities)'. Moreover 'the whole internal structure of the nation itself depends on the stage of development reached by its production …'[4] Presumably the alternative, against which Marx argues at length, was a view that cultural or racial differences, placed on a hierarchical and developmental scale, accounted for the differential development of individual nations compared with others, and indeed for the propensity of some to triumph over others as history 'develops' or 'ascends'. In persuading readers of his thesis – that inter-state and intra-state relations depend crucially on the level of development of productive forces – Marx delineates three forms of ownership (of productive resources and of resulting products), leading up to the development of modern private property and of industrialised production in a money-economy.

The first of these is said to be 'tribal ownership', when 'a people lives by hunting and fishing, by the rearing of cattle or, in the highest stage, agriculture'. Following the analytical priority given to production, as previously claimed, Marx comments:

> The division of labour is at this stage still very elementary and is confined to a further extension of the natural division of labour existing in the family. The social structure is, therefore, limited to an extension of the family: patriarchal family chieftains, below them the members of the tribe, finally slaves. The slavery latent in the family only develops gradually with the increase of population, the growth of wants, and with the extension of external relations, both of war and of barter.[5]

This slavery inherent in the family is explained elsewhere in the text. In that discussion Marx's analytical purpose is evidently to draw out the notion of a division of labour and to explain that historically there has been an '*unequal* distribution, both quantitative and qualitative, of labour and its products, hence property'. The first instance of this ubiquitous social form and historical fact – slavery – is then located by Marx in 'the natural division of labour in the family and the separation of society into individual families opposed to one another'. However, this raises certain questions which he does not deal with, in *The German Ideology* or elsewhere. The first is the force of the term 'natural' in this kind of discussion, and the second is the depiction of women and children as victims of men.

While Marx describes this early form of slavery as 'crude', he does not hasten to ascribe this epithet to categories in his own analysis. Given his evident anxiety to develop a social theory of human life as almost wholly developmental in terms of human ambition and intellect, and very little indebted to presumably immovable 'natural' limitations or barriers, his forays into naturalising discourse are notably rare. On the one hand, he would probably have been offending very few people at the time by naturalising the family in this way and drawing it out of the realm of changing social relationships and variable cultural constructs. But, on the other hand, he (again with Engels) took care to promise, in the *Communist Manifesto*, that there would be a new relation between the sexes when communists had broken through the exploitation inherent in the 'bourgeois' economic system. Marx, however, simply did not say anything about what this new relationship was going to be like.

This narrative strategy is highly risk-averse and characteristic of what could be characterised today as masculinist attitudes. As attitudes today descend from those of the past, it does not cause me that much difficulty assigning them in some minimally meaningful way to Marx, even if the context of contemporary sexual politics would be largely (though not, I think wholly) foreign to his thoughts. My point is that read politically as the work of a conventionally gendered heterosexual male, the passage makes sense: a genuflection to the eternal character of reproduction, conveniently and restfully conceptualised as a 'family' relationship, combined with a nod to the sexist oppression of women, and to exploitative practices towards children, as manifested by male heads of household (in whatever class). Indeed this was extensively documented in Marx's time, whether in factual reports or crusading novels. Given that sexual politics, and childcare concerns, were not Marx's specific analytical focus, it is perhaps surprising that these topics rate a mention at all. These things certainly were not a primary focus for the 'German ideologists' either, whose strategy in these matters was not all that different, no doubt for similar reasons.

Marx's main complaint about the 'German ideologists' was that they organised a bogus history of humanity, purportedly derived from 'concepts'. Those concepts, so Marx argued, merely tracked their conventional and confused predilections and thus fogged any possibility of a truly radical understanding of contemporary society. In pursuing this critique Marx necessarily had to offer alternative principles (contemporary, historical and general inferences concerning 'production'), and alternative factual illustrations (which in this text are really just sketches). Ultimately in *The German Ideology* he got down to sexual and reproductive basics in arguing that the 'production of life, both of one's own in labour and of fresh life in procreation ... appears as a double relationship: on the one hand as a natural, on the other as a social relationship'.[6] While the text develops a notion of the 'social' as a 'mode of cooperation', which necessarily varies with the specific stage of the 'mode of production', today's reader might reasonably wonder, once again, what exactly is intended when he uses the concept 'natural'? Marx concludes, *contra* the 'German ideologists', that the '"history of humanity" must always be studied ... in relation to the history of industry and exchange', and that in Germany 'it is impossible to write this sort of history, because the Germans lack "evidence of their senses"' owing to their preoccupation with what they deem 'consciousness'.[7]

Presumably the quotes that Marx placed around 'history of humanity' indicate a certain distance from that kind of conceptualisation, and indeed that sort of activity in the first place, and the ones around 'evidence of their senses' suggest that the 'German ideologists' are so muddled by idealism that they do not see what is actually happening in their own and neighbouring societies. None the less just as Marx needs to offer an alternative account of history in what he deems to be empirical terms, focusing on productive activities and relationships, so he also needs to offer an alternative account of 'consciousness' and its development – however little he was actually interested in this, and however ironic and distanced his delivery. This he does in an abbreviated recapitulation of his pre-historical sketch, and in doing so he digs a little deeper into sexuality and reproduction, conceived as 'natural' in some unspecified sense, and into consciousness and culture, conceived as specifically human and potentially developmental, though only when linked with production.

Here we learn that 'the division of labour ... was originally nothing but the division of labour in the sexual act', though Marx does not explain precisely what this 'division' is, what act(s) he has mind, and what he understands by 'sexual'. This ambiguity is followed by 'the division of labour which develops spontaneously or "naturally" by virtue of natural predisposition (e.g., physical strength), needs, accidents, etc., etc.'[8] While Marx may have thought quite correctly that this type of empirical reference to reproduction, and his supposedly plausible supposition about pre-historic 'tribal' relationships, would anchor their account in a factuality that no one could reasonably question, this is no bar to re-opening these issues today, or indeed to conceptualising them as issues for debate rather than evidence for some proposition. What could possibly count as a basis for any inference about activities and relationships in pre-history is certainly the subject of controversy at present,[9] and what relevance such accounts have for any arguments or conclusions concerning contemporary social relationships is a further matter of debate. One wonders whether Marx would have dabbled in this area at all, had he not constructed his remarks in answer to a kind of history, and a pattern of historical enquiry, of which he clearly disapproved. *Capital*, for instance, is notably free of this type of speculation; where there are presumed eternal verities in question, such as the specifically human (rather than animal) character of labour-power, Marx in that text – not written in answer to the 'German ideologists' – tends to offer ahistorical generalisations, rather than what are very nearly 'just-so' stories. In *The German Ideology* these stories are then propped up with allusions to tribal societies as an imputed guide to the past (now a very suspect notion, too).

The presumed level of 'biological basics' as 'first historical acts' does not figure in *Capital*, either. While I have attributed much of the substantive discussion of *The German Ideology* to Marx's necessary interaction with the German ideologists' agenda and views – as the genre of critique would dictate – I none the less conclude that in that text Marx interrogates himself on the general themes of nature and culture, men and women, reproduction and the family, and that his views and values, and most importantly his silences and evasions, become manifest.

One huge silence is on the subject of men as men, simply because Marx deploys 'man' in a characteristic (but now suspect) generic manner, presuming an application to people of both sexes. As with other (male) authorities, this apparent gender-neutrality, or more properly sex-blindness or presumed androgeny, dissolves when 'wife' appears and when family-centred narratives of reproduction state or assume a child-rearing (rather than strictly child-bearing) role for women as 'mother'. Typically in these accounts, little if anything is noted about or prescribed to 'fathers' other than duties as head of household and economic provider which, by apparent implication, 'wife' and 'mother' do not or cannot fulfil, at least 'normally' or 'generally'. The 'division of labour' ascribed by Marx to 'the sexual act', from which by implication the class struggle – and indeed all important historical development and change – eventually proceeds, might rest ambiguously in a conspiracy of silence between authors (male) and readers (presumed male). What is it supposed to portend when it appears to identify male/female, man/woman reproductive biology as the origin of other 'divisions'? It might be left there, in this zone of convenient ambiguity, were it not for the worrying (for men) discussion of the origin of inequality, placed not directly in the sexual act, but rather located in the 'family', in which 'wife and children are the slaves of the husband'. What male characteristics – eternal? malleable? – account for the motivation to create this slavery and the – general? inevitable? – 'success' of the institution, as *The German Ideology* tells the story?

Attributing this (im)balance of power in gender-relations to naturalised attributes of 'physical strength' is today unthinkingly careless but unsurprisingly near-universal; it is of course likely that further presumptions about maleness as opposed to femaleness, and about a fixed or changing boundary between immovable nature and malleable culture, are lurking behind the rather hasty gallop through prehistory that Marx has left us. This is to say that on the one hand Marx is not that much better at posing issues in sexual politics than most male social theorists are today. But on the other hand, his drift away from naturalising limitations on human development and change – whether those limitations come from supposed biological and physical 'basics' such as 'race', or from supposed rationalities inherent in eternal or self-developing 'concepts' – and his espousal of an increasingly self-conscious developmental trajectory for important activities in human social life – are at least a possible point of departure for social constructionist, and political activist, theorisations of gender. To make progress in that direction, though, something is going to have to be said about sexual and reproductive differences, and therefore something reasonably definite about men.

Men and women in *Capital*

As indicated above, *Capital* is a rather different kind of text from *The German Ideology*. It is basically the work of Marx, rather than something closer to a kind of collaboration with Engels, and while it is a critique, the object of attack was not the 'German ideologists' but the 'political economists', most particularly David Ricardo and subsequent authorities of the British school. More importantly it was a published text, seen through three German editions (and a French translation) by the author himself, and while not perfectly free of loose ends in textual terms, it is certainly a work that has been substantially polished. Again, as indicated above, the text has a rather different take on what might be termed 'bedrock' arguments, tending towards plausible but ahistorical generalisations, rather than the perhaps less plausible but more vivid just-so story about prehistory that figures in *The German Ideology*. The following passage gives the flavour of the ahistorical generalisation; insofar as this narrative does not issue in an account of 'family' life, or indeed the sexual act, as the originary moment in conceptualising human labour, the signifier 'man' could perhaps be genuinely androgenous for author and reader:

> Labour is, first of all, a process between man and nature, a process by which man, through his own actions, mediates, regulates and controls the metabolism between himself and nature. He confronts the materials of nature as a force of nature. He sets in motion the natural forces which belong to his own body, his arms, legs, head and hands, in order to appropriate the materials of nature in a form adapted to his own needs. Through this movement he acts upon external nature and changes it, and in this way he simultaneously changes his own nature. He develops the potentialities slumbering within nature, and subjects the play of its forces to his own sovereign power. We are not dealing here with those first instinctive forms of labour which remain on the animal level.[10]

Worryingly, and typically, we are not told what 'forms of labour' are 'on the animal level'. It might be tempting to ascribe reproductive and birth labour to this level, as consonant with the naturalising presumptions and discourse of *The German Ideology* detailed above, but then it is not at all clear in the discussion in *Capital* whether Marx is keeping to the 'dual-systems' view that *The German Ideology* makes explicit: labour is both labour outside the body on nature, and labour inside the body (as it were) in sexual and reproductive activities. On the one hand, this omission *might* save Marx from a charge that he unthinkingly focuses on a masculinist concept of labour, whilst leaving reproduction and childcare (and further 'family' dependencies) in a feminised realm; on the other hand, the fact that any significant discussion of procreation and inter-generational social life is omitted lends credence to the complaint that he really does see the world in masculinised terms that relegate rather unexamined 'family' activities to women generally and mothers in particular.

While *Capital* develops a number of themes currently conceptualised under gender studies and sexual politics, and in particular considers these in industrialised societies dominated by commodified exchange-relations (otherwise known as 'the capitalist mode of production'), it also contains passages in which Marx notably revisits the narratives of prehistory, as developed in *The German Ideology*. The treatment in *Capital* is much briefer: 'Within a family and, after further development, within a tribe, there springs up naturally a division of labour caused by differences of sex and age, and therefore based on a purely physiological foundation.'[11] Again, and typically, there is no discussion to tell us exactly what this 'purely physiological foundation' is, and what differences of 'sex and age' there (necessarily?

generally?) are. And just as briefly, readers are catapulted out of a realm of naturalisation and stasis into a realm of mutability and development when Marx considers a transition from capitalist exploitation to a 'higher form' of social relations, conceptualised without attributing much significance at all to a public/private boundary:

> It was not however the misuse of parental power that created the direct or indirect exploitation of immature labour-powers by capital, but rather the opposite, i.e. the capitalist mode of exploitation, by sweeping away the economic foundation which corresponded to parental power, made the use of parental power into its misuse. However terrible and disgusting the dissolution of the old family ties within the *capital*ist system may appear, large-scale industry, by assigning an important part in socially organized processes of production, outside the sphere of the domestic economy, to women, young persons and children of both sexes, does nevertheless create a new economic foundation for a higher form of the family and of relations between the sexes.[12]

While slavery within the family is attributed in the above passage to the exploitation that is foundational to the capitalist economic system, it is not clear how this relates to any primordial division of labour such that slavery was inherent in the 'first' family form. Nor is it clear what power-relations are going to be attributed to and within the 'higher form of the family', other than some parental power over children. What is clear is that the discourse has moved away from 'the father', who figured in *The German Ideology* (against a significantly unmentioned mother). 'Husband' and 'wife' from *The German Ideology* seem also to have dropped away in the proposed new 'relations between the sexes'. This lack of terminological specificity could be an advantage, or it could leave areas of great significance exactly as they were. How new is new?

Once again, my point is not to hold Marx to a theoretical agenda that has been generated largely (though not wholly) since his time, but rather to note that his terminological swings and rather exceptional lack of curiosity are symptomatic of a strategy. The strategy was to gain support and not create enemies, and to have the argument both ways: an unspecified realm of naturalisation, and an open realm of possibility. In both cases the strategy suits masculinised presuppositions, as naturalisations tend to assign polymorphous talents and capacities to men, and monomorphous duties and encumbrances to women. The open realm of possibility is therefore much more open, given an absence of further specification, to men than to women. The extent to which this strategy was fully conscious in Marx's mind is not really the issue; the issue for us today is reading Marx in dialogue with both an imputed audience, one whose presumptions may not have changed all that much since the publication of *Capital* in 1867, and also with a present-day theoretical and political agenda, one concerning sex and gender, childcare and domestic partnerships, sexuality and partnership, which is certainly different.

In that light it is quite interesting to examine some of Marx's bolder passages in *Capital* concerning women. These are quite difficult to read nowadays for a rather different reason, namely that – as is almost a cliché – there are many feminisms. Read against one kind of mid- to late-twentieth century feminism, Marx's comments and presumptions are patronisingly sexist; but read against another feminism of our day, Marx actually emerges as in some (limited) sense a feminist of his time. The latter is a difficult argument to make, and not one that could be pushed very far. In the biographical record, as indeed in the texts examined above, Marx does not link his work overtly to any feminism of his day, whether of a theoretical or a practical character, beyond his support of, and participation in, the workers' movement, which itself had a mixed record on this score. In some senses, as we know from mid- to late-twentieth century feminist history, a link to feminism would have been possible; indeed by Marx's later years, and certainly in Engels's, this kind of move was virtually required within the socialist movement. However, it is also known Marx had many suspicions of campaigns and individuals supportive of women and issues they espoused in that frame.

Marx's immediate objections to feminism were the class character of the activists (largely middle and upper class) and the class analysis of their proposals, judged against his ever-ready conceptualisation of proletarian interests as the unified interests of a single class. Where the participants and proposals were acceptably proletarian, however, Marx could evidently see little gain for the movement (in his conceptualisation, obviously) in separate agendas or organisations. These issues surfaced in conjunction with the International Working Men's Association, and later with August Bebel's *Woman under Socialism* (1883) and Engels's work in *The Origin of the Family, Private Property and the State* (1883).[13] In sum, it is quite difficult to make Marx out to be a feminist in an activist sense, much less a feminist with any view about men. My argument here is that reading what he says specifically about women in *Capital* is a fruitful exercise only when done in conjunction with a generously nuanced view of the nineteenth-century feminist scene, and an even more generous allowance for complacency with regard to any theorisation of men/husbands/fathers etc., of which he had considerable personal experience. Here are a few examples of his comments in print:

> Before the labour of women and children under 10 years old was forbidden in mines, the *capital*ists considered the employment of naked women and girls, often in company with men, so far sanctioned by their moral code, and especially by their ledgers, that it was only after the passing of the Act that they had recourse to machinery … In England women are still occasionally used instead of horses for hauling barges, because the labour required to produce horses and machines is an accurately known quantity, while that required to maintain the women of the surplus population is beneath all calculation.[14]

The above passage illustrates one of Marx's themes in *Capital*, which is the way that an increasingly mechanised factory system absorbed and exploited the labour of women and children. He treats them together as persons of 'slight muscular strength, or whose bodily development is incomplete, but whose limbs are all the more supple', and concludes that the 'labour of women and children was therefore the first result of the capitalist application of machinery!'[15] This counters an argument which Marx thought current: that machinery 'saves' labour and promotes 'civilisation'. By quoting official sources extensively he was concerned to portray the horrors of the factory-system as intrinsic to the capitalist mode of production, bound to get worse, and egregiously uncivilised by 'bourgeois' standards of gentility. Women were conceptualised here in Marx's work in physiological terms as physically weaker than men; this is controversial now but at least has a kindly, caring air about it of protecting the vulnerable, albeit from the economic system, not from 'men' as such. Presumably the overall argument is that exploitation is not good for men, either, but that egregious exploitation of 'women and children', who are (said to be) weaker, makes the general point more tellingly.

That theme surfaces later in Marx's discussion where he quotes, with evident approval, a public health report concerning the introduction of an industrial system into agriculture, and its effects again on women and children.

'Married women, who work in gangs along with boys and girls, are, for a stipulated sum of money, placed at the disposal of the farmer by a man called the "undertaker", who contracts for the whole gang. These gangs will sometimes travel many miles from their own village; they are to be met morning and evening on the roads, dressed in short petticoats, with suitable coats and boots, and sometimes trousers, looking wonderfully strong and healthy, but tainted with a customary immorality and heedless of the fatal results which their love of this busy and independent life is bringing on their unfortunate offspring who are pining at home.' All the phenomena of the factory districts are reproduced here [Marx comments], including a yet higher degree of disguised infanticide and stupefaction of children with opiates.[16]

In a footnote to this passage Marx adds: 'Infants that received opiates "shrank up into little old men", or "wizened like little monkeys". We see here how India and China have taken their revenge on England.'[17]

Interestingly these passages capture both female independence in the labour-market as an upside, and female vulnerability (or is it moral weakness?) as a downside. Childcare in relation to adult employment also surfaces, but without much suggestion, other than the catch-all 'family' in Marx's texts. Or rather it surfaces in Dr. Hunter's words in his public health report, which Marx quotes: 'happy indeed will it be for the manufacturing districts of England, when every married woman having a family is prohibited from working in any textile works at all'. Marx seems to quote this approvingly, but says nothing further on the subject.[18] Men are intriguingly missing from this discussion, though Marx does give a general reference to Engels's *The Condition of the Working Class in England* (1845); Engels does not solve childcare issues in any very startling way either, in that early work, though he does portray the distress felt by out-of-work males when their female partner is employed outside the home, and they (males) are left with the children.[19] The contrast between the two writers is interesting, in that Engels ventures onto the masculine side of the gender binary and sexual politics, right into the home and family life (albeit with a certain naivete and lack of personal experience), whereas Marx seems to feel some restraint in holding back from either endorsing conventionality too openly and explictly, or from involving himself too much in discussions about the history and future of gender and parental relationships. Possibly the explanation, whether reflecting personal nervousness or intellectual strategy, was to keep his analytical focus on the 'public' face of material goods and services, without complicating this unduly by bringing in what, from a masculinised perspective, are 'other issues'.

It cannot be claimed that the inter-relation between women, mothers, men, fathers, children and employment/unemployment in industrialised societies has been resolved to all that much satisfaction anywhere in the world, either theoretically or practically, though there are certainly notable gradations in benefits, attitudes, opportunities and perceptions far too complex to go into here. My point in this discussion is that it is untrue to say that Marx never noticed these things, nor that his approach and conclusions can be captured in any very simple way. Moreover the silences of his texts (not unusually in this respect) do theorise men implicitly, and conventionally. In the above discussions men are, by implication, physically strong, sexually aggressive and absent (or at least distant) fathers on the breadwinner-outside-the-home model. As a general conceptualisation this is hardly surprising, and it is reflective of a contemporary image which was, no doubt, in an ambiguous relation to varied ways that individuals behaved; what is perhaps at least slightly disappointing is the lack of curiosity in conceptualising this problem, which evidently grated on Marx to a degree, especially considering his own anguish as a father, which we have from correspondence, and his own jovial role as *pater familias*, at least as this appears in surviving memoirs.[20]

Family slavery resurfaces in *Capital*, though in an economically determined context, not in one determined by 'nature' and the beginnings of culture, as in *The German Ideology*. Marx comments:

> Machinery also revolutionizes ... the agency through which the capital-relation is formally mediated ... our first assumption was the capitalist and the worker confronted each other as free persons ... But now the capitalist buys children and young persons. Previously the worker sold his own labour-power ... Now he sells wife and child. He has become a slave-dealer. Notices of demand for children's labour often resemble in form the inquiries for Negro slaves ...[21]

This, of course, portrays men as victims of the economic system, but also once again as slave-masters within the family, both as husband and as father. Male sexuality is never raised as a topic of discussion, in this (pre-capitalist or capitalist) world (as it were) or the next (socialist) one; Marx's strategy in *Capital* in considering both the primordial world of reproductive instincts and the socialist world of social rationality and absence-of-struggle, is to portray reproductive sexuality as divided albeit egalitarian in 'the act', and early childcare as women's work (rather than men's, even in domestic partnership). Unsurprising as this is, re-reading Marx can help to re-raise issues like these in the contemporary context rather than to close them down in familiar ways. Perhaps unexpectedly, for instance, he ventures a developmental sketch on female sexuality. Though a quotation, again from a public health report, the context is explicitly approving:

> 'Each moulder [of bricks] … supplies his subordinates with board and lodging in his cottage. Whether members of his family or not, the men, boys and girls all sleep in the cottage … all on the ground floor, and badly ventilated. These people are so exhausted after the day's hard work, that neither the rules of health, of cleanliness, nor of decency are in the least observed … The greatest evil of the system that employs young girls on this sort of work, consists in this, that, as a rule, it chains them fast from childhood for the whole of their after-life to the most abandoned rabble. They become rough, foulmouthed boys, before Nature has taught them that they are women. Clothed in a few dirty rags, the legs naked far above the knees, hair and face besmeared with dirt, they learn to treat all feelings of decency and shame with contempt. During mealtimes they lie at full length in the fields, or watch the boys bathing in a neighbouring canal.'[22]

And similarly:

> In some branches of industry, the girls and women work through the night together with the male personnel … 'young girls and women are employed on the pit banks and on the coke heaps, not only by day but also by night … These females employed with the men, hardly distinguished from them in their dress … are exposed to the deterioration of character, arising from their loss of self-respect, which can hardly fail to follow from their unfeminine occupation'.[23]

These passages raise questions about childhood/adulthood and heterosexuality, and particularly sexual difference, that are again unresolved in Marx, and still unresolved in contemporary society.[24] While it might seem that Marx's comments merely evoke Victorian values of fragile femininity and female purity, it is also a reasonable supposition that there were differing views on these matters in Marx's time, even though the overall framework for discussion – when there was discussion – was not that of present-day sexual politics. Giving some consideration to just this openness and variability of context is essential to a rich and productive reading of Marx. This issue takes me to two different kinds of criticism that have been mounted since the 1880s. I shall consider passages from works by Michèle Barrett and Jeff Hearn, not because they exhaust the field, but because the two represent very different critical strategies, and allow me to draw two quite contrasting conclusions.

Two concepts of criticism

In a commemorative article 'Marxist-Feminism and the Work of Karl Marx' (in a volume marking the centenary of Marx's death) Barrett berates Marx for his 'naturalism' in regard to the family (as detailed in the passages from *The German Ideology* quoted above), and sexism in regard to his general assumption that wage-labourers are male. Barrett says that he devalues women wage-workers as little other than 'a threat to the male worker', because factories replaced male labour with that of women and children (as detailed in the passages from *Capital* quoted above). Marx has 'unreflectively sexist presuppositions', according to Barrett, and therefore 'assumes as a baseline that there is a (pre-given) housewife engaged in domestic labour in the home'. Barrett concludes that this 'is hardly an unspeakable crime', but that 'it is not what we might expect from a mind that did not rest at appearances'.[25]

Given Barrett's assumptions, these conclusions are probably fair enough, but this is really to raise the question, what exactly are her assumptions? I sense that they are rather different from mine, as a strategy for reading Marx. It seems to me, first of all, that Barrett is trying to read Marx as an authorial mind, rather than to read his texts. While texts can hardly be read at all without some sense of who the author is, and why the text was written,[26] it certainly does not follow that texts have to be seen as a window on the author's views, and little else. Even if these texts were read as merely a window on 'what Marx thought', it seems to me that Barrett's reading promotes an interpretation of the authorial mind as singular and certain in having just one view. With a more exploratory reading, and with a strategy of filling in the silences with more than one possibility, it seems to me that a more complex and more interesting authorial Marx can be usefully, if provocatively, constructed. In short, I think we are looking at selective quotation and ungenerous interpretation. This is curiously mirrored in Barrett's treatment of nineteenth-century feminism, in that she rightly does not accept that Marx can be exonerated for his 'feet of clay' on feminist issues by declaring that he lived in a 'pre-feminist' culture.[27] And she argues, also rightly, that the currency of feminist ideas in the nineteenth century should not be underestimated. Unfortunately, however, her own deployment of feminism reflects neither any specifically nineteenth-century quality to these ideas, nor any diversity within this putative nineteenth-century context. While it is my intention to argue methodologically here, and not specifically to get Marx off any hook, least of all a feminist one, none the less it does seem to me that, viewed against a more complex and diverse 'take' on feminist ideas and movements of the nineteenth century, Marx begins to look slightly better.

As there are many feminisms today, so there were many in the nineteenth century. It is by no means agreed that the liberal feminist campaign to get equal opportunities for women in the labour market, nor the socialist feminist campaign to bring power to working-class women, nor the radical feminist campaigns to end oppression in a so-called private or domestic sphere – all of which are invoked by Barrett – were individually or severally the dominant doctrine and practice in Marx's time. All these issues were there, of course, but it is arguable that in practical political, and in at least somewhat theoretical terms, a very significant feminism of the time assumed, somewhat contrarily, that women were inherently domestic, with responsibilities for child-bearing, child-rearing, home-making, and similar considerations that worked against waged employment outside the home – which was said to be a realm for men. Moreover this often took on an overtly moralistic character, with arguments that women had a special purity, quite unlike men's character, and indeed that women had responsibilities for keeping men's activities in check – particularly where alcohol was involved. Rather than see Marx as an author inexplicably in the grip of Victorian *sexual* values (given that he detested Victorian *social* values), it might be interesting to see him reflecting some version of Victorian *feminist* values, albeit ones that have largely faded from view today, or at least largely faded from the view of academic writers, who are not often gripped with interest in women's views on the political right. Feminist history can be constructed in highly different ways, depending on the writer's purposes and politics; Barrett's purpose seems to have been to cut Marx loose from Engels on 'the woman question', and to pick over his work for 'howlers' (her word).[28] While I do not share Barrett's view that Engels is all that much better,[29] I none the less welcome debate. However, I think that Barrett has impoverished Marx quite considerably, and deliberately, by narrowing the historical contextualisation down unduly in terms of feminist history, and by narrowing Marx down as an authorial consciousness to the point where he seems brain-damaged.

It can be useful to prise texts loose from the authorial mind somewhat, and that is very largely what I have tried to do in the chapters in this book. On the one hand, I have no problem with producing a more interesting authorial Marx as a matter of interpretive generosity (why focus on 'howlers'?) and exploratory contextualisation (bringing in an unfashionable feminism). On the other hand, I have also tried to create dialogue between texts of the past and texts of the present by distancing the author and foregrounding the commentator, hence the critical strategy of lining my readings of Marx up with my readings of contemporary sexual politics.

This is more like the strategy employed by Jeff Hearn in a highly critical yet productive reading of Marx's texts that he undertakes in *The Gender of Oppression*. Rather than taking Marx to task for failing to meet a contemporary agenda, Hearn explores the discursive strategies deployed by Marx in passages concerning reproduction and the family, on the one hand, and the material production of useful goods and services, on the other. My emphasis was on the former area – reproduction and the family – as a way of arguing that these texts are actually rather more interesting than they might at first appear, whereas Hearn's is on the latter – material production of useful goods and services – as a way of linking the two areas together. Rather than simply cast doubt on Marx's conceptualisations of reproduction and the family, which is easy enough to do, Hearn probes into Marx's characterisations of both reproduction and production, contrasting them with Mary O'Brien's 'focus on "reproductive labour" and [Catharine] MacKinnon's on "sexuality"'. Doing this, he argues, disrupts 'taken-for-granted conventions of production-based (male-dominated) marxisms'.[30] It is not that Marx 'said the wrong things about reproduction and domestic labour', as it were, but rather that he left the patriarchal character of the very definitions and value-hierarchies involved in these activities untroubled.

This is to say not just that Marx reads quite a lot directly off 'sexual difference' when he (briefly) remarks on reproduction, childcare and domestic labour, but further that he also reads quite a lot *covertly* off sexual difference, when he makes 'productive' activities crucial in historical change and political progress. These activities are not merely reflective of sexual difference, in that they are commonly coded male or masculine, but rather they are constitutive of sexual difference in countless ways, not least in the child-rearing and educational presuppositions and practices that produce men and women as identifiably and consistently different. This makes them 'different' for the job market, and licences the job market to view them differently. That there is a conceptual separation at all between 'public' and paid labour, on the one hand, and 'private' and domestic labour, on the other hand, is in Hearn's view a patriarchal strategy. He concludes that '[e]ither the notion of labour needs to be enlarged to incorporate *all* such aspects of material being, or it needs to be complemented by a firmer notion of material being that is beyond and outside narrow "works".'[31] This opens issues up (by making both gender and labour problematic), rather than closing them down (by taking them both for granted as unrelated).

Marx is thus illustrative of the way that malestream theorists leave so much unexamined and thus seem to licence the conventional naturalising discourses that *make* men and women what they are with respect to the division of labour (paid or unpaid) in society, and with respect to interpersonal power-relations in other kinds of relationships. Given his revolutionary views on social relations, though, it seems surprising now that the 'categories of sex and sexuality' did not occupy Marx, who stuck firmly to the 'economic categories' in his critique. Not all his contemporaries were quite so blind to gender, and to issues of men in relation to women.

Yet Marx is also rather typical in the way that overtly gendered discourse creeps into his theorisations, both at the level of (pre) historical conceptualisation (as in *The German Ideology*) and at the level of contemporary political controversy (as in *Capital*, vol. 1), at least in terms of the authorities that he quotes with approval. While there is no doubt that Marx never aimed to become the theorist of 'slavery in the family' (which he mentions in *The German Ideology*), it is also true that he never aimed to become the theorist of 'slavery in the economy' (which he mentions in *Capital*, vol. 1), or at least only the 'wage-slavery' on which his theory turns. While Marx paid some attention to the compatibility of capitalism with pre-capitalist economic practices, such as chattel-slavery,[32] he did not make the connection back to 'the family' and gender-relations more broadly, as only a very few male radicals did, from time to time, when noting that for women, marriage had aspects of slavery.

In relation to men and masculinity, however, the puzzle remains … why was Marx not more disturbed at the posited connection between men as such (at least during some historical period) and the enslavement of women and children under male heads of households? Why would this role have been innate? Or was it developed? Did it decline? Perhaps it is rather like asking *why* 'men' developed surplus production and the self-expanding spiral of capitalist expansion and exploitation. Marx never actually asks *why* 'men' (or rather *some* 'men') develop their productive forces to the point where a drive for productivity strains against the fetters of the property, legal and political system.[33] Unsurprisingly, therefore, he does not offer an answer to that question, or to issues concerning the origin of masculinist oppression. That is probably all to the good. However, it is not particularly good that he left so much about gender, which he called 'relations between the sexes', hanging in such an untheorised and unexplored way, with only brief comments and enigmatic quotations for the record.

Notes

1 For two recent examples where Marx 'surfaces' in important ways, see Evans, *Sexual Citizenship*; and Grant, *Fundamental Feminism*.
2 For detailed consideration of the hermeneutical issues arising from the Marx–Engels 'partnership', and from *The German Ideology* in particular, see Terrell Carver, *The Postmodern Marx* (Manchester: Manchester University Press, 1998), pp. 97–107, 163–79.
3 Karl Marx and Frederick Engels, *Feuerbach: opposition of the materialist and idealist outlooks* [*The First Part of 'The German Ideology'*] (London, Lawrence & Wishart, 1973), pp. 31–2.
4 Marx and Engels, *Feuerbach* [*German Ideology*], pp. 19–20.
5 Marx and Engels, *Feuerbach* [*German Ideology*], p. 20.
6 Marx and Engels, *Feuerbach* [*German Ideology*], p. 33.
7 Marx and Engels, *Feuerbach* [*German Ideology*], p. 33.
8 Marx and Engels, *Feuerbach* [*German Ideology*], pp. 34–5.
9 See, for example, Shanks and Tilley, *Social Theory and Archaeology*.
10 Karl Marx, *Capital*, vol. 1, trans. Ben Fowkes (Harmondsworth: Penguin, 1986), p. 285.

11 Marx, *Capital*, vol. 1, p. 471.
12 Marx, *Capital*, vol. 1, pp. 620–1.
13 For a discussion of Bebel and his work, see Anne Lopes and Gary Roth, *Men's Feminism: August Bebel and the German socialist movement* (Amherst, NY: Humanity/Prometheus, 2000); for a discussion of Engels, see pp. 227–51 below.
14 Marx, *Capital*, vol. 1, p. 517.
15 Marx, *Capital*, vol. 1, p. 517.
16 Marx, *Capital*, vol. 1, p. 522.
17 Marx, *Capital*, vol. 1, p. 522 n. 51.
18 Marx, *Capital*, vol. 1, p. 522.
19 Frederick Engels, *The Condition of the Working Class in England*, ed. Victor Kiernan (Harmondsworth, Penguin, 1987), p. 168.
20 See David McLellan, *Karl Marx: his life and thought* (London: Macmillan, 1973), pp. 274–5, 330.
21 Marx, *Capital*, vol. 1, p. 519.
22 Marx, *Capital*, vol. 1, pp. 593–4.
23 Marx, *Capital*, vol. 1, pp. 368 and 368 n. 61.
24 For a discussion of 'age of consent' legislation in analytical and historical terms relating to both sexes and varied sexualities, see Matthew Waites, 'Sexual citizens: legislating the age of consent in Britain', in Terrell Carver and Véronique Mottier, eds, *The Politics of Sexuality: identity, gender, citizenship* (London: Routledge, 1998), pp. 25–35.
25 Michèle Barrett, 'Marxist-Feminism and the Work of Karl Marx', in Betty Matthews, ed., *Marx: 100 years on* (London: Lawrence & Wishart, 1983), pp. 210–14.
26 I discuss the relationship between biography as a genre and the historical contextualisation of authors in the political theory canon in *Gender is not a Synonym for Women*, pp. 2–3; see also my 'Methodological issues in writing a political biography', *Journal of Political Science* 20 (1992), pp. 3–13.
27 Barrett, 'Marxist-Feminism', pp. 199, 216–17.
28 Barrett, 'Marxist-Feminism', pp. 214–15.
29 See pp. 232, 247–8 below.
30 Jeff Hearn, *The Gender of Oppression: men, masculinity and the critique of Marxism* (Brighton: Wheatsheaf, 1987), pp. 98–9.
31 Hearn, Gender of Oppression, p. 100.
32 Marx, *Capital*, vol. 1, pp. 345, 377.
33 Marx mocks political economists and politicians who constructed just-so stories to explain this, but merely presumes, in his own theoretical constructions, that it simply happens (and thus 'man' creates history); see, for example, Marx, *Capital*, vol. 1, pp. 873–4.

CHAPTER TEN

Engels: men behaving naturally

Strategies and intersections

Friedrich Engels wrote his short book *The Origin of the Family, Private Property and the State* (1884) just after the re-publication of August Bebel's *Women and Socialism* (1879, 2nd edn 1883). That book, now little known, was already a (banned) success and very soon one of the best-selling and most influential socialist tracts of the nineteenth century. It is likely that Engels's title comes from a line in Bebel's book.[1] Having got his start as a polemical and highly political journalist, Engels was well used to writing ripostes, in some cases inflammatory and satirical, and in other cases more rigorous and serious-minded. *The Origin of the Family* may be one of the latter, and unlike his already well known *Anti-Dühring* (1878–9),[2] for instance, it is possible that it rather belies its original format as a riposte altogether, because Bebel and his book get no mention. Alternatively it may be that Engels was not writing a riposte or a supplanting account, and was happy instead with his positioning as a kind of addendum or footnote to Bebel's more radical work.[3] Certainly the latter argument would be more persuasive if had Engels featured Bebel's work in his own, though there may have been political risks here – Bebel's work had been immediately and successively suppressed under the anti-socialist laws in Germany, whereas Engels's more heavy-weight scholarly study was not. Rather than self-censor it for publication in the 'theoretical' monthly of German socialism, Karl Kautsky's Berlin-based *Die neue Zeit*, Engels published it in Switzerland, from whence it was clandestinely distributed. Bebel's tract is no longer widely read, and it seems to have faded nearly as fast as it flowered, not least because Marxist historiography has triumphed over it in producing an Engels-centred account of socialist theory and practice (and so marginalising Bebel).

Engels's 'light touch' strategy in not foregrounding Bebel's work in *The Origin of the Family* was perhaps to spare the worthy trade-unionist Bebel any discouragement, as he was very much an ally and friend rather than a rival and threat, like the academician Dühring. Bebel subsequently and modestly bowed to Engels's (supposed) greater expertise in theoretical matters, and so never mounted any counter-challenge.[4] Perhaps there was for Engels an element of being caught off-guard, and of damage-limitation as well, in that he already had a clear agenda for intervention on 'major' theoretical questions to do with philosophical foundations, method, history, class struggle and revolution, on which he aimed to set people straight. The 'woman question', on which he had had some experience, however (cf. *The Communist Manifesto* and some very early writings – and cartoons[5]), was never a central interest, nor included prominently in any previous overview of substantial issues for Marxists. It may be that Engels was not keen to publicise the matter all that much and thus to make it a central question of the age, since it would necessarily distract, in his view, from the central and singular focus on class politics (which we now see as masculinised) that Marxists had always argued was their mark of distinction. Moreover it might pose awkward questions of organisation, even *separate* organisation in some sense, that from the (male) leadership's perspective could only be unwelcome and divisive. Certainly the text of *The Origin of the Family* overall is rather concerned to add women to the conception of history, philosophy and politics that Engels attributed to Marx, and that he himself had expounded in his various works and introductions to the master's writings since 1859 – but then to stir the mix as little as possible.

Even merely 'adding' women raises the issue of gender, that is, ways that sex and sexuality become power-relations in society.[6] Such discussions are bound to raise issues of sexuality (typically through comments on marriage in some form and 'the family') and about men as men, being the 'other half' of gender-relations. Engels rose splendidly to the task, and indeed *The Origin of the Family* is remarkable for its sweep, taking the story of human reproductive and caring relationships from their earliest origins through to a post-capitalist future that he identified as socialism. It was very widely circulated in German and in translation, and by 1891 it was in its fourth edition.

Certainly the terms of the title – 'family', 'private property', 'state' – would have had a familiar, safe ring to them for male socialists and trades unionists, to whom the book was primarily directed. Engels, knowingly I think, did not repeat the 'woman' signifier of Bebel's title (*Die Frau und der Sozialismus*), with its overt reference to the 'woman question' and the issues raised in, and by, the feminist movements of the time, diverse as they were, inside and outside of socialism.

In short, Engels was the safe (male) pair of hands through which Marxism could meet any challenge, and if it needed any amendment or revision, he was the one authorised to make any changes. Engels not only lived his relationship with Marx, when the master was alive, he was also the first biographer of that relationship, as well as Marx's literary executor (though not the sole owner of his papers), and from those unimpeachable credentials he brooked no rivals in speaking for Marx, nor during his own lifetime did any emerge. He went from 'second fiddle' and 'junior partner' to quite another role, that of near co-author and posthumous collaborator, though his self-acknowledgement in that regard was characteristically self-effacing.[7] Only now, with full publication of Marx's manuscripts and scholarly tracking of Engels's treatment of them, is this becoming an issue that cannot be avoided or explained away.[8]

And changes there were in *The Origin of the Family*. Engels adapted Marx's concept of 'material' production to include human reproduction, and attempted to build on this revision an apparatus of twin-track 'determination' in history, involving sex-oppression, as well as class-oppression. Moreover this was also the occasion on which Engels made public his incorporation of Charles Darwin's 'great discovery' into the actual conception of history bequeathed by Marx from the pre-Darwinian 1840s, and indeed to build it into Marx's historical account of the transitions from one epoch to another that had been elaborated in published form (by both Marx and Engels, separately) in 1859.[9] Bebel's intervention on the 'woman question' was thus the occasion for no small revision to the 'outlook' which Engels attributed to Marx, but of which he was now in sole charge, Marx having died just the year before the first publication of Engels's little book.

Ritually Engels linked his own work with unpublished manuscripts on anthropology that Marx had left behind, though without actually claiming that those writings were in any sense drafts of a work (by Marx), or indeed of Engels's actual work as he conceived it, and as eventually published. The manuscripts themselves, while acknowledged at the outset, were not specifically cited in Engels's text, and so the work has come down in the interpretive tradition as Engels's alone. Moreover scholarly analysis has shown that Engels's claim, both vague and extravagant in terms of an overlap in content or imprimatur for the ideas, does not stand up to scrutiny. It is clear that Marx was interested in Engels's main source, Lewis Henry Morgan, but it is not particularly clear why or what he thought about it.[10] What the interpretive tradition has not grappled with very extensively, though, are Engels's revisions and amendments to the 'guiding thread' that Marx had left behind in 1859, and had then briefly cited in the first volume of *Capital* (1867), in order to help readers understand his published critiques of political economy, the economic theory of the day.[11]

This reluctance to address Engels's remarkable revisions to the very fundamentals of Marxism (and to rewrite one of Marx's most famous texts, as rehearsed yet again by Engels in *Anti-Dühring*) must be due to an association between those amendments, and the 'woman question', gently transmuted by Engels into 'family', 'private property' and 'state' in his title and in the structure of his short book. No (male) commentator on Marxism has taken *The Origin of the Family* as methodologically central to Marxism and to understanding Marx.[12] Rather the work has occupied a place well down the line in the *Engels* canon, with its (shocking?) content recounted, but not critically assessed, and certainly not promoted to pride of place over Marx's 'Preface' to *A Contribution to the Critique of Political Economy* (1859) – on the place of epochal 'modes of production' in history – or over the jointly written *Manifesto of the Communist Party* (1848) – on the nature of class struggles. Other late works by Engels, e.g. *Ludwig Feuerbach and the End of Classical German Philosophy* (1886), did not attempt anything so ambitious, rather the reverse, in fact, as Engels argues there that Marx's philosophical position can be traced back developmentally, in a smooth sweep, to the philosophical and political controversies of the 1840s, in which Engels was himself involved.

The Origin of the Family thus has two strikes against it. One is that it complicates what was otherwise a settled and (reasonably) simple story of historical 'determination' by an identifiably singular factor (production, albeit of its means and relations) – as opposed to the obviously dual-factor 'production' and 'reproduction' of *The Origin of the Family*. The other is that it raises issues to do with women which the (presumptively male) leadership were only to happy to shelve, preferably in a book whose title gave scant advertisement to the feminist cause, and whose argument, read as a whole, did not support separate organisations for women nor take sex-oppression in class society more seriously than class-oppression. In short Engels is the feminists' Marxist; but left to his own devices, he was not much of a feminist by argument or action. *The Origin of the Family* thus poses problems for Marxism, in terms of its fundamental tenets, but those problems have rarely, if ever, been addressed outside the feminist context, and given the airing they evidently merit.

Engels's book also poses problems for feminism, though these were explicitly taken up at length, and in depth, only in the 1980s. The main issues were the validity and utility of a 'dual-systems' approach that would find social 'determination' in gender dynamics, *and* in class dynamics, equally or at least even-handedly. Moreover the status and content of pre-historical accounts as such came under scrutiny in this literature, as Engels had made bold claims in this area and had constructed a highly readable, and widely read, discussion. Lastly the extent to which Engels's vision of a socialist future corresponded to any widely shared feminist ideals came under scrutiny. Was his claim that most gender-oppression would vanish, once class-oppression had been expunged through proletarian revolution, well supported with theory or sadly facile in practice? Was he really in a position to theorise 'woman' and 'women's experience' at all? Had he in fact articulated a sufficiently nuanced, and in particular emotionally sensitive, vision of future familial and sexual relations?

As a feminist text Engels's work suffered from minority status – few works (perhaps no works?) by men could, by definition, count as central and essential feminist reading. While there is no particular reason why Marxism should not have been more influential in second- and third-wave feminism than, say, psychoanalysis – and just as many reasons why both traditions carried heavy baggage of feminist-unfriendly, not to say misogynist associations – none the less few commentators would say that Marxism has counted for more in feminist thought than psychoanalytic theory. In general feminist history, feminist research and feminist theory do not take Engels all that seriously (Marxist-feminists to the contrary, of course), and when they do, the upshot is that he is insufficiently interested in gender to deliver on his promises, or to show exactly how someone (more feminist) could do so.

Despite this, Engels's *The Origin of the Family* has become a minor point of reference for feminist theory, even if it is not in itself a feminist classic. For some it is evidence why feminists should reject Marxism, or even Marx's work, and for others it is the foundation of a Marxist feminism, its deficiencies notwithstanding. Michèle Barrett comments:

> Scarcely a Marxist-feminist text is produced that does not refer somewhere to Engels's argument, and if one had to identify one major contribution to feminism from Marxism it would have to be this text.[13]

More strongly, I would argue that any text that self-identified as Marxist-feminist, or which figured as such by treating gender and class in tandem as determining social structures, would strike an odd note if it did not cite and then revisit Engels's *The Origin of the Family*. Over the years it has been regularly re-issued in English with appropriately updated introductions linking it to contemporary feminist politics, as well as to Marxist scholarship.[14]

Few commentators, feminist or otherwise, would defend very much of the anthropological material cited by Engels or very many of the anthropological points he makes independently. Too much has happened in the intervening years, both in terms of empirical research and fieldwork, and in terms of the scope and presumptions of anthropology itself, to sustain the certainties through which Engels wrote his text. The text is rightly described by Barrett as 'flawed and disputed'.[15] Moreover the kind of Marxism through which Engels conceived his account, and to which he aimed to contribute in *The Origin of the Family* in a quite fundamental and foundational way, has itself been subject to several generations of critique, rooted in issues to do with science, causation, knowledge, determinism, class, leadership and revolution. *The Origin of the Family*, in Marxist terms, has fallen somewhat to one side in all these Marxist critiques, without – as has been mentioned above – ever becoming truly central, or perhaps as central, as it should have been, given its relationship to the 'materialist interpretation of history', the foundational concepts of production and labour, and Marxist predilections for developmental historical periodisations.

In terms of gender studies more broadly, and in particular, with reference to studies of men and masculinities, Engels's work should have a lot to offer. He gives a gendered account of men (as men) in the famous sections on pre-history which cover the development of sexual and family relationships, something in which men figure by definition and with which, in practice, they are still involved. He also writes Darwinian concepts of sexual selection into this account, which necessarily make claims about male behaviour (and the 'nature' of men as men), an area in which males have an important stake in self-knowledge, never more so than today, given feminist and other challenges.[16] And his account of private property and government in the historical and contemporary age is itself gendered (and not merely generic), in that he details the roles of both men (as men) and women in bringing those institutions about, and in enjoying (or suffering) the consequences. Why, then, is Engels's *The Origin of the Family* not one of the foundational texts of men's studies?

Unfortunately, it takes some considerable work of analysis to make Engels's views on these matters apparent. In common with other texts Engels's *overtly gendered* account of men tends to slip into the background, as he also rather typically states his views and conclusions in apparently generic and gender-neutral terms. That is, Engels's text moves rather easily from an overtly gendered concept of man to an apparently de-gendered one, without alerting anyone very markedly to the difference. He is hardly alone in this, as the analytical distinction has only recently been developed, and is not yet widely appreciated, by any means.[17] None the less, despite remarking on men in overtly gendered terms, and theorising their nature and behaviour in explicitly drawn ways, Engels is hardly a gender pioneer in men's studies, precisely because he does so little argumentatively with what he exposes to view. His text has no purchase on any *critique* of men as men, nor any exposure of generic man as male (rather than female). Nor is there any evident suggestion that politically or personally he would have had any sympathy for such a notion (few men do, even now). Rather Engels derived considerable political and personal benefit, as men still do, from not raising transformative issues in any very serious way, and for reinforcing this complacency through a discursive strategy that 'flickers' between overtly gendered accounts of men as husbands and fathers, and covertly gendered accounts of 'man' as generic and gender-neutral. The overall effect is thus to rehearse certain naturalised and naturalising presumptions about men, but without making them at all problematic with reference to culture and change. Politically this then leaves men where they were, secure in their 'nature', and immune from the challenges posed by feminisms, and by transformative thinking about what manners maketh man, and what masculinities are acceptable.

Engels's *The Origin of the Family* has been taken seriously by at least one men's studies scholar, somewhat in the hope that Marxism will be taken seriously within gender studies, just as some feminists have found theoretical and political mileage in a critical engagement with Marx and Marxists. Jeff Hearn has argued that transformative thinking about labour could follow from the suggestion in *The German Ideology* (a manuscript work of 1845–6 by Marx and Engels) that human labour is materially productive and species-reproductive.[18] Working from a feminist standpoint position on maternal labour, Hearn suggests a revisioning of human labour as both emotionally nurturing and technologically developmental.[19] The 'other' to this conception is the narrow view of labour, inscribed within modern economics, as mere factor of production, a commodity with a market-value, albeit one rather inconveniently located in human bodies and brains, rather than in raw materials and machinery. The advantage of taking this earlier location for dual-systems theory, that is, a view that Marxism incorporates a gendered concept of labour related to human reproduction, is that *The German Ideology* does not pose issues about pre-history and anthropology in quite the explicit way that the later text, *The Origin of the Family*, poses so directly and at considerable length. Moreover Engels's later work is inscribed within overt presumptions about social theory that incorporate a positivist view of science within a deterministic view of human behaviour, or at least his outlook seems to tip more that way than towards the more speculative and hermeneutic discourse of the 1840s. *The German Ideology* bravely calls for empirical studies to fill out the conceptual framework that the joint authors have sketched in, but an identification of some notion of factual illustration for the 1840s with the positivistic notions of science that Engels himself developed only later during the 1860s and 1870s would surely be anachronistic.[20]

The upshot is that Engels's *The Origin of the Family* is an undiscovered text for men's studies and theoretical work on masculinities, as indeed are numerous classics in all fields of social studies written by male authors.[21] Generally these are replete with overtly stated yet unexamined presumptions about 'what men are like' (as men), and why that aspect of 'human nature' is simply factual, natural and cannot be made problematic. An important discursive strategy that ensures this outcome is the 'flickering' that the texts incorporate between overtly gendered and apparently de-gendered conceptualisations of 'man'. This not only naturalises gendered behaviour as necessarily (because 'biologically') inherent in the 'male of the species' but also then generalises this to humans as such through the (supposedly) generic concept of 'man', in which much of this masculinised behaviour is said to inhere 'in the species'. Of course at certain moments in these texts the feminine 'other' pops up, notably when the mechanics (literally) of pregnancy, parturition and lactation are in view, not to mention the 'need' (of men, of course) for sexual partners and domestic 'partnership'. Engels's text is a particularly thorough portrayal of this typical and effective discursive strategy, and it is with this in mind that I revisit his arguments in *The Origin of the Family*.

Novelising history

There are numerous objections on any number of grounds to any given proposition or argument in Engels's *The Origin of the Family*.[22] Rather than rehearse these, my strategy here will be rather different, namely revealing not just what the work says about men and masculinity (in Engels, masculinity is profoundly singular), but showing what role men play in his revised version of Marxism. My claim is that the work as a whole tells a story, and that piecemeal criticism misses the underlying point. Much of the significance of Engels's text, and of others like it, is only recoverable through narrative analysis, and in that respect Engels's work bears re-reading almost as a kind of novel. No doubt this does considerable violence to Engels's intentions, but not so much, I think, to the way that his readers made sense of what he had written.[23] Moreover this approach does make his text a useful illustration of the point that in talking about women, one talks about men (and vice versa), even if the authorial and discursive strategies do not make this apparent, or indeed play it down. Gender is organised around a binary, and in asserting what is the case on one side, there is no escape from some implication for what obtains with respect to the other.

The historical approach to sexuality was as unpopular in conservative quarters in the 1880s as it had been in the 1840s when the *Manifesto of the Communist Party* was written by Engels and Marx. Indeed it is surprising even now how naturalistically rather than historically sexuality is still conceived, despite the appearance of influential, even landmark works in history and sociology, not to mention considerable feminist energy devoted to the subject.[24] In *The Origin of the Family* Engels continued his critique of 'the bourgeois family', begun many years before and notably present in the *Manifesto of the Communist Party*:

> Transformation of the family! Even the most radical of the radicals flares up at this infamous proposal of the communists.
>
> What is the basis of the contemporary bourgeois family? Capital and private gain. It is completely developed only for the bourgeoisie; but it finds its complement in the enforced dissolution of the family among the proletarians and in public prostitution.
>
> The bourgeois family naturally declines with the decline of its complement, and the two disappear with the disappearance of capital ... Bourgeois phrases about the family and child-rearing, about the deeply felt relationship of parent to child, become even more revolting when all proletarian family ties are severed as a consequence of large-scale industry, and children are simply transformed into articles of trade and instruments of labour.
>
> But you communists want to introduce common access to women, protests the whole bourgeoisie in chorus.
>
> The bourgeois sees in his wife a mere instrument of production. He hears that the instruments of production are to be utilised in common and naturally cannot think otherwise than that common use is equally applicable to women.
>
> He does not suspect that the point here is to transform the status of women as mere instruments of production ... Our bourgeois, not content with having the wives and daughters of the proletariat at their disposal, not to mention legally sanctioned prostitutes, take the greatest pleasure in reciprocal seduction of married women.
>
> Bourgeois marriage is really the community of married women ... In any case it is self-evident that with the transformation of the current relations of production, the community of women emerging from those relations, i.e. sanctioned and unsanctioned prostitution, will disappear.[25]

While daring, in a kind of add-on way, this discussion was notably negative in detailing what was wrong but saying little about how to put it right, and the same is true of Marx's even earlier pronouncements on the position of women and the communist transformation of sexual relationships.[26]

Formally Engels aimed to survey the entire history of sexuality, reproduction of the species, and production of goods and services in all societies, however 'primitive', in order to produce a history of political forms leading up to the modern 'bourgeois' state. In common with other nineteenth-century accounts his approach involved the demarcation of historical stages, causal explanations for change, and an assumption of progress in the development of civilisation. As a Marxist he foresaw the resolution of the conflicts he detailed through the eventual victory of proletariat over their class oppressors. But unusually in his own time he considered women to be further oppressed, and moreover argued that this oppression was the historical product of a fundamental change in human relationships. Startlingly he claimed that the imposition of male domination over women made them the first oppressed class. As a historical product, that oppression was judged by him to be remediable and transitory. Thus the story Engels told was ostensibly about changes in the relation of one sex to another, with a promise of further change as the class struggle develops. It is a complicated account that I will be examining here in detail.

The status of Engels's writing as history or anthropology is somewhat misleading anyway, though overwhelmingly it is viewed as a major contribution to the former and the sole contribution to the latter within the canon of classical Marxism. In important ways, though, it is much more like a historical novel – *The Forsyte Saga* comes continually to mind – as one follows Engels's projection of nineteenth-century values back into the distant past, and his ruling device of generational upsets. Narrative analysis involves following the twists and turns of the plot, as Engels constructed it, 'men' and 'women' being his main characters, and this will, I hope, provoke renewed interest in the text. But another reason why the text is interesting is that it prompts us to reflect on the consequences of foregrounding 'women' as narrative subject and analytical object, as Engels does. Men appear in his account only secondarily in contrast to his focus on the oppression of women, yet women's oppression is inexplicable for Engels without them. He clearly found that he needed to say little about men in order to make his narrative work. The assumptions about them that he employed were so obviously simple and 'factual' that they required little explanation. Women, of course, were more problematic for him, and doubtless in his view for (presumptively male) readers as well. Thus his narrative is preoccupied more with material concerning women than with a discussion of men, who were, none the less, the agents of domination. This has the effect of covertly reproducing conventional 'men's history' from a supposedly generic perspective (emphatically not a history of men as men), whilst appearing to be a history focused on women. Thus Engels's theorising about women proceeds against a background of unexamined assumptions concerning men, and the fact that he made women problematic obscures the fact that he treated men unproblematically. His story is actually driven by men, but they appear somewhat fleetingly and mechanically in the narrative. Men's studies and studies of masculinities, by contrast, have attempted to 'bring men in', this time as men, but in an appropriately critical framework, informed by feminist work and politics.[27]

Engels was not simply an unwitting victim of 'traditional' assumptions and values. Rather his narrative was itself a traditional exculpation of conventional hegemonic or dominant masculinity, conceived as monotonic and universal. This masculinity was important to him politically, as political action which did not validate those norms and conventions was virtually unthinkable. Despite the superficial feminism of *The Origin of the Family* he never associated himself with women's struggles *as women*. To do so would have lost him such political allies as he had, and gained him little in the way of usable political clout.

Moreover conventional masculinity was important to Engels personally, as episodes in his self-development and later relationships were constructed from characteristically masculine 'scripts'. Examination of early letters and drawings reveals what might be termed 'a secure gender identity' that never rubbed against the class-based radicalism that he adopted early on and adapted but little throughout his political career. In life he was quite capable of sympathising with 'the oppressed' and 'workers of the world', but then complaining vituperatively about his servants, who were always female.[28] As argued above, the extent to which Engels's work should be taken as evincing feminist sympathies in any depth seems very limited. How then does *The Origin of the Family* attempt to reconcile a view that women are peculiarly oppressed by men with an unexamined and naturalised masculinity that was conventional, even 'bourgeois'? While this was not Engels's project in writing the work, it is – analytically speaking – an intriguing question.

Getting on with the plot

Engels made it his business to consider the condition of women in pre-history, in contemporary 'primitive' societies where technology was little developed, in the history of recorded civilisations up to the present, and in the communist society he envisaged for the post-capitalist future. Moreover he amended the materialist conception of history – the theory he attributed to Marx and which he himself espoused – to cover the stages of development of the family. This he interpreted very loosely as both kinship arrangements dividing tribes into clans *and* the organisation of households to include parents and children.

According to Engels's materialist conception the determining factor in history in the last resort was the production and reproduction of human life. He added an important gloss on production and reproduction, saying it was of a *twofold* character: the production of the means of subsistence, including food, shelter and tools; and the production of human beings themselves, which takes place within what he variously termed 'the family', 'groups based on ties of sex' and 'the family system'. The family was further subject to natural selection and to the sexual behaviour that Engels thought was characteristically different in men and women. Both kinds of production – labour on the one hand, procreation on the other – were said to condition the social institutions of any given country during any given historical epoch. And conflicts traceable to production *and* procreation were said to account for major historical change as one epoch succeeds another.[29]

It appears that Engels has established two autonomous lines of explanation for the social order: economic relations and family relations, the class war and the sex war. But it is difficult to reconcile this theoretical preamble with the story that he actually told, which informed us that the 'old society' of pre-history was built on groups based on ties of sex, but domination of the social order by those family relations was itself an *appearance*: 'the less the development of labour, and the more limited its volume of production, and, therefore, the wealth of society, the more preponderatingly does the social order appear to be dominated by ties of sex'.[30]

While it is true that Engels referred to the old society as based or built on those ties, his portrayal of historical change presented the family as dominant in society only when the alternative kind of production, namely for exchange rather than subsistence, had not itself developed beyond the merely rudimentary production of subsistence. Historical change was thus not explained by development in the family system. And the development, if such it was, in the 'ties of sex' considered by Engels was reactive, rather than autonomous. The old society burst asunder, he opined, when assaulted by newly developed social classes, whose members were not tied by sex but instead by economic interests founded on productive labour which the property system came to reflect and enforce. The property system then came to dominate the family system, he concluded.[31]

In the old society the production and distribution of subsistence goods was ordered by sex and clan. In the new society relations between the sexes and the rearing of children were entirely dominated by the property system, antagonistic interests and the class struggle. Thus it is difficult to believe that Engels took his theoretical dualism seriously when one factor (labour) accounted for the most significant of all changes in the other (the family) and not the reverse, when the most significant historical change was not traced to one factor (the family) but explained by the other (labour), and when the most significant instance (the old society) in which the family was said to have had a determining role was declared to be one in which this only *appeared* to be the case. Here we have an instance of taking up a position ... in order to put it down again. Tracing social change to reproductive labour would have epitomised labour as female, particularly in the absence of any determinedly interpretive work on men's actual or possible roles in 'childwork'.[32] Engels was neither equipped to do this – his liaisons produced no offspring (that we know about for sure)[33] – nor particularly interested in such matters, as his letters and papers reveal no special concern with children or even 'family life' in any practical way.

Making love *and* war

So far it is not clear that the categories 'reproduction of human beings', 'ties of sex' and 'the family' are doing any work in Engels's analysis. But perhaps they might help in making sense of the sex war within the overall context of the class war that he discerned in history. If so, this might temper any criticism that his outlook was not just Marxist but 'masculinist' or simply 'male' in virtue of the priority assigned to physical work outside the body and exclusion of emotional and body-centered activities from analytical importance.[34] At this point the reader should also be warned of numerous questionable assumptions in the text beyond those amounting to a gendered characterisation of labour. Some of the categories employed by Engels derive from the writings of Lewis Henry Morgan (*Ancient Society, or Researches in the Lines of Human Progress from Savagery, through Barbarism to Civilization*, 1877) and J.J. Bachofen (*Das Mutterrecht* [*Mother Right*], 1861); and some derive from Marx. The mixture and modifications, of course, were uniquely Engels's.

Engels assumed that all 'civilised' peoples have a structure of kinship terms and marital patterns which developed through distinct, necessary stages from a common, original form. Moreover he assumed that the practice of currently existing but 'primitive' societies provides evidence that unobserved stages in the development of the kinship and marital structures of civilised peoples existed in the expected stages. And he assumed that unobserved, primitive stages of marital patterns can be deduced from the language of primitive peoples when their kinship terms appear to conflict with their actual marital practices.[35]

More crucially Engels introduced assumptions about natural selection and sexual behaviour. He assumed that natural selection was behind successive alterations in kinship restrictions on marital partners and that sexual behaviour in males differs from that in females in important respects, which he could easily identify.[36] According to Engels all marital and kinship structures developed from an original condition of promiscuous intercourse, leading to group marriage according to generations, then to mutual community of husbands and wives within a definite family group, and after that to what he termed the pairing family, which he then distinguished from modern monogamy. This proceeded as natural selection (so he opined) worked to the benefit of those clans in which marriage amongst relatives was forbidden: first between near relations and then remoter relations in an ever-widening circle of exclusion.[37] This marks a major introduction of Darwinian analysis into Marxist historical periodisations, which had previously invoked Marx's historical typology (in the 1859 'Preface' to *A Contribution to the Critique of Political Economy*) of 'communal', classical slave-owning, feudal, and modern commodity-producing forms of production, or his brief comments in *Capital*, vol. 1, suggesting a technology-based (or more strictly, substance-based) categorisation of stone age, bronze age, iron age as the major epochs in history.[38]

The result of this development in Engels's thought, pushing Marxist historical typologies in the direction of Darwinian sexual selection, was that men, whom he assumed are the sexual predators, were denied 'access' (a euphemism for what?) to more and more women, so it was men who began to obtain partners by abduction and purchase. Thus within the pairing family and modern monogamy Engels claimed that polygamy and infidelity remained men's privileges, while they then demanded strict fidelity from their wives and cruelly punished adultery when it occurred during the period of cohabitation. Moreover he assumed that the sexual nature of women was such that once the promiscuous sexual relations of the jungle (*sic*) had lost their 'naive' character, women found a pattern of promiscuity degrading and oppressive. He suggested that they longed for chastity and for the right to temporary or permanent marriage with just one man as a 'deliverance'. Thus he cast them as the opposite of sexual predators, as the partner sought rather than the one who seeks, without giving evidential reasons for this characterisation.[39]

Women are credited by Engels with the 'advance' away from promiscuous behaviour towards monogamy. But in his view they were tricked, since men contrived to oppress them. This happened when men were unfaithful and deprived women of the stable relationships that Engels assumed that they desired. How men could find adulterous women was not detailed, since Engels's account was limited to his version of male motivation – the pleasure of multiple partners. Marital relations were therefore stable to the extent that men found further pursuit of sexual partners a distraction from the time that they could spend having sex with the one they already had. Needless to say the presumed imbalance in intellectual power or moral character between men (who were clever but devious) and women (who were good but naive) was not explored, either.[40] This is precisely what gives Engels's text its novelistic quality: characterisation is simply ascribed, as needing no explanation … which in the case of individual characters in a novel (whatever their symbolic or stereotypical status otherwise) is not needed. In a work of social theory, however, we are owed some account as to why a characterising generalisation is the right one.

Engels assumed that the three forms of marital relations he had identified – group marriage, the pairing family and stable monogamy

– were developments characteristic of three stages of economic development – savagery, barbarism and civilisation.[41] This represents yet another Marxist periodisation of history, derivative as it is from Morgan. But the relationship between the forces of natural selection and sexual behaviour (which supposedly accounted for the development from group marriage to the pairing family) *and* the economic development in stages from savagery to barbarism (by means of cattle-breeding and agriculture) was not explored.[42] Were those two factors (labour – in different, developmental guises – and procreation) linked together? If so, how – and why? If not, which one explained which aspect of this complex transition?

The upper stage of barbarism attracted Engels's particular interest, because it was there that he looked for the origins of 'civilisation'. For Engels this was ultimately the capitalist economy and its corresponding family form – modern monogamy and the nuclear household. Crucial to an understanding of Engels's position is his view that the pairing family (and the preceding forms of group marriage) were matrilineal. It was clear, he said, that descent was traceable only on the maternal side. The female line alone was recognised, since natural fathers cannot be determined with certainty. The exclusive recognition of a natural mother, he assumed, signified high esteem for women. Though the marriage tie in a pairing family might be easily dissolved by either party, the children would then belong solely to the mother. Within the household the women would come wholly or mostly from one kinship group which men then joined. Female children would remain and male children would marry outside the household and matrilineal clan.[43]

Moreover Engels assumed that the primitive communistic household, within which group marriage and the pairing family were supposed to have functioned, implied the supremacy of women in the house, because they ruled the common stores, and men did the providing under female supervision. Women thus had a free and highly respected position among savages and barbarians.[44] The overthrow of this mother-right must have come, on Engels's argument, with the development of new sources of wealth deriving from outside the home. The savage warrior and hunter had been content to occupy second place in a household where division of labour between men and women had regulated the distribution of property, giving superior rights and status to women. Herds and other new sources of *surplus* wealth turned this upside down, causing women's housework to lose significance compared with men's new efforts outside the domestic economy. Where wealth had once been contained within the female province – the house, clothing, ornaments, culinary implements including boats and weapons – the new economy won surplus goods through cattle-rearing, metalwork, weaving and tillage. Engels assumed this to be men's work and the goods to be men's goods. Moreover he presumed that the results remained the man's property if he were required to leave, while the woman retained the fixed household possessions. Engels provides no evidence justifying these presumed differences between women and men.[45]

As men's wealth grew, so their status increased, and there arose a stimulus for them to overthrow matrilineal reckoning of kinship and inheritance. According to Engels a 'divorced' father would want his children (who must stay with their mother and matrilineal clan) to inherit his own goods, and would accept no doubts about paternity, because with pairing marriage his paternity was more nearly certain. In consequence men established the patriarchal family and then eventually modern monogamy, in which men declared themselves supreme. On Engels's view modern monogamy included the hypocritical privilege of infidelity – for men only.[46] The overthrow of mother-right, Engels wrote, was the world-historic defeat of the female sex. It was also the victory of private property over common ownership. More strongly, he added: 'the first class antagonism which appears in history coincides with the development of the antagonism between men and woman in monogamian marriage, and the first class oppression with that of the female sex by the male.' How some men went on to oppress others as well through the economic system was then outlined by Engels, starting with slavery.[47]

Civilisation and its (female) discontents

Before noting what Engels assumed about bourgeois and proletarian monogamy, including the related and somewhat novelised matters of adultery, hetaerism, cuckoldry, prostitution, 'boy-love', exclusive domination of the family by the husband, wifely rebellion and women 'wearing the breeches', it is important to consider an assumption he made about the relationship between the division of labour (including the overall amount) and social status. Engels assumed that the *division of labour* between the two sexes was determined by causes entirely different from those that determine the *status* of women (and men?) in society. In the communistic household, where Engels assumed women were held in high esteem because of the matrilineal kinship system and because of their supervisory role in the necessarily domestic economy, women (in some cultures if not all) were burdened with excessive toil. This in no way conflicted, so he said, with high status and real respect for women in society. The lady of civilisation, whom Engels said was estranged from real work, was surrounded by sham homage, making her infinitely lower socially than the hard-working woman of barbarism, who was regarded as a 'real lady'.[48]

Engels's assumption about civilised monogamy was that it arose out of the concentration of wealth in the hands on one person – a man – and out of his desire to bequeath this wealth to his own children exclusively. Monogamy was the supremacy of the man over the woman, and the individual family was the economic unit of society. This was the first form of the family based on economic conditions, not on natural ones, since it represented for Engels the victory of private property over original, naturally developed common ownership. The new sources of wealth arose, so he assumed, out of productive activities organised within the framework of private property, which seems to have arisen out of an individualistic – and male – desire for each man to secure his own property for his natural children. Engels was himself somewhat nervous about the obvious anachronism here concerning the 'the man of property', now a rather Galsworthian image.[49]

Engels assumed that bourgeois marriage, as an institution, engendered hetaerism and prostitution as men hypocritically pursued a sexual freedom supposedly ruled out by monogamous marriage. When women, neglected by their husbands, took paramours, they were (once again) severely punished, and the domination – sexual, physical and economic – of the bourgeois male over his household was assured.[50] This was incompatible with Engels's view of romantic sex love, which could become the rule only among the proletariat. There the economic foundations of monogamy were removed, because there was 'a complete absence of all property' and therefore 'no stimulus here whatever to assert male domination'. Instead, personal and social relations different from those of a bourgeois marriage came into play, so he believed, particularly when large-scale industry transferred women from the house to the labour market and factory, and often made them the breadwinner of the family. Since many sexual unions were not legally sanctioned, and since proletarians lacked access to the law (which cost money), the woman regained the right of separation. Engels's conclusion was that male domination disappears – except, perhaps, for some of that brutality towards women which became firmly rooted, so he assumed, with the establishment of modern monogamy.[51]

That passage throws an interesting light on Engels's successive sexual relationships with the proletarian Burns sisters Mary and Lizzie, whom he supported in Manchester in a household separate from his bachelor quarters. Mary died in 1863, and unusually there are no surviving photographs of her, and practically nothing is known about their relationship. On her death Engels berated Marx by letter for insufficient condolences concerning the loss, yet it is possible that the evidently embarrassed Marx had actually read the situation well enough in his first rather off-hand reactions: it had not struck him that Engels cared so deeply. Though Engels later lived with Lizzie in London after his retirement from business in 1869 (at the age of 49), and while in residence with him she 'kept house', he did not marry her until she was on *her* deathbed in 1878. Was Engels when a bachelor defiantly flouting the conventions of bourgeois morality by living with an unmarried woman?[52] Or was he not conforming all too typically to another bourgeois convention, whereby discrete liaisons and 'housekeeping' arrangements with socially inferior women were preferable to marriage across the forbidden boundary of class?[53] A working-class Frau Engels would certainly have been very unpleasing to the bourgeois family in Germany to which Engels belonged, and whose property was partly in his charge while he was alive and an obvious item in his will should he pre-decease a spouse. Notably he did not take Lizzie to meet his blood relations in Germany when they travelled together on the Continent.[54]

Perhaps Engels's relationships led him to the conclusions detailed above concerning the domestic life of proletarians. But I think it more likely that his romanticised views were ones that his privileged circumstances allowed him to hold. They also conveniently distanced him personally from the oppression of females that he located within marriage as a bourgeois institution, whilst allowing him to enjoy an unexamined asymmetry in power between himself and his domestic partners. It seems likely that both Mary and Lizzie Burns were life-long illiterates.[55]

In *The Origin of the Family* Engels was equivocal on the subject of domestic duties, since he implied some residual division of labour by sex. He referred explicitly to a woman's 'family duties', but exactly what these were, and what consequences they entailed for women and their public employment, are matters that he did not raise. He was not, therefore, an early theorist of the 'double shift'. Nor did he discuss whether or not men have some domestic duties and the consequences that this might entail. He was therefore not an early theorist of gender equality, either. In personal correspondence throughout his life he played the demanding male, jesting at his own domestic helplessness in order to secure the services of a female servant, unmarried female relative (such as his younger sister Elise) or suitable divorcée (Louise Kautsky Freyberger) to make fires and darn socks.[56]

Theoretical, personal, political

Thus there is very little in Engels's *The Origin of the Family* that inspires much confidence today, though it must also be noted that it is difficult to see what can be said about pre-history that is not a re-tracing of modern ideas and concerns.[57] By making women problematic, Engels became canonical for Marxist-feminism. Whilst the work has been subjected to various criticisms, including feminist ones, my claim is that as a whole it tells a story recoverable through narrative analysis. An important though little researched aspect of the story is that it is about men. This is not readily apparent, because men are theorised in Engels's text through a theorisation of women.

Hence it is my point that Engels did not make men problematic. Instead, he dissolved any problems that there might be with men into a developmental naturalism that effectively excused them all politically – as men. Thus, for Engels, in pre-history biology made men oppressors and women victims, but in historical times the class struggle made the bourgeoisie the oppressors and the proletariat the oppressed. Engels's transmutation of pre-historical naturalism into historical politics left men where they always were and validated a masculinity of convenience, much like the one he lived out. More importantly it left dominant masculinities and dominating males quite untouched. Until we have credible ways of theorising those masculinities, it will be as easy as ever to excuse men's oppressions within the family, private property, the state – or wherever.

Engels's text has been vastly influential, but not for the right reasons. Studies of pre-history and historical teleologies are not as convincing as they once were (or least that is my hope), given that we are rightly focused today more on processes than on origins, and more on contingency than on over-determination. His feminism is just what we might expect from a man: full of knowingness about women, and near-deliberate recalcitrance about men. In so far as Marxism can be identified with a reductionist determinism (whether of one or two fundamental factors), Engels's revisions in *The Origin of the Family* have not been much debated. In so far as Marx's own views can be identified with a theoretical outlook that is more nuanced, and less deterministic, Engels's sketchy discussion (a tissue of assumptions, really) looks even less satisfactory. As Gayle Rubin said, 'Eventually, someone will have to write a new version of *The Origin of the Family, Private Property and the State*, recognizing the mutual interdependence of sexuality, economics and politics ...'[58] Altogether *The Origin of the Family* as it stands is a triumph of assertion and self-assertiveness over all else. In particular it tells us a great deal about one man in particular – Friedrich Engels.

The text also tells us a great deal about how masculine hegemony is maintained in the gender order. While it does not endorse masculine domination and marginalisation of women directly (indeed it makes quite the opposite claim), it emphatically reinscribes this through a subtle discursive strategy, namely that of naturalising the masculine qualities that reflect this oppression in the first place. This is subtly done, almost unnoticeably, as this naturalising is already familiar to readers at the outset, and in fact it takes a great deal of work to make these beliefs about men problematic at all, so relentlessly are they – always and already – inscribed in 'nature' as gendered beings. Engels has only to allude to the 'obvious', and the point is made. Given that he appears to be extending every courtesy and helping hand to women through his (apparently) feminist project of equality and transformation, his position in gender politics is secured. Unfortunately his discursive strategy secures the existing gender order far more than a transformative one, precisely because of the way that he characterises men.

Notes

1 Lopes and Roth, *Men's Feminism*, pp. 29–39, 73, 82 n. 55.
2 The title in full was *Herr Eugen Dühring's Revolution in Science*, with fully intended irony. On, the early Engels, see Terrell Carver, *Friedrich Engels: his life and thought* (Basingstoke: Macmillan, 1989), pp. 31–9; on *Anti-Dühring*, see pp. 241–4.
3 Lopes and Roth, *Men's Feminism*, pp. 73–5.
4 Lopes and Roth, *Men's Feminism*, p. 82 n. 55.
5 Carver, *Friedrich Engels*, pp. 10–12, illustration no. 10 (between pp. 120–2), 145–8, 244–5; Terrell Carver, *Marx and Engels: the intellectual relationship* (Brighton: Wheatsheaf, 1983), pp. 78–95.
6 Terrell Carver, 'A political theory of gender: perspectives on the universal subject', in Vicky Randall and Georgina Waylen, eds, *Gender, Politics and the State* (London: Routledge, 1998), pp. 18–24.
7 Carver, *Marx and Engels*, pp. 118–51, 152–8; Carver, *The Postmodern Marx*, pp. 163–80.
8 Terrell Carver, '"Marx-Engels" or "Engels v. Marx"', *MEGA-Studien*, 1996/2, pp. 79–85.
9 Karl Marx, 'Preface' to *A Contribution to the Critique of Political Economy*, in Karl Marx, *Later Political Writings*, ed. and trans. Terrell Carver (Cambridge: Cambridge University Press, 1996, repr. 2002), pp. 160–1; these transitions are critically discussed in Terrell Carver, *Marx's Social Theory* (Oxford: Oxford University Press, 1982), pp. 38–57.
10 Lawrence Krader, intro. to *The Ethnological Notebooks of Karl Marx: studies of Morgan, Phear, Maine, Lubbock* (Assen and New York: Van Gorcum and Humanities Press, 1972); Carver, *Marx and Engels*, pp. 144–5.
11 Carver, *Marx's Social Theory*; Karl Marx, *Capital*, vol. 1, pp. 175–6 n. 35.
12 The modern *locus classicus* for this version of Marxism, and this reading of Marx, is G.A Cohen, *Karl Marx's Theory of History: a defence* (Oxford: Oxford University Press, 1978), which does not take up the question of Engels's revisions to this 'outlook' in *The Origin of the Family*.
13 Barrett, 'Marxist-feminism and the work of Karl Marx', p. 214.
14 This begins with the English translation (Chicago, IL: C.H. Kerr, 1902); see also Frederick Engels, *The Origin of the Family, Private Property and the State*, intro. Eleanor Burke Leacock (London: Lawrence & Wishart, 1972); and Friedrich Engels, *The Origin of the Family, Private Property and the State*, intro. Michèle Barrett (Harmondsworth: Penguin, 1985).
15 Barrett, 'Marxist-feminism and the work of Karl Marx', p. 214.
16 Engels's 'biological' and Darwinian framing (never mind his lifelong heterosexism) could make the text an interesting object of critique from

the gay male standpoint, but to my knowledge no one has taken this up directly.
17 Pateman, *The Sexual Contract*, pp. 1–18; Carole Pateman, 'Beyond the sexual contract?', in Geoff Dench, ed., *Rewriting the Sexual Contract* (New Brunswick, NJ: Transaction, 1999), pp. 1–9; Carver, '"Public Man"', pp. 673–86.
18 See the discussion of this text, pp. 223–4 above.
19 Hearn, *The Gender of Oppression*, pp. 59–118.
20 Carver, *Friedrich Engels*, pp. 232–52.
21 This is, of course, the premise of the present volume.
22 Terrell Carver, review of *Engels Revisited: New Feminist Essays*, ed. Janet Sayers, Mary Evens, and Nenneke Redclift, in *History of Political Thought* 9 (1987), p. 180.
23 Kim Lane Scheppele, 'Foreword: telling stories', *Michigan Law Review* 87 (1989), pp. 2073–98; Don Lavoie, *Economics and Hermeneutics* (London: Routledge, 1990).
24 Michel Foucault, *History of Sexuality*, 3 vols, trans. Robert Hurley (Harmondsworth, Penguin Books,1984/86/88); Scott, *Gender and the Politics of History*.
25 Karl Marx and Friedrich Engels, 'Manifesto of the Communist Party', in Marx, *Later Political Writings*, pp 16–17; Engels's authorial relationship to the *Manifesto* is discussed in Carver, *Marx and Engels*, pp. 78–95.
26 Karl Marx, 'Economic and Philosophical Manuscripts' (1844), in *Early Writings*, trans. Rodney Livingstone and Gregor Benton (Harmondsworth: Penguin, 1975), pp. 346–7.
27 Segal, *Slow Motion*, pp. 274–319; Connell, *Masculinities*, pp. 39–42.
28 Carver, *Friedrich Engels*, pp. 146–8, 152–3, 159, 169, 182–3.
29 Frederick Engels, *The Origin of the Family, Private Property and the State*, in Karl Marx and Frederick Engels *Selected Works in One Volume* (London and Moscow: Lawrence & Wishart and Progress Publishers, 1980), pp. 449–50.
30 Engels, *Origin of the Family*, pp. 449–50.
31 Engels, *Origin of the Family*, pp. 449–50.
32 Hearn, *Gender of Oppression*, pp. 149–87.
33 See Carver, *Gender is Not a Synonym for Women*, pp. 81–100, for a discussion of Engels's actual and reported roles with respect to the paternity (attributed to Marx in 1962) of Frederick Demuth, the son of Marx's (and later Engels's) housekeeper, Helene Demuth.
34 Hearn, *Gender of Oppression*, pp. 98–101.
35 Engels, *Origin of the Family*, pp. 458–9, 466–80.
36 Engels, *Origin of the Family*, pp. 474, 484–5.
37 Engels, *Origin of the Family*, pp. 474, 485.

38 Marx, 'Preface', in *Later Political Writings*, pp. 160–1; Marx, *Capital*, vol. 1, p. 286 n. 6.
39 Engels, *Origin of the Family*, pp. 484–5.
40 Engels, *Origin of the Family*, p. 485.
41 Engels, *Origin of the Family*, p. 502.
42 Engels, *Origin of the Family*, p. 461.
43 Engels, *Origin of the Family*, pp. 484–8.
44 Engels, *Origin of the Family*, pp. 481, 484–8.
45 Engels, *Origin of the Family*, pp. 485–8.
46 Engels, *Origin of the Family*, pp. 485–8.
47 Engels, *Origin of the Family*, pp. 494–5.
48 Engels, *Origin of the Family*, pp. 481–2, 568–71.
49 Engels, *Origin of the Family*, pp. 485–8.
50 Engels, *Origin of the Family*, pp. 499–500.
51 Engels, *Origin of the Family*, pp. 499–500.
52 Barrett, 'Marxist-feminism', pp. 215–16.
53 Carver, *Friedrich Engels*, p. 159.
54 Carver, *Friedrich Engels*, p. 158.
55 Carver, *Friedrich Engels*, pp. 158–9.
56 Carver, *Friedrich Engels*, pp. 148, 165.
57 Shanks and Tilley, *Social Theory and Archaeology*.
58 Gayle Rubin, quoted in Scott, *Gender and the Politics of History*, p. 202.

Conclusion

I had a dual purpose in *Men in Political Theory*. Firstly I aimed to utilise the feminist-framed men's studies and masculinities literatures to investigate selected classic texts, to see what would happen when the 'gender lens' is deployed in this way. Secondly, I aimed show the depth and richness of these works (surprising, as ever, even after centuries of commentary) by drawing them into our times and politics, as political theorists are trained to do. Overall these discussions, varied as they are, were intended to be lively and fun, and I hope that sometimes, at least, I have succeeded. I realise that some discussions will seem sparsely 'framed' and telegraphic, and that I have made assertions (and revealed omissions in my reading) that specialists on each author will find irritating. I can only beg their patience and rely on their indulgence, hoping that they take the view that different readings can testify to the strength of an author's vision, rather than necessarily to some weakness in the reader.

The gender lens works differently for men and things masculine than it does for women and things feminine. While masculinism and gender inequality works to subordinate women as such, it is crucial for the way this works that a further hierarchy among men is defined, described, naturalised and defended. I hope that these chapters have presented some evidence for this, and have analysed some of the ways in which this works. To construct these hierarchies, theorists also require a view of knowledge, truth, certainty, evidence and order, which can itself be investigated. My approach to these issues in a text is also framed with views on its authorship, context, transmission and further hermeneutical considerations. I have emphasised the need to engage with all these things, before attempting a fine-grained reading.

This has made the opening sections of some chapters into rather long preambles before the excitement of sexual difference and gender politics emerges, but I hope that I have shown that the philosophical and hermeneutic discussions were worthwhile, and that I did not linger unduly.

My focus has been on selected texts, rather than with building up a picture of an author and his views, from what remains of an *oeuvre*. As most commentators on political theory today (though certainly not all) present the subject through canonically suitable texts, and then contextualise an author in as much detail as need be, I have followed this procedure, and have not attempted to attribute a unified intellect to, say, Aristotle, and then perforce to find a unity in his texts. I am rather hopeful that even if my readings of, say, the two Rousseau classics considered here, fit ill with what specialists find in the larger *oeuvre* (and in his case, it is very large indeed, and not all yet published), then perhaps I have served a purpose in stimulating their enquiries and engagement. The texts studied here are often used to generate simple and indeed simplistic ideas, usable in political conflict, restoration and transformation. My objective was to make these ideas rather more complex in their political currency. Delivering 'man' up to further scrutiny, I hope that I have helped to establish an effectual mode of political critique, not just of texts, but of lived realities.

In sum, the obvious conclusion is that, 'yes', political theory is already about men, but I hope that I have shown that the masculinised dynamics of politics depend on concepts of 'man' that are inflected with other factors. These vary from an attribute of supposed 'de-genderedness' to markers of race/ethnicity, class, sexuality and culture that are intriguingly and often bizarrely deployed. My emphasis on metaphor throughout has been crucial to utilising the gender lens and to drawing out the gender politics in each text. The distinction we are encouraged to make between the 'literal' or 'straightforward' in terms of an argument or doctrine, and the 'merely metaphorical', which can supposedly be disregarded, is a genuine barrier to the exploration of texts, and of life, as we attempt to make sense of it. My concentration on metaphors, particularly those of animals and machines, through which the gendered aspects of human life are explicated and communicated, has, I hope, paid off, and not irritated readers as a 'side issue'. While this way of reading texts does not speak directly to those concerned with traditional problems (legitimacy, equality, consent, obligation, public/private, rebellion etc.) on the terms that they are used to, I hope that a focus on (all) language as trope will re-open some of these discussions and contribute to our skill in handling them. Metaphors are words, and they help us do things.

In detail, I hope that I have brought:

- more drama to *The Republic* and less grief to 'Plato' in terms of his presumed political 'teaching';
- more critical sensitivity and less credence to what Aristotle says about 'observation' and 'nature', particularly when he addresses human differences;
- more astonishment to the gospels as the story of Jesus unfolds, with increased sympathy for those whom he obviously annoyed;
- more scepticism to Augustine's view of himself, his political use of sexualities and his 'fit' with other authors in the canon;
- more variety and colour to the way that Machiavelli is read, by reading his men *as men*, rather than generically as 'man';
- more depth to Hobbes by taking his mechanical materialism to its limits as science fiction, and revealing the machine-like qualities of modern masculinity;
- more clarity to our understanding of Locke's *Two Treatises* and the politically productive contradictions thereof;
- more enthusiasm for turning Rousseau on his head and deconstructing the fantasies from which hierarchies of sexual difference arise;
- more impatience with Marx's slender and undynamic forays into gender theory; and
- more anger at Engels's naturalising and patronising approach to gender politics.

Having read the chapters, noted the literatures and followed the methodology, readers will find the outlook transferable, I hope, to further thinkers and other contexts. There is no shortage out there of intellectual artifacts and real-life dilemmas.

Bibliography

Annas, Julia, *An Introduction to Plato's Republic*, Oxford: Clarendon Press, 1981.
Aristotle, *The Politics*, trans. Ernest Barker, Oxford: Oxford University Press, 1946, repr. New York: Oxford University Press, 1962.
Aristotle, *The Politics*, trans. Jonathan Barnes, ed. Stephen Everson, Cambridge: Cambridge University Press, 1988.
Ashcraft, Richard, *Revolutionary Politics and Locke's Two Treatises of Government*, Princeton, NJ: Princeton University Press, 1986.
Astell, Mary, *Some Reflections on Marriage* [1700], in Marie Mulvey Roberts and Tamae Mizuta, eds, *Perspectives on the History of British Feminism, the Wives: the rights of married women*, London: Routledge/Thoemmes Press, 1994.
Augustine, *The Confessions*, trans. Maria Boulding, Hyde Park, NY: New City Press, 1997.
Barkawi, Tarak, 'Peoples, homelands and wars? Ethnicity, the military and battle among British imperial forces in the war against Japan', *Comparative Studies in Society and History*, 46 (2004), pp. 134–63.
Barker, Philip, *Foucault: a critical introduction*, Cambridge: Polity Press, 1994.
Barrett, Michèle, 'Marxist-feminism and the work of Karl Marx', in Betty Matthews, ed., *Marx: 100 years on*, London: Lawrence & Wishart, 1983.
Blasius, Mark, *Gay and Lesbian Politics: sexuality and the emergence of a new ethic*, Philadelphia: Temple University Press, 1994.
Brod, Harry (ed.), *The Making of Masculinities: the new men's studies*, Winchester, MA: Allen & Unwin, 1987.
Brown, Peter, *Augustine of Hippo: a biography*, new edn, Berkeley, CA: University of California Press, 2000.
Brown, Peter, *The Body and Society: men, women and sexual renunciation in early Christianity*, New York: Columbia University Press, 1988.

Butler, Judith, *Gender Trouble: Feminism and the Subversion of Identity*, London: Routledge, 1990.
Carver, Terrell, *Friedrich Engels: his life and thought*, Basingstoke: Macmillan, 1989.
Carver, Terrell, *Gender is not a Synonym for Women*, Boulder, CO: Lynne Rienner, 1996.
Carver, Terrell, *Marx and Engels: the intellectual relationship*, Brighton: Wheatsheaf, 1983.
Carver, Terrell, '"Marx-Engels" or "Engels v. Marx"', *MEGA-Studien*, 1996/2, pp. 79–85.
Carver, Terrell, *Marx's Social Theory*, Oxford: Oxford University Press, 1982.
Carver, Terrell, 'Men and IR/men in IR', in Louiza Odysseos and Hakan Seckinelgin, eds, *Gendering the 'International'*, Basingstoke: Palgrave, 2002.
Carver, Terrell, 'Methodological issues in writing a political biography', *Journal of Political Science* 20 (1992), pp. 3–13.
Carver, Terrell, 'A political theory of gender: perspectives on the universal subject', in Vicky Randall and Georgina Waylen, eds, *Gender, Politics and the State*, London: Routledge, 1998.
Carver, Terrell, *The Postmodern Marx*, Manchester: Manchester University Press, 1998.
Carver, Terrell, '"Public man" and the critique of masculinities', *Political Theory* 24 (1996), pp. 673–86.
Chadwick, Henry, *Augustine*, Oxford: Oxford University Press, 1986.
Cohen, G.A., *Karl Marx's Theory of History: a defence*, Oxford: Oxford University Press, 1978.
Cohn, Carol, 'Gays in the military: texts and subtexts', in Marysia Zalewski and Jane Parpart, eds, *The 'Man Question' in International Relations*, Boulder, CO: Westview, 1998, pp. 129–49.
Cohn, Carol, 'Sex and death in the rational world of defense intellectuals', *Signs* 12 (1987), pp. 687–718.
Connell, R.W., *Gender and Power: society, the person and sexual politics*, Cambridge: Polity Press, 1987.
Connell, R.W., *Masculinities*, Cambridge: Polity Press, 1995.
Connolly, William, *The Augustinian Imperative: a reflection on the politics of morality*, new edn, Lanham MD: Rowman & Littlefield, 2002.
Coole, Diana H., *Women in Political Theory: from ancient misogyny to contemporary feminism*, 2nd edn, London: Harvester/Wheatsheaf, 1993.
Cooney, Sharon, 'A revolution in the household: Locke's Reconstitution of the Family', unpublished paper presented to the American Political Science Association 1995 Annual Meeting.
der Derian, James, *Virtuous War: mapping the military—industrial—media—entertainment network*, Boulder, CO: Westview, 2001.

di Stefano, Christine, *Configurations of Masculinity: a feminist perspective on modern political theory*, Ithaca, NY: Cornell University Press, 1991.

Dunn, John, *The Political Thought of John Locke: an historical account of the argument of the 'Two Treatises of Government'*, Cambridge: Cambridge University Press, 1982.

Edwards, Tim, *Erotics and Politics: gay male sexuality, masculinity and feminism*, London: Routledge, 1994.

Eisenstein, Zillah, *The Radical Future of Liberal Feminism*, Boston, MA: Northeastern University Press, 1986.

Elshtain, Jean Bethke, *Augustine and the Limits of Politics*, Notre Dame, IN: University of Notre Dame Press, 1995.

Elshtain, Jean Bethke, *Public Man/Private Woman: women in social and political thought*, 2nd edn, Princeton, NJ: Princeton University Press, 1993.

Engelhardt, Jr., H. Tristram, *The Foundations of Bioethics*, 2nd edn, New York and Oxford: Oxford University Press, 1996.

Engels, Frederick, *The Condition of the Working Class in England*, ed. Victor Kiernan, Harmondsworth: Penguin, 1987.

Engels, Frederick, *The Origin of the Family, Private Property and the State*, intro. Eleanor Burke Leacock, London: Lawrence & Wishart, 1972.

Engels, Frederick, *The Origin of the Family, Private Property and the State*, in Karl Marx and Frederick Engels, *Selected Works in One Volume*, London and Moscow: Lawrence & Wishart and Progress Publishers, 1980, pp. 449–583.

Engels, Friedrich, *The Origin of the Family, Private Property and the State*, intro. Michèle Barrett, Harmondsworth: Penguin, 1985.

Evans, David T., *Sexual Citizenship: the material construction of sexualities*, London: Routledge, 1993.

Farr, James, '"So Vile and Miserable an Estate": the problem of slavery in Locke's political thought', *Political Theory* 14 (1986), pp. 263–89.

Filene, Peter, 'The secrets of men's history', in Harry Brod, ed., *The Making of Masculinities*, Winchester, MA: Allen & Unwin, 1987, pp. 103–20.

Foucault, Michel, *History of Sexuality*, 3 vols, trans. Robert Hurley, Harmondsworth, Penguin Books, 1984/1986/1988.

Frayling, Christopher, and Wokler, Robert, 'From the orang-utan to the vampire', in R.A. Leigh, ed., *Rousseau after Two Hundred Years*, Cambridge: Cambridge University Press, 1982, pp. 109–24.

Goldsmith, M.M., *Hobbes' Science of Politics*, New York: Columbia University Press, 1966.

Goldstein, Joshua S., *War and Gender: how gender shapes the war system and vice versa*, Cambridge: Cambridge University Press, 2001.

Grant, Judith, *Fundamental Feminism: contesting the core concepts of feminist theory*, London: Routledge, 1993.

Guy, John, *Tudor England*, Oxford: Oxford University Press, 1988, repr. 1991.

Hearn, Jeff, *The Gender of Oppression: men, masculinity and the critique of Marxism*, Brighton: Wheatsheaf, 1987.

Hearn, Jeff, *Men in the Public Eye: the construction and deconstruction of public men and public patriarchies*, London: Routledge, 1992.

Hearn, Jeff, and Collinson, David, 'Unities and differences between men and between masculinities', in Harry Brod and Michael Kaufmann, eds, *Theorizing Masculinities*, Newbury Park, CA: Sage, 1994, pp. 97–118.

Heyd, David, *Genethics: moral issues in the creation of people*, Berkeley, CA: University of California Press, 1992.

Hobbes, Thomas, *Leviathan*, ed. C.B. Macpherson, Harmondsworth: Penguin, 1968, repr. 1985.

Hobbes, Thomas, *Leviathan*, ed. Richard Tuck, Cambridge: Cambridge University Press, 1991.

Holy Bible, New International version, Grand Rapids, MI: Zondervan Bible Publishers, 1996.

Hooper, Charlotte, *Manly States: masculinities, international relations, and gender politics*, New York and Chichester: Columbia University Press, 2001.

Jones, Adam (ed.), *Genocide and Gendercide*, Nashville, TN: Vanderbilt University Press, 2004.

Jones, Kathleen B., *Compassionate Authority: democracy and the representation of women*, London: Routledge, 1993.

Kates, Gary, *Monsieur d'Eon is a Woman: a tale of political intrigue and sexual masquerade*, new edn, Baltimore, MD: Johns Hopkins University Press, 2001.

Katz, Jonathan Ned, *The Invention of Heterosexuality*, New York: Dutton, 1995.

Krader, Lawrence, *The Ethnological Notebooks of Karl Marx: studies of Morgan, Phear, Maine, Lubbock*, Assen and New York: Van Gorcum and Humanities Press, 1972.

Kuhn, Thomas S., *The Structure of Scientific Revolutions*, 3rd edn, Chicago, IL and London: University of Chicago Press, 1996.

Landes, Joan, *Women and the Public Sphere in the Age of the French Revolution*, Ithaca, NY: Cornell University Press, 1988.

Locke, John, *Two Treatises of Government*, ed. Mark Goldie, London: Dent, 1993.

Locke, John, *Two Treatises of Government*, ed. Peter Laslett, Cambridge: Cambridge University Press, 1988.

Lopes, Anne, and Roth, Gary, *Men's Feminism: August Bebel and the German socialist movement*, Amherst, NY: Humanity/Prometheus, 2000.

Machiavelli, Niccolò, *The Discourses*, ed. Bernard Crick, trans. Leslie J. Walker, S.J., Harmondsworth: Penguin, 1976.

Machiavelli, Niccolò, *The Prince*, ed. Quentin Skinner and Russell Price, Cambridge: Cambridge University Press, 1994.

Machiavelli, Niccolò, *The Prince*, trans. and ed. Robert M. Adams, New York: Norton, 1977.

Marso, Lori Jo, *(Un)Manly Citizens: Jean-Jacques Rousseau's and Germaine de Staël's subversive women*, Baltimore, MD and London: Johns Hopkins University Press, 1999.

Marx, Karl, 'Economic and Philosophical Manuscripts' (1844), in *Early Writings*, trans. Rodney Livingstone and Gregor Benton, Harmondsworth: Penguin, 1975, pp. 279–400.

Marx, Karl, *Capital*, vol. 1, trans. Ben Fowkes, Harmondsworth: Penguin, 1986.

Marx, Karl, 'Preface' to *A Contribution to the Critique of Political Economy*, in Karl Marx, *Later Political Writings*, ed. and trans. Terrell Carver, Cambridge: Cambridge University Press, 1996, repr. 2002, pp. 158–62.

Marx Karl, and Engels, Frederick, *Manifesto of the Communist Party*, in Karl Marx, *Later Political Writings*, ed. and trans. Terrell Carver, Cambridge: Cambridge University Press, 1996.

Marx Karl, and Engels, Frederick, *Feuerbach: opposition of the materialist and idealist outlooks* [*The First Part of 'The German Ideology'*], London, Lawrence & Wishart, 1973.

McLellan, David, *Karl Marx: his life and thought*, London: Macmillan, 1973.

Megone, Christopher, 'Potentiality and persons: an Aristotelian perspective', in Mark, G. Kuczewski and Ronald Polansky, eds, *Bioethics: ancient themes in contemporary issues*, Cambridge, MA: MIP Press, 2000.

Monoson, Sara, *Plato's Democratic Entanglements: Athenian politics and the practice of philosophy*, Princeton, NJ: Princeton University Press, 2000.

Myers, Peter C., 'Locke on the Constitution of the Liberal Family', unpublished paper presented at the American Political Science Association 1997 Annual Meeting.

Nathanson, Paul, and Young, Katherine K., *Spreading Misandry: the teaching of contempt for men in popular culture*, Montreal and Kingston: McGill-Queen's University Press, 2001.

Nietzsche, Friedrich, *The Viking Portable Nietzsche*, trans. Walter Kaufman, New York: Viking, 1968.

Okin, Susan Moller, *Women in Western Political Thought*, Princeton, NJ: Princeton University Press, 1979.

Pappas, Nickolas, *Routledge Philosophy Guidebook to Plato and the Republic*, New York and London: Routledge, 1995.

Pateman, Carole, 'Beyond the sexual contract?', in Geoff Dench, ed., *Rewriting the Sexual Contract*, New Brunswick, NJ: Transaction, 1999, pp. 1–9.

Pateman, Carole, *The Sexual Contract*, Cambridge: Polity Press, 1988.

Pitkin, Hannah Fenichel, *Fortune is a Woman: gender and politics in the thought of Niccolò Machiavelli*, new edn, Chicago, IL: Chicago University Press, 1999.

Plato, *The Republic*, trans. and ed. Robin Waterfield, Oxford: Oxford University Press, 1993.

Plato, *The Republic*, trans. Tom Griffith, ed. G.R.F. Ferrari, Cambridge: Cambridge University Press, 2000.

Rorty, Richard, *Contingency, Irony and Solidarity*, Cambridge: Cambridge University Press, 1989, repr. 1995.

Rousseau, Jean-Jacques, 'Discourse on the Origins of Inequality among Men', in *The Discourses and other early Political Writings*, ed. and trans. Victor Gourevitch, Cambridge: Cambridge University Press, 1997.

Rousseau, Jean-Jacques, *The Social Contract and other Later Political Writings*, ed. and trans. Victor Gourevitch, Cambridge: Cambridge University Press, 1997.

Sayers, Sean, *Plato's Republic: an introduction*, Edinburgh: Edinburgh University Press, 1999.

Scheppele, Kim Lane, 'Foreword: telling stories', *Michigan Law Review* 87 (1989), pp. 2073–98.

Schochet, Gordon J., *Patriarchalism in Political Thought: the authoritarian family and political speculation and attitudes especially in seventeenth-century England*, Oxford: Blackwell, 1975.

Schwartz, Joel, *The Sexual Politics of Jean-Jacques Rousseau*, Chicago, IL: University of Chicago Press, 1984.

Scott, Joan Wallach, *Gender and the Politics of History*, rev. edn, New York: Columbia University Press, 1999.

Seery, John E., *Political Theory for Mortals: shades of justice, images of death*, Ithaca, NY: Cornell University Press, 1996.

Seery, John Evan, *Political Returns: irony in politics and theory, from Plato to the antinuclear movement*, Boulder, CO: Westview, 1990.

Segal, Lynne, *Slow Motion: changing masculinities, changing men*, London: Virago, 1990.

Seidman, Steven, *Queer Theory/Sociology*, Cambridge, MA: Blackwell, 1996).

Shanks, Michael, and Tilley, Christopher, *Social Theory and Archaeology*, Cambridge: Polity Press, 1987.

Shanley, Mary Lyndon, 'Marriage contract and social contract in seventeenth century English political thought', in Jean Bethke Elshtain, ed., *The Family in Political Thought*, Amherst, MA: University of Massachusetts Press, 1982.

Shapiro, Michael J., 'Metaphor in the philosophy of the social sciences', *Culture and Critique* 2 (1985–86), pp. 191–214.

Sinfield, Alan, *Cultural Politics, Queer Reading*, London: Routledge, 1994.

Skinner, Quentin, *The Foundations of Modern Political Thought, vol. 1: The Renaissance*, Cambridge: Cambridge University Press, 1978.

Snyder, R. Claire, *Citizen-Soldiers and Manly Warriors*, Lanham, MD: Rowman & Littlefield, 1999.
Stevens, Jacqueline, *Reproducing the State*, Princeton, NJ: Princeton University Press, 1999.
Strauss, David Friedrich, *The Life of Jesus Critically Examined*, London: SCM Press, 1973.
Strong, Tracey B., *Jean-Jacques Rousseau: the politics of the ordinary*, Thousand Oaks, CA: Sage, 1994.
Tatchell, Peter, *We Don't Want to March Straight: masculinity, queers and the military*, London: Cassell, 1995.
Thucydides, *The History of the Peloponnesian War*, trans. Richard Crawley, New York: Dutton, 1950.
Tronto, Joan C., *Moral Boundaries: a political argument for an ethic of care*, London: Routledge, 1993.
Vogel, Ursula, '"But in a Republic, men are needed": guarding the boundaries of liberty', in Robert Wokler, ed., *Rousseau and Liberty*, Manchester: Manchester University Press, 1995, pp. 213–30.
Waites, Matthew, 'Sexual Citizens: legislating the age of consent in Britain', in Terrell Carver and Véronique Mottier, eds, *The Politics of Sexuality: identity, gender, citizenship*, London: Routledge, 1998, pp. 25–35.
Waldron, Jeremy, *God, Locke, and Equality: Christian foundations in Locke's political thought*, Cambridge: Cambridge University Press, 2002.
Weeks, Jeffrey, *Coming Out: homosexual politics in Britain from the nineteenth century to the present*, rev. edn, London: Quartet, 1990.
Weeks, Jeffrey, *Sex, Politics and Society: the regulation of sexuality since 1800*, 2nd edn, London: Longman, 1989.
Weiss, Penny A., *Gendered Community: Rousseau, sex and politics*, New York: New York University Press, 1993.
Weithman, Paul, 'Augustine's Political Philosophy', in Eleonore Stump and Norman Kretzmann, eds, *The Cambridge Companion to Augustine*, New York: Cambridge University Press, pp. 234–52.
Wingrove, Elizabeth Rose, *Rousseau's Republican Romance*, Princeton, NJ: Princeton University Press, 2000.
Wittgenstein, Ludwig, *Philosophical Investigations*, trans. G.E.M. Anscombe, 2nd edn, Oxford: Blackwell, 1958.
Wokler, Robert, *Rousseau*, Oxford: Oxford University Press, 1995.
Zarkov, Dubravka, 'The body of the other man: sexual violence and the construction of masculinity, sexuality and ethnicity in Croatian media', in Caroline O.N. Moser and Fiona C. Clark, eds, *Victims, Perpetrators or Actors? gender armed conflict and political violence*, London: Zed, 2001.
Zerilli, Linda M. G., *Signifying Woman: culture and chaos in Rousseau, Burke, and Mill*, Ithaca, NY: Cornell University Press, 1994.

Index

Aquinas, Thomas, Saint 65
Aristophanes, 13
Aristotle 6, 13, 34–57, 82, 132–3, 253, 254
Augustine, of Hippo, Saint 1, 7, 65, 80–104, 254

Barrett, M. 221–3
Bebel, A. 216, 227–9
Brod, H. 3
Brown, P. 94–100
Burns, E. 246
Burns, M. 246
Butler, J. 4

Cohn, C. 150
Connell, R.W. 3, 147–8
Connolly, W. 84, 88–93
Coole, D. 2–3

der Derian, James 148
di Stefano, C. 144–6

Elshtain, J.B. 84, 85–88, 89
Engels, F. 9, 64–5, 206, 216, 218, 227–51, 254

Foucault, M. 97

gender 4
  masculinities 2, 3, 21–6, 31–2, 36, 44–5, 51–4, 68–73, 105–27, 165–73, 183–8, 191–7, 212–13, 232–5, 252–3
  woman 2, 22, 26–31, 40, 44, 46, 53–4, 71, 131–2, 189–90, 237–8
  see also sex; sexualities

Hearn, J. 3, 221, 223–4, 234
Hegel, G.W.F. 65, 86
Hobbes, T. 7–8, 61, 64, 77, 81, 82, 83, 86, 101, 130–52, 254
Hooper, C. 149

Jesus 7, 58–79, 254

Kuhn, T. 38–9

Lenin, V.I. 83
Locke, J. 8, 83, 86 101, 146, 153–76, 197–8, 254

Machiavelli, N. 7, 64, 81, 105–29, 254
Marx, K. 9, 64–5, 205–26, 228–31, 235–6, 241–2, 254
More, T. 63–4

nature 43–4, 45–8, 49–55, 181–2, 214
  Darwinian 9, 50, 229, 241
Nietzsche, F. 88–9, 91

Okin, S.M. 2

Pateman, C. 2, 161
Plato 5–6, 11–32, 34–6, 37–8, 53–4, 59, 62, 63, 64, 82, 83, 123, 182–3, 254

Rawls, J. 89
Rousseau, J.J. 8–9, 82, 84, 86, 87, 177–204, 254

sex 177–81
  reproduction 41–2, 43, 206–7
  see also gender; sexualities
sexualities 94–102
  female 178, 220
  gay 73
  male 242–4
Shapiro, M.J. 139

theory, political 1–2, 80–5, 252–4
  feminist 1–2, 32, 73, 105, 131, 153–5, 199, 216–19, 231–2, 252
  women 1, 5, 80
Thucydides 21, 59–60, 61–3

Wittgenstein, L. 18, 87
Wollstonecraft, M. 19, 80

Lightning Source UK Ltd.
Milton Keynes UK
UKOW041311150213

206344UK00004B/97/P